Abrahamson
  America arms for
a new century

America Arms for a New Century

The problem of military organization has two aspects, a dynamic aspect and a political aspect. The measure of military force required to meet any given emergency is purely dynamic, while the form of military institutions must be determined on political grounds, with due regard to national genius and tradition. There can be no sound solution of the problem if either of these fundamental aspects is ignored.

"The Organization of the Land Forces
of the United States, *ARWD* (1912),
I, 76

America Arms for a New Century

The Making of a Great Military Power

JAMES L. ABRAHAMSON

THE FREE PRESS
A Division of Macmillan Publishing Co., Inc.
NEW YORK

Collier Macmillan Publishers
LONDON

The Free Press
A Division of Macmillan Publishing Co., Inc.
866 Third Avenue, New York, N.Y.   10022

Collier Macmillan Canada, Ltd.

Library of Congress Catalog Card Number: 80-69716

Printed in the United States of America

printing number
1   2   3   4   5   6   7   8   9   10

Library of Congress Cataloging in Publication Data

Abrahamson, James L.
  America arms for a new century.

  Bibliography: p. 237-244.
  Includes index.
  1. United States—Military policy. 2. United
States—History, Military. 3. United States—
History, Naval. I. Title.
UA23.A4295   355'.00973   80-69716
ISBN 0-02-900190-0   AACR2

To Thomas Everett Griess

Contents

Acknowledgments

MY PRINCIPAL INTELLECTUAL DEBTS are to three former teachers. In his lectures on "War and Society" Peter Paret awakened me to the dynamic relation between a society and its military institutions. Barton Bernstein taught me to read more critically, and his seminar on "American Liberalism" helped me understand civilian attitudes toward war, the armed forces, and America's role in world affairs. With David Kennedy, who guided my doctoral dissertation, I began my study of the army's reformers, and in his seminar on the "United States and World War I," I first perceived the complex nature of the late-nineteenth-century military renaissance. Subsequently encouraging me to broaden my horizon to include both naval reform and civilian thought, he also helped me achieve much of whatever felicity of expression may grace this work.

During preparation of this manuscript others came to my aid. Colin Jones of The Free Press wisely guided my revisions and provided a quiet encouragement that built confidence and lightened every step. To my immense benefit, my colleague Andrew J. Bacevich, Jr., one of the modern army's soldier-scholars, also read the entire manuscript. For whatever shortcomings survived their careful inspection and thoughtful criticism, I am entirely responsible. Miss Deborah Bittle skillfully typed the final draft, and Marigold patiently endured the long hours I devoted to research and writing.

There are other debts as well. The librarians and archivists of the Manuscript Division of the Library of Congress, the National Archives, the Hoover Institution on War, Revolution and Peace, the Naval Historical Division, the Huntington Library, and the Sutro Library gave invaluable help. Florence Chu of Stanford University's Main Library and Charlotte Snyder of the United States Military Academy Library deserve special praise for their efficient handling of the host of items obtained for me on Inter-Library Loan.

In a quite different sense, the real heroes of this study are the turn-of-the-century army and navy officers who took time to reflect upon the ways in which their world was changing and what the nation might consequently demand of them. Their efforts pointed toward a modest and realistic adaptation of the nation's military policies to the national mood, the international situation, and a developing industrial society. Those men have too long suffered the neglect of historians.

Above all others, however, stands Thomas E. Griess—whose act of faith made possible all that follows.

Preface

A GENERAL INTEREST in progressivism and in the relation between military and social reform originally prompted me to write this book, which tries to look at how, in the four decades preceding the close of the First World War, American army and navy officers viewed their nation's steady achievement of great-power status and how those officers reacted to developments that transformed American national life during that period. The book assesses the military's awareness of trends that were reshaping both domestic conditions and the world order, and it looks, too, at officers' perceptions of the likely effect that transformation was to have on American military institutions and policies. Also examined are the assumptions, the values, goals, and events that governed army and navy responses to change and the relation between military and civilian reform. That examination permits some judgment on the extent to which military reformers saw themselves as adapting the armed services to new situations over which they had no control or as advocates of new national policies requiring the enlargement of the military establishments. Throughout, I use the word military to refer to the armed forces in general; military is inclusive of both the army and the navy.

The years from the Grant through the Wilson administrations define a period of profound change in American life; this book seeks to explain the military officers' relation to that transformation. Of course, transformation is a frequent theme in American history, so much so that few periods in the nation's past have escaped characterization as transitional.[1] Still, it can be said that the four decades or so preceding the conclusion of the Great War do mark that period during which the nation first felt the full and sometimes harmful implications of modernization: technological innovation; pursuit of organizational efficiency; wide use of inanimate sources of power to magnify output; extensive commercial activity; an increasingly urban society; substantial improvements in literacy and the means of communication with the consequent expansion of intellectual horizons and the substitution of cosmopolitan attitudes for localism.[2] In the case of the United States, the victory of modern ideals created conditions in which new technology produced a vast outpouring of goods that expanding railways carried throughout the nation and outward-looking businessmen sought to sell in new markets overseas. Technology similarly gave a more commercial character to agriculture, creating a surplus and making farmers too dependent upon distant markets, the means to reach them, and a ready supply of capital. Rural Americans and immigrants from Europe and Asia flocked to the nation's growing and often squalid cities, and improvements in literacy and communications carried new urban values into the countryside. In addition to a vast enlargement of the urban working class, America's factories spawned a new group of managers and technicians and before the turn of the century propelled the United States into first rank among the world's economic powers.[3]

Most Americans found that transformation unsettling. Increasingly less able to control their own affairs, rural Americans felt threatened by the new urban centers, which managed the marketing of rural produce, regulated the supply of capital to small-town banks, produced the new manufactured goods undermining the status of local artisans, directed the sales organizations that limited the scope of village shopkeepers, and even manipulated the sources of news and opinion. Many urban folk felt equally troubled. Frustrated by their inability to move into the ranks of the self-employed, urban workingmen sensed the economic vulnerability of those forced to sell their labor to others. Businessmen too felt endangered as improvements in technology and transportation opened formerly secure local markets to the often cutthroat competition of distant producers. Urban areas became the focus of social conflict as economic conditions, new values, and a large alien population produced severe social tension. In the face of change, the old elite sensed its loss of influence, and old institutions seemed unable to control events. Government especially, as it seemingly fell victim to corruption and the selfish manipulation of powerful groups, forfeited the respect of the public and denied citizens a sense that they controlled the nation's affairs or that government promoted the general welfare.

In the late years of the nineteenth century, many Americans consequently resisted modernization, blaming its harmful effects on the machinations of some evil, conspiratorial group. Those Americans responded to their fear and frustration by seeking to preserve some approximation of an old order that rapidly receded beyond their grasp. Farmers attributed their problems to the greed of middlemen, bankers, industrial monopolists, or railroad magnates. Workers condemned the wage system itself, felt alienated from their employers, and charged that owners conspired to deny them a living wage and used the power of government to break their protests and force them into poverty. While assailing the irreligion and materialism of the age, the old elite sought salvation through purification of government and urged their fellow citizens to return public affairs to men from the "best families"—those with inherited wealth, education, and few ties to the new industrialization. And men and women from many walks of life joined to blame the new immigrants for the class tension, bad government, and radical ideas thought to be undermining American life.

While all those "enemies" and many of the schemes for their overthrow contributed in some measure to the early-twentieth-century reform of national life, the regeneration drew its spirit and form from a new class that sought transcendence rather than preservation. Seeking to adapt American society to the forces of modernization rather than to destroy the agents of change, the members of that new class struggled to harness innovation and turn its power to desired ends, in so doing substituting centralized direction for local control. New, permanent bureaucracies applying established rules directed public and private organizations and replaced the personal and informal methods of the past. Skilled managers, technicians, specialists, and experts of all kinds staffed the hierarchic organizations that dominated national life and consequently curtailed the power of both the old elite and the entrepreneurs who had begun the industrial transformation. Committed to conservation and efficiency, that new class employed comprehensive, long-range planning and social engineering to achieve predetermined commercial or political ends and to control both the pace and the direction of change.

America Arms for a New Century argues that reform-minded military officers made up a part of that new class furthering the process of modernization in America. Along with the more perceptive of their fellow citizens, many members of the army and navy recognized that national and international developments had brought the nation and its armed forces to a turning point. Like other Americans concerned with related aspects of the nation's transformation, the late nineteenth century found army and navy officers debating the meaning of the changes and the nature of an appropriate response. Some tried to hold fast to the past; others sensed the need to reform and strike out in new directions. The latter triumphed, and they encouraged a reorganization and redirection of the military services that gave the armed forces the same bureaucratic character typical of the public and private organizations beginning to control national life. For the military profession, those officers sought the same autonomy, authority, and prestige being accorded the specialists directing the other new bureaucracies. As efficiency could only follow a rational determination of ends, army and navy officers advocated the coordination of foreign and military policies and emphasized comprehensive planning and peacetime training to ensure the services' ability to accomplish their likely tasks. Generally avoiding the pursuit of institutional self-interest, collusive cooperation with big business, and advocacy of warmongering interventionism or imperial expansion, the military reformers advanced modest programs that recognized and relied upon the advantages inherent in America's geographic and political situation and its great industrial and financial power. Having briefly experienced the problems of an overactive globalism during the decade after the war with Spain, military officers focused their attention on the Western Hemisphere and defense of North America, and they depended upon less violent means to secure American interests outside the nation's traditional sphere. Stressing efficiency, organization, planning, expertise, and social engineering, military officers gave the armed forces a modern character, adapting both the army and the navy to the changed nature of warfare and to America's new world position without, however, seeking an impossible absolute security or failing to balance the social and economic costs of the military establishment against both the possible harm of remaining less than fully prepared and the probability of an attack upon the United States.

While America and its military establishment came of age in the decades preceding the Great War, the officers who guided that modernization assumed a modest, adaptive, and conservative approach and remained fully aware of the domestic as well as the international dimensions of military policy. Their approach to reform suggests a pattern suitable for emulation by subsequent generations of military leaders.

West Point, New York   J.L.A.
January 1981

PART I

The Military Renaissance

Other work than waging war may incidentally devolve upon an Army . . . , but when other work is its only work, and the only one for which it is fitted, the so-called Army is but a police force.

Lieutenant John Bigelow, Jr., USA
"Discussion," *JMSIUS,* IV (1883), 406

CHAPTER 1

The Turning Point

T HE OBITUARIES CONTAINED no obvious omission.[1] Emphasizing the recent World War, they traced in passing the path that had led Hunter Liggett from West Point to France and to command of more soldiers than any previous American general save Pershing. Both the *New York Times* and the *Army and Navy Journal* quickly noted the decade of frontier duty that had followed Liggett's graduation in 1879 and only briefly recounted his turn-of-the-century service in Cuba and Mindanao, his later assignment to the War College and the General Staff, and his prewar duties in the American-governed Philippines. Liggett's postwar direction of the forces based at Coblenz, home of America's army of occupation while President Wilson negotiated the peace he hoped the League of Nations would permanently secure, and Liggett's preretirement command of the new Ninth Corps, with headquarters in San Francisco, received equally scant attention. The centerpiece of each article, the apparent highlight of forty-two years' service, was clearly wartime command of the American First Army in its climactic assault on the Hindenburg Line, a post Liggett had won by his skillful handling of the First Army Corps during the second Marne campaign, the reduction of the St. Mihiel salient, and the opening of the Meuse-Argonne offensive.

3

Focusing on the general's contribution to victory in 1918, the two sketches failed to recognize that far more than a lifetime separated the army that Major General Liggett left in 1921 from the force that Cadet Liggett prepared to join as he entered the Military Academy in the summer of 1875, almost two years before President Grant left office. Those two armies had existed in quite different worlds, and the traditional, backward-looking character of the latter had little in common with the modern force from which Liggett retired. The obituaries thus neglected perhaps the most notable aspects of Hunter Liggett's career: He had entered the army at a turning point in its history; his duties had revealed the path taken by the army as it moved from that point of departure; and his forty-two years' service had witnessed the army's transformation.

As Lieutenant Liggett trekked westward in the autumn of 1879, he headed for the Montana Territory and the Fifth Infantry, which had established itself at Fort Keogh in the Division of the Missouri's Department of Dakota as a consequence of the 1875–76 war with the Sioux. Fifty-eight of his sixty-seven West Point classmates made a similar journey, reporting to one of the infantry or cavalry regiments scattered across the trans-Mississippi West. With the minuscule American army of fewer than twenty-seven thousand officers and men dispersed among 142 small garrisons, the Class of 1879 would not reunite in the foreseeable future. So dispersed, the West Pointers immersed themselves in the routine that had engaged American officers for nearly a century. Regarding themselves as civilization's advanced guard, generations of army officers had performed duties more appropriate to a constabulary than a military force. They had explored the unknown, assisted commerce, escorted settlers, and sought to keep the peace on the frontier. For the army and the American Indian, performance of that most traditional of the army's tasks regularly led to conflict, and during the next decade, Lieutenant Liggett played his part in that perennial struggle.[2]

Aside from the danger, performance of that mission also subjected Liggett and his fellow officers to a frontier life of almost unrelieved discomfort and monotony. Except during the rare periods of actual warfare, the soldiers spent their days in a dreary round of guard duty, road building, cutting timber for fuel and barracks, raising vegetables to supplement the army ration, escorting civilians and convoys across the Great American Desert, searching for deserters—itself a commentary on the quality of frontier army life—and, only rarely, drilling or target practice. As sergeants supervised most of those duties, the officers passed much of each day in gambling on cards or billiards, hunting—according to one frontier officer the "principal recreation" at Fort Sill in the Oklahoma Territory—and drinking. Except for periodic leaves, often of several months, only an assignment to a Washington bureau, to the Military Academy as an instructor, or to one of the schools of application as a student broke that routine for the officers at the many posts too rugged or too exposed to permit female companionship.[3]

At the more established posts, however, the ladies of officers' row often pooled their china, silver, and linen to present formal dinners—especially for Christmas, Independence Day, weddings, visiting generals, and the unexpected "stray visitor from the outside world." Seeking to approximate the civilized life they had known before joining their husbands on the frontier, the officers' wives also organized post bands, which played for dress parades and entertained at balls and concerts, and presented minstrel shows and other theatricals. In addition, some posts established small libraries, and periodical literature quickly passed from hand to hand until it disintegrated. As one officer recalled, "Life in garrison was somewhat monotonous."[4]

Scattered among small garrisons throughout the nation, supported by a skimpy budget of forty million dollars, and still preoccupied by guerrilla warfare on the frontier, the army to which Lieutenant Liggett reported in 1879 was already becoming an anachronism. Even as he learned the skills of frontier warfare, thoughtful officers could foresee an early end to Indian hostilities. In William T. Sherman's annual report for 1883, for instance, the commanding general described Indian warfare "as substantially eliminated." The following year, the reports of the army's departmental and divisional commanders revealed to Secretary of War Robert T. Lincoln "no disturbance to cause the firing of a single musket," prompting the secretary to remark upon the "unprecedented quiet among the Indians." By the close of the decade, the army's new commanding general noted the passing of an era and described the century-long struggle to "subdu[e] the warlike tribes of Indians" as "nearly accomplished."[5]

The imminent victory on the frontier did more than close a long chapter in the army's history; it also raised troubling questions about the army's future. Officers probably agreed with the editor of the *United Service,* who feared that a nation long "accustomed to think of the army as chiefly concerned with Indian matters" would be unable to "conceive of any use to which the army can be put when once the Indian has ceased to trouble." Quartermaster General Samuel B. Holabird's fear that the army would thus disappear along with warlike Indians apparently prompted worried discussions among officers concerned about the possible abolition of the army.[6]

Army officers knew, of course, that their service had other uses: defending the coasts; repelling invasion; and, in extremis, preserving domestic order. Such responsibilities came to civilian notice, however, only in moments of crisis, of which there had been few between the struggle for independence and the recent Civil War. By the time Lieutenant Liggett joined his regiment, a recurrence of sectional conflict seemed improbable, and even army officers doubted the likelihood of invasion. In 1880, for example, General Sherman described the latter notion as "simply preposterous."[7]

Defense of the coasts seemed another matter. A host of nations had sufficient naval strength to bombard coastal cities or to conduct limited incursions, perhaps as a means of forcing the resolution of some hypothetical diplomatic impasse. However uncertain the prospect of such an attack, army officers felt an obligation to look to the nation's coastal defenses. They did not care for what they saw.

Except as weakened by age and disrepair, the army retained essentially the same system of fortifications, begun in 1817, that had guarded the coasts during the Civil War. In 1865 that system had nevertheless comprised smoothbore cannon of enough power and range to destroy enemy warships and, at most vulnerable points on the nation's coasts, vertical-walled, brick and stone forts of sufficient strength to protect artillerymen from naval bombardment. That system had then been, recalled General Schofield, "among the best in the world." By 1875, however, largely because Congress then completely stopped appropriating money for fortifications, physical decay and technological innovation had rendered that formerly powerful system, claimed West Point's Professor Peter S. Michie, "absolutely more dangerous to the defenders than to the enemy." Converting to rifled ordnance, the world's principal navies in the meantime acquired guns of sufficient accuracy and power to pound a masonry fort to rubble, and protecting the hulls of their new steam-powered warships with iron plates, those navies could accomplish that destruction while nimbly maneuvering beyond the range of smoothbore cannon, whose projectiles could in any case now do little harm. During that period of rapid technological evolution, the rotting of wooden gun carriages had dropped much of America's ancient coastal ordnance to the ground, and Congressional parsimony had blocked construction of rifled coastal guns and their emplacement on disappearing carriages located within dispersed batteries protected by concrete and low earthen embankments. Even third-rate naval powers like Chile could consequently use their modern cruisers to threaten American seaports with destruction.[8]

Having swept aside those obsolete coastal batteries, an invader would face an army that was ill-equipped, weakened by decentralization in structure and operation, irrationally administered, inappropriately trained, unsure of its purpose, and lacking an effective system of reinforcement. Each year since the Civil War had reduced its capacity for conventional conflict. The "new" weapons and uniforms approved in the 1870s represented only modest modifications of Civil War items. To arm infantry and cavalry units, for example, an 1872 board had selected single-shot, breech-loading weapons that fired metallic cartridges. As such weapons had seen service in the Civil War, they represented less a major departure than a minor improvement of older models. Though less tactically significant, Lieutenant Liggett's soldiers also received the familiar Union blue uniforms until stocks were exhausted in 1880.[9] Finding his soldiers uniformed and equipped like Civil War veterans, Liggett soon discovered they were also led by Civil War heroes, his own chain of command reading like an honor roll of the war's generals: Nelson A. Miles; Alfred H. Terry; Philip H. Sheridan; William T. Sherman.[10]

The uniforms, equipment, and leaders of the frontier army were not the only relics of the past. Having no tactical unit larger than a regiment, the army lacked the organizational cohesion of its Civil War counterpart. The "division" in which Liggett served was a geographic expression with largely administrative functions. Certainly, it never took the field as a military unit. Even regimental commanders seldom assembled their entire force, and the units never engaged in maneuvers like those held annually in Europe. Staff colleges might have compensated for the lack of field experience with larger units, but the army had none in the 1870s. Consequently, only the Civil War veterans knew how to employ large formations.[11] Should some unforeseen crisis call for the emergency creation of an expanded force, the army had no system for mobilizing and training the men. As in the past, it would rely upon hastily trained civilians whose large numbers might compensate for lack of experience.[12] At the highest levels, too, the army's organizational structure had returned to prewar patterns less suited to combat than to such routine administrative tasks as pay, procurement, construction, and the provision of personnel, legal, and medical services. No central

agency studied the army's possible use in war. No commanding general
had the authority to ensure that the administrative bureaus adhered to a
common plan or prepared the army for anticipated duties.[13] Such decentralization and lack of planning left the army no choice but to respond to any new crisis in an ad hoc fashion, substituting improvisation
for careful analysis and purposeful preparation.

Although few officers thought it likely that a major invasion would
test that lack of preparation, and almost no one expected any requirement to raise a large expeditionary force for use beyond the nation's
borders,[14] the army had nevertheless clearly reached a turning point.
Success in the guerrilla warfare of the frontier spelled the end of its duties there, and a long list of deficiencies cast doubt on the army's capacity to defend the coasts, its most likely role in a conventional conflict. As
Colonel August V. Kautz warned the military and civilian readers of
Century Magazine, the army's duties were "destined soon to change."[15]
Just how much Hunter Liggett would soon learn.

William Sowden Sims first took the Naval Academy entrance exami-
nations in 1875, the year that Hunter Liggett successfully passed into
West Point. Having been a poor student, however, Sims failed on his
first attempt, finally entering Annapolis with the Class of 1880, which
commenced its studies in the summer before Grant left office.

Like Liggett, Sims entered a service bound to its past, unsure of its
future, but certain of the approach of a turning point in its history. In
the forty-two years following his graduation Sims rose from midshipman to admiral and to wartime command of all American naval forces
in Europe. Promotion and high command in the World War are, however, the least important parallels in the two officers' uncommonly successful careers. More significantly, Sims, like Liggett, saw his service respond to its unsettled situation, and his assignments both illustrated
and embodied the transformation of the United States Navy.[16]

In June 1880, Midshipman Sims reported aboard the *Tennessee,*
flagship of the North Atlantic Squadron. Sims's assignment to a squadron may suggest that his ship formed part of a trained naval task force
capable of maneuvering, perhaps as part of a fleet, in close combat with
an opposing naval force. No such formation then existed in the American navy, whose squadrons instead consisted of heterogeneous collections of whatever vessels happened to be stationed on one of the oceans
in which the United States maintained a naval presence.[17] Rather than

train together, an activity for which their diversity of size, speed, range, motive power, weaponry, and maneuverability rendered them unfit, the ships of each squadron operated independently under its admiral's general supervision rather than his direct command. Like the army's divisions, the navy's squadrons were less combat units than geographically defined administrative echelons.

The independent operation of each squadron's ships stemmed in part from the nature of the navy's mission, which, except for the Civil War, had been the promotion and protection of American overseas commerce. Dispersed over the world's oceans in small, shallow-draft vessels, naval officers amassed data on ports and navigation and gathered information on new commercial opportunities. Although few pirates still roamed the seas to require naval protection for merchant ships, thus deployed the navy could rapidly respond when local authorities or an outbreak of violence in some foreign port threatened to disrupt trade. The United States consul or American businessman in some Latin American or Far Eastern port had learned that the mere presence of an American ship of war produced a quieting effect and protected American interests.[18] In a sense, America's army and navy shared a common mission; both brought American commerce and civilization to not always appreciative populations.

Strangely perhaps, that mission also imposed upon young Sims a life in certain respects not unlike Liggett's. For life aboard an American warship on foreign station, like life on the frontier, contained much that was routine and monotonous and not a little physical discomfort. Except for leaves and shore duty, often while the ship underwent repairs, only the time in port interrupted long periods at sea with only water, fish, an occasional bird, and a few officers for company. While at sea the ship might engage in hydrographic work or render aid to a merchantman, but American men-of-war accomplished little target practice and even more rarely participated in squadron maneuvers—or evolutions. Only eight years out of Annapolis in 1882, young Bradley A. Fiske began to find the navy "an extremely uninteresting place for a man who had already learned virtually all there was of the naval profession, and who could see no prospect ahead except a tiresome alternation of monotonous cruises at sea and profitless tours on shore."[19]

When in port, the officers took in the sights, often making extensive journeys inland, enjoyed the hospitality provided by local officials, United States consuls, and other ships, or engaged in diplomacy—often with some commercial object in view. Thus separated from their families for long periods, naval officers, like their landbound brothers, often took to drink. "We had a great deal of leisure," recalled Fiske, "too much, in fact; so I am surprised now that we kept as good as we did." Moreover, "the conduct of some of us was not such as our parents would approve."[20]

At the highest organizational levels, too, parallels existed between the two services. A series of quasi-independent bureaus also controlled the navy, building and repairing its ships, purchasing its supplies, recruiting, assigning, and paying its personnel, and providing legal and medical services. In periods of continuity, when routine dominated naval life, those bureaus performed their duties to good effect. To forecast or to respond to new situations, however, the navy relied upon ad hoc boards appointed for short periods and confined to specific problems. No general staff studied the future or ensured that the bureaus worked in harmony as they prepared the navy to meet it.

Nor, except for the skills required to handle a single ship and its weapons, did the navy prepare its officers. Assigned to ships that operated singly, naval captains learned little about maneuvering with other vessels. In command of squadrons that rarely assembled, the service's admirals had little practical experience in the control of naval formations. Having no war college to impart even theoretical knowledge, the navy left its officers either to ignore the study of war or to pursue it independently, as they elected.[21]

Sims's initial assignment aboard the *Tennessee* illustrates another aspect of the navy he entered. During the previous fifteen years, naval science had undergone a revolution: Iron and steel plates replaced wooden hulls, permitting the construction of larger, less vulnerable warships; steam engines supplemented and then replaced sails, and screw propellers superseded sidewheels, vastly improving speed and maneuverability; breech-loading, rifled guns firing projectiles capable of piercing the new metal hulls displaced smaller caliber, smoothbore, muzzle-loading cannon, dramatically increasing the destructive power of the world's navies. During that period of change, the United States Navy stagnated. The Congress authorized but ten new ships, two iron-plated torpedo boats and eight small steam vessels. In 1880, one of the latter, the wooden frigate *Trenton,* was the American navy's finest ship. Sims's ship, a wooden-hulled steam vessel that was also fully rigged for sailing, was even less advanced. Launched in 1865, the *Tennessee* posed no serious threat to the modern frigates or battleships of the principal foreign navies.[22]

David Dixon Porter, hero of the Civil War and the navy's senior admiral since 1870, described his entire force in similar if more forceful terms. Characterizing the American fleet as "all on paper," Porter told Congress that most of its vessels "no more represented ships of war than a person in the last stages of consumption represents an able-bodied man." The force of cruising vessels ostensibly poised to raid enemy commerce and protect America's own merchant ships in the event of war had but twenty-six warships capable of going to sea. Of those, only eighteen had sufficient "speed to pursue or power to escape from a swift cruiser." The scores of other cruising vessels on the navy's lists were deteriorating, antiquated hulks. In Porter's opinion, the navy consequently could not perform two of its wartime missions: raiding an enemy's commerce or protecting American traders. The other wartime task, helping the army guard the nation's coasts, fell to the twenty-four monitors, for the most part laid up and rotting in various shipyards. With few exceptions relics of the Civil War, Porter described the monitors as "simply useless." Capable of an average speed of only six knots, they could not "go to sea without being towed, and their armor would not withstand even small rifled guns." Their own obsolete cannon could not penetrate "four-inch armor at a distance of 500 yards," a shortcoming characteristic of many of the navy's guns. In an 1882 report, Secretary of the Navy William E. Chandler confirmed that his service had "not one modern high-powered cannon." Although the recent conversion of some Civil War era smoothbore cannon had provided the navy with a few useful weapons, altogether they constituted but 6 percent of the navy's inventory of 2,664 cannon. In sum the United States Navy reminded Admiral Porter of the "ancient Chinese forts on which dragons were painted to frighten away the enemy."[23]

When Sims entered the navy, Admiral Porter's doubts concerning the service's ability to accomplish its wartime duties were but one of the worries that forced naval officers to ponder the future of their service. By the start of the century's last quarter, they had even begun to question the navy's need to perform its traditional peacetime duties: the protection and the promotion of America's overseas trade. In the years before the Civil War, when the navy had first defined its role in support of the merchant marine, American ships had carried more than three quarters of the nation's foreign trade, a share that had peaked above 80 percent in the 1840s. But the failure of American builders quickly to adopt new maritime technology based upon steam and iron and Britain's willingness to subsidize its own carriers had initiated a decline in the United States merchant fleet, whose share of American commerce had fallen well below 70 percent by 1860. During the Civil War, the flight of American carriers to foreign flags in hopes of avoiding the depredations of Confederate raiders like the famed *Alabama* accelerated the descent. By the end of hostilities American ships consequently carried but a quarter of the nation's overseas trade, and that share had fallen to 17 percent the year Sims entered the navy.[24]

The gradual disappearance of American-owned merchant ships from the world's oceans produced in thoughtful naval officers feelings akin to the alarm felt by the army's leaders at the prospect of the Plains Indians' imminent defeat. Since the Civil War expansion of the navy to more than six hundred ships armed with some five thousand guns, the fortunes of the service had declined with those of the national merchant marine, leading naval officers like Lieutenant J. D. J. Kelley to conclude: "If there were no merchant marine there would be no need for a navy either to foster commerce or to police and survey the seas." The American navy might one day then consist of "coast-defence vessels manned by . . . such artillerymen as had their sea-legs." Another junior officer satirized both aspects of the turning point facing the navy by the 1880s. For a Naval Institute essay contest, Master Carlos G. Calkins reconstructed the drama played out whenever foreign naval officers visited an American warship in some distant port. Calling attention to the American navy's lack of a peacetime mission, those officers invariably first asked: "Why do you come here, where no merchant vessel ever shows your flag?" After examining the American vessel, they inevitably remarked on its technological inferiority by inquiring: "How did you get here in such an antiquated and clumsy craft?"[25]

The navy clearly faced a turning point; there existed little demand for its traditional peacetime services, and it lacked the capacity to perform its likely wartime tasks.

To this point the description of the changed situation facing the army and navy has concerned essentially national developments. The decline of the American merchant marine and the army's imminent mastery of the West suggested to thoughtful officers that the United States would have little future use for military forces fit only for policing the seas and pacifying Indians—the services' traditional peacetime responsibilities. Technological innovation, moreover, had demonstrated the inability of either service to perform its most important wartime task— guarding America's coasts, whether from forts along the shoreline or from ships at sea. Surely the loss of a mission and the stark physical decay of the nation's military equipment would alone have convinced most officers that the services had reached a turning point. Foreign developments, however, also pointed to a similar conclusion.

Evidence from abroad indicated that the very nature of warfare was changing, convincing many officers of the end of America's era of free security. Referring to the Franco-Austrian conflict of 1859 and to Prussia's defeats of Austria (1866) and France (1870), Lieutenant Arthur L. Wagner concluded that modern wars "arise quickly and cannot be long foreseen." Moreover, future conflicts would be of too short duration "to enable an unprepared nation to build up its military strength while struggling with its foe."[26]

The speed with which modern wars reached their decisive phase stemmed largely from the same developments in science, transportation, communication, manufacturing, and administration that were transforming Western societies. On the one hand, technological sophistication meant that nations could no longer improvise ships, forts, and guns in an emergency. Because modern weapons took months, perhaps years, to build, they must be prepared before war threatened—even before an obvious enemy appeared on the horizon. On the other, even a poor and unpopulous nation that prepared such weapons in advance, trained men in their use, and created systems for the mobilization and concentration of its forces could possess, warned Colonel Henry Boies, "an almost invincible power, before which numbers and wealth and ordinary elements of national strength may be swept away like chaff."[27]

To naval captain William T. Sampson the lesson seemed obvious; "preparation for war that is deferred until war is imminent will result in certain defeat." In order to deter an attack or to prevent a decisive early defeat, the United States, which had industrial resources in abundance, must divert a modest portion of its national strength to the preparation of well-trained, well-equipped military forces. Such preparation, of course, involved considerable expense; that much military officers acknowledged. The costs of a "sudden, sharp, and decisive" defeat were, however, twofold. Not only must the United States repair its own losses, it must expect to pay an indemnity—according to Lieutenant Eugene Griffin, now "one of the essential articles of a treaty of peace. As war becomes more expensive yearly, *the cost of defeat increases proportionally.*"[28]

Adequate military preparation for modern war also had a human dimension: a reserve of men already trained to use the sophisticated new weaponry. Until the nineteenth century's last quarter American mili-

tary officers had given little thought to that problem; the veterans of
the Civil War supplied just such a reserve. By the 1890s, however, General Schofield judged them "no longer physically able to bear arms,"
and army officers began to encourage federal support for improvements
in the states' militia. So long as military officers remained confident
that no European power had the maritime capacity to transport any very
large number of troops in a single movement, however, the service's requests for trained reserves remained modest. First priority went to modern equipment for the regulars, small increases in the size of the active
forces, improvements in their training, and the reorganization of tactical units and administrative agencies.[29]

While military officers contemplated the significance of the suddenness of modern warfare, they also turned their attention abroad to consider the conditions that seemed to make international conflict more
likely. As they did so, American officers studied current history, analyzed international crises, and drew from each conclusions about the inadequacies of their own nation's military preparations.

Naval writing, for example, revealed the powerful influence of the
1873–74 *Virginius* affair. To naval officers, the incident demonstrated
the diplomatic and naval dangers of relying upon an antiquated naval
force. In 1873, a Spanish gunboat patrolling the Caribbean in search of
ships attempting to smuggle arms and men to Cuban insurgents seized
the filibustering ship *Virginius,* which illegally flew the American flag.
After a hasty court-martial in Santiago, the Spanish summarily shot fifty-three of the unfortunate ship's passengers and crew, some of whom
were Americans. Despite the ship's illegal activities, the American public considered the speedy executions totally unwarranted, and it raised
an immediate outcry. Fearing war with Spain, the American government hastily assembled its decrepit navy at Key West, where it eyed the
superior Spanish fleet in Cuba.[30]

Following that experience, naval officers generally agreed with naval
lieutenant Robley D. Evans that the *Virginius* affair had shown the
American navy to be a "sham." Evans described the activities of the
American fleet as "making faces at the Spaniards," whose modern
force contained seven armored ships. Evans also declared that his fellow
officers were "dreadfully mortified" at the state of America's wooden
ships and outmoded guns; "two modern vessels of war would have done
us up in thirty minutes." Lieutenant Seaton Schroeder agreed. Comparing the Spanish flagship to his own vessel, he wrote that "none of

her IX-inch smooth-bores could send a shell through the armor plate of the Spaniard."[31]

Army writers, while also cognizant of the implications of the *Virginius* incident, made more frequent reference to the 1880 Chilean bombardment of Callao, Peru, during the War of the Pacific, and to the 1882 British bombardment of Alexandria, a step in the reduction of Egypt to the level of a protectorate. Those two engagements provided two important parallels and an obvious conclusion. In each case the naval forces had modern armored ships with high-powered rifled guns, like America's potential enemies, and the harbor defenders employed older smoothbore cannon fired from masonry forts, similar to those in the United States. The fate of Peru and Egypt thus demonstrated to army officers what a major power might do to America's coastal cities. By a similar logic the frequency of such international incidents suggested a growing likelihood of American involvement in war.[32] Foreign affairs as well as national developments thus led military officers to conclude that their services were in the midst of a crisis.

During the forty-two years that Hunter Liggett and William S. Sims served in the armed forces, officers of both services responded to that crisis. Liggett, Sims, and their fellows defined its nature, debated the appropriate responses, and with the support of their civilian superiors set the armed forces on new paths. Through a process similar to that transforming American society, the military establishment abandoned traditional assumptions, discarded old methods, and replaced them with values and institutions of a decidedly modern character. To relate the full extent of that transformation will require several chapters, but even the bare outlines of the two officers' careers, which commenced during the Grant era and were closing as Wilson left office, suggest the character of the coming change. For each man's service encompassed the period of transformation, and both their careers embodied the new trends.

The most obvious changes in that process are quantitative. Hunter Liggett left an army some nine times larger than the one he entered, and it disposed of a budget almost thirty times bigger than that of 1879. As measured by the increased number and quality of the navy's ships, Sims saw his service climb from a rank alongside Chile to parity with Great Britain, long the world's premier naval power. During those same years, the navy expanded from less than ten thousand officers and men supported by expenditures of almost thirteen million dollars to a force of nearly one hundred thousand disposing of appropriations approaching a half billion dollars.[33]

More significant by far, however, are the qualitative changes. Three times Liggett went abroad to Cuba and the Philippines, where the United States exercised its power in the imperial fashion of its European peers. For five years he served the newly created General Staff, which sought to coordinate the administrative bureaus and then to plan purposefully for the future. Both activities challenged the army's traditionally defensive and continental orientation and its usually ad hoc response to new situations. Liggett also witnessed army efforts to rationalize its organization by creating tactical divisions and by concentrating its forces at a few large posts where commanders might train their soldiers in new methods and maneuver their units as parts of larger formations. As president of the War College, Colonel Liggett sat at the apex of the army's new system of officer education, a group of schools that tested the professional competence of the officer corps, gave officers theoretical instruction in the methods of modern warfare, and filled students with a sense of the army's new role and place in society. In the World War, as a division, corps, and army commander, General Liggett participated in the previously unthinkable: intervention in the affairs of Europe in close association with a military alliance. He commanded troops that fought with machine guns, airplanes, tanks, and motorized transport—none of which had existed four decades earlier. Returning to the United States after occupation duty in Germany, Liggett became directly responsible for one of the corps areas whose units were to provide a framework for the rational mobilization and training of the millions of men necessary for any future expedition abroad.[34]

In Sims's case, too, the qualitative changes illustrated by his own career seem the most important dimension of his service. A reformer in the progressive and muckraking mold, Sims, during the course of his career, waged one long battle with the bureaus that controlled the navy.[35]

He began that struggle in the mid-1890s while serving as an intelligence officer aboard the *Charleston*, then assigned to the Asiatic Station. During that time Sims initiated his subsequently bitter attacks on bureau-designed ships that showed too little appreciation for the demands of modern naval warfare and upon the bureaucratic inertia that delayed such reforms as the introduction of superior gunnery techniques developed by the seagoing officers of the navy's line. Sims was also a longtime advocate of a naval general staff, which he thought would enable the navy's line officers to wrest control of the service from the deskbound technicians who directed the Washington bureaus. That campaign culminated on the eve of American intervention in the World War with the establishment of a rather weak version of such a body.

As a young officer in a wooden-hulled, sail-powered navy devoted to the protection and promotion of commerce, Sims observed two other important changes: In the 1880s the navy finally adopted steel and steam, the protected cruiser *Philadelphia*, built in 1888, being the first ship of that new navy on which Sims served. During the nineteenth century's last quarter, the navy also redefined its peacetime mission and commenced a corresponding reorganization of its naval forces. No longer would the ships of a squadron cruise singly, in peacetime primarily involved in the affairs of underdeveloped nations and in war engaged in close defense of the coasts or ship-versus-ship duels with enemy cruisers.

Before Sims retired, the navy sought to facilitate accomplishment of all its goals by creating a battleship fleet capable of winning control of the seas. As captain of the *Minnesota*, one of four ships in a division of battleships, and commander of a flotilla of thirty destroyers, Sims had a hand in that change, helping develop techniques for the safe maneuvering, day or night, of ships that operated at high speed in close formation in all kinds of weather and creating an American fleet capable of contesting with an enemy's main force for control of the sea.

Always a thinker and a "paper man" who responded more to his intellect than his instincts, Sims also became an early advocate of naval education. His career-long study of naval science and warfare continually helped him break free of the past and the traditional methods that blinded others to change. And while a student at the new Naval War College, he received training that directly contributed to his success with the Atlantic Destroyer Flotilla. Twice Sims served the college as its president, and he forcefully urged the navy to consider attendance as a prerequisite for nomination to high command.

During his years with the destroyer flotilla, Sims also contemplated the navy's lack of an efficient system for expanding its forces in the event of a major conflict. He consequently prompted the creation of the reserve flotilla, a partial solution to that problem.

Selection as commander of United States Naval Forces Operating in European Waters seemed the logical climax of a career devoted to redefinition of the navy's mission, the preparation of naval forces capable of accomplishing new tasks, and the creation of the educational, organizational, and administrative systems necessary to support both the new forces and the new mission. In another way as well Sims's wartime assignment reflected how far the navy had come; in the late nineteenth century no one would have contemplated American naval involvement in the affairs of Europe in close cooperation with Great Britain.

By the time Wilson left office, the old army and the old navy had in almost every respect ceased to exist, replaced by new services fully reflecting the fundamental transformation of American society. The officers who shaped the nature of the services' evolution were those who shared Hunter Liggett's "zeal and ability, his hunger for learning, and his assiduous study of his profession." They also had, as Elting Morison said of William Sims, the ability to "imagine reality." They could consequently recognize the forces changing the world in which they lived, grasp the implications of those changes for the armed forces, and define the response required of the army and navy to adapt each to an unfolding future seen only in the mind's eye.[36]

CHAPTER 2

The Debate over Missions

ALTHOUGH THE ARMY and navy ultimately responded in a similar manner to the crisis each faced by the last quarter of the nineteenth century, the intraservice debates of that decade and the next revealed profound disagreement over the proper reaction to both each service's imminent loss of its raison d'être and the sheer physical decay of its equipment. Some officers looked to the past and sought changes likely to give new vitality to the missions that had occupied their service during the preceding century. Others focused on contemporary developments and found guideposts to reform in indications that the United States had entered a new era.

Those two responses implied creation of quite disparate military organizations suited to quite different tasks. Army and navy leaders who looked to the past for guidance would prepare the services for continued performance of such essentially nonmilitary tasks as controlling Indians, quelling civil disorder—whether at home or abroad—and promoting America's overseas trade. Such duties required armed forces fitted for the intimidation of civilians and nonindustrialized societies, the latter task sometimes performed in cooperation with the other major powers. Should that cooperation break down and a major power become a military threat to the United States, those officers who looked to the past

would rely upon America's physical isolation, vast size, and great resources to deter an attack or ensure eventual victory—even if preparation for great-power conflict were delayed until the very eve of war. In
contrast, army and navy officers who anticipated the commencement of
a new era of great-power rivalry sought to arm, organize, and train their
services for contests with those states possessing the most powerful new
weapons. Believing that military readiness alone could prevent disaster
in such a struggle, those officers argued that the principal peacetime
duty of each service must become development of the nation's military
potential and preparation of its armed forces against the possibility of
war with a major power.

     That possibility had little influence on the first phase of naval mod-
ernization, which instead resumed construction of a "peace navy"
suited to the continued protection and promotion of American overseas
commerce.[1] Tradition and the rationale of two naval advisory boards
easily account for the initial rehabilitation along those lines.
     Except for brief periods, the United States had always maintained a
peace navy, and many late-nineteenth-century naval officers accepted
the assumptions that had justified creation of a commercially oriented
force following the War of 1812. Apparently sharing the Enlighten-
ment belief that free trade would both economically benefit all nations
and serve as an instrument of international peace, those officers assumed that the United States would inevitably become a great trading
nation, a goal the navy would help achieve by building ships designed
to protect America's overseas commerce and by deploying them where
they could promote mercantile growth. As Great Britain, whose interests often coincided with those of the United States, dominated the sea
lanes between the United States and Europe, whose powers maintained
order in their ports, the American navy had few duties there. The violence against which United States trade required protection arose instead in the ports and waters of nonindustrialized states, and in those
regions the nation's consuls and businessmen often sought the presence
of a Western ship of war to prevent local disorders and the violation of
treaty privileges. While patrolling such distant areas, moreover, the
United States Navy could promote American commerce by opening
new ports and gathering information on possible new markets.[2]
     As measured by European standards, none of those activities re-
quired a powerful battle fleet. Rather than great battleships, the peace-

time promotion of commerce demanded a host of smaller vessels capable of cruising the world's oceans for extended periods. There, in cooperation with the European navies, the ships of America's squadrons would intimidate economically undeveloped nations and ensure the free flow of international trade.

In the event of war with another great power—a development considered highly improbable—swift American cruisers would quickly destroy the enemy's merchant marine and thus deliver a devastating economic blow. Protected by size and distance, the United States would meanwhile build a battle fleet capable of gaining control of the seas—if commerce raiding alone had not already forced an opponent to sue for peace. A navy designed primarily for its commercial uses in peace would thus suffice to bring victory in the unlikely event of war.[3]

The majority report of the first Naval Advisory Board, appointed in 1881 to provide Secretary of the Navy William H. Hunt with recommendations for the rehabilitation of America's crumbling fleet, reflected the influence of that peace-navy tradition. Virtually ignoring war and defense of the coasts, the majority based the navy's modernization upon a

> proper consideration [of] the various requirements of the different squadrons for surveying, deep-sea sounding, the protection and advancement of American commerce, exploration, the protection of American life and property endangered by wars between foreign countries, and service in support of American policy in matters where foreign governments are concerned.

Only the latter two tasks even hinted at a truly military use of naval power, and the board derived from the listed objects its recommended construction of an "unarmored" fleet of seventy cruising vessels protected only by thin iron or steel plates but strong enough to guarantee American access to the ports of the nonindustrialized world.[4]

Although the board's majority acknowledged the danger of basing defense of the coasts upon Civil War ironclads that did "not compare favorably with those of foreign nations in size, speed, armor, or armament . . . ," those officers nevertheless suggested a defensive augmentation of only five rams and twenty-five torpedo boats. Those new craft, America's geographic isolation, and the use of the navy's cruising fleet in raids upon an opponent's commerce would, the majority hoped, "hold a naval enemy in check until armored vessels [those with large-caliber guns and heavy iron plates] can be supplied to perfect the defense and undertake offensive operations." The heavy ironclad's propensity to rapid obsolescence and American industry's inability to construct the heavy guns they required also served to justify the majority's decision to regard armored ships as virtually irrelevant to "the work of the United States Navy."[5]

In 1881 the navy's work as an ally of American commercial expansion captured little public support. Other developments, however, were already laying the foundation for a resurgence of popular interest in naval reform. The worldwide expansion of Europe's trade and investment, the propensity of its principal powers to territorial acquisitions, and French efforts to construct a canal through Panama threatened to undermine American access to Latin American markets and even suggested a future European assault on that region's political independence. East Asia, a long-standing object of American missionary and commercial interest and another possible outlet for America's goods, had already become the target of an intense European imperial rivalry that threatened to close the region to American trade. The nation's swelling industrial capacity and presumably growing need for foreign markets served to exacerbate fears of further European expansion. Resurrection of the United States Navy might somehow thwart European imperialism just as a stronger navy appealed to the heightened sense of national pride apparent long before the turn-of-the-century clash with Spain.[6]

If the public's interest in a larger navy remained incipient, many in Washington were already drawn to plans for rehabilitation of a commercially oriented peace navy. Protectionist Republicans, embarrassed by the Treasury's large and growing surplus, could use expenditures on new ships to counter Congressional pressure for tariff reduction. Within the executive, both navy secretary Hunt and his predecessor, Richard W. Thompson, had advertised the navy's aid to "mercantile interests" and its ability to promote "the most amicable commercial relations" with "all quarters of the globe." Secretary of State James G. Blaine had similar objects in view, particularly in Latin America. With Republicans in control of both the White House and Congress and apparently aware of the link between national policy and naval power, the time seemed right for the navy's rehabilitation.[7]

The sheer size of the board's program, one hundred new ships, of which sixty-eight vessels costing over twenty-nine million dollars "should now be built," nevertheless filled both Congress and the administration with consternation. A hot summer of committee hearings and debate led frustrated congressmen to authorize but two steel cruisers, for which they appropriated no money, and to request the new naval secretary, William E. Chandler, to appoint a second advisory body.[8]

Although its membership varied, this new Naval Advisory Board, presided over by Commodore Robert W. Shufeldt, endured for six years, and it not only gave advice on the navy's size and the character of its ships but also submitted designs for newly authorized vessels and supervised their construction from contract to acceptance trials. Despite a near total change in membership—only Lieutenant Edward W. Very also served the earlier body—the Shufeldt board proceeded along quite similar lines, recommending a peace-navy policy and a cruising fleet of seventy unarmored vessels. Having learned a lesson from the first board, however, Shufeldt's group described the seventy-vessel force as only an ultimate goal, one to be reached by annual increments over a ten-year period. Like its predecessor in virtually ignoring defense of the coasts, the Shufeldt board cryptically suggested construction of a single ram—if there was "prospect of war"—and refurbishment of four old monitors.[9]

That time the advocates of a peace navy won the support of Congress, which on March 3, 1883, approved three protected* cruisers, the U.S.S. *Atlanta*, *Boston*, and *Chicago*, and a dispatch boat, the U.S.S. *Dolphin*. Popularly known as the "White Squadron," those ships were to have steel hulls, breech-loading rifled guns, steam power—and sails! The latter enabled the cruising vessels of a nation without overseas coaling stations to remain at sea for long periods. And peace-navy concepts still dominated naval building programs when Congress again authorized new ships. In March 1885 it voted two more unarmored cruisers, the U.S.S. *Charleston* and *Newark*, and two new gunboats, the U.S.S. *Yorktown* and *Petrel*—ships designed largely for the navy's peacetime role as guardian of commerce.[10]

While adequate for the peacetime intimidation of nonindustrialized peoples and wartime attacks on enemy merchantmen, the navy's new ships lacked the armor and armament to engage successfully the armored ships forming the backbone of European fleets. During the early eighties, then, peace-navy concepts continued to shape American naval policy, to determine the navy's wartime strategy, and to guide America's shipbuilding programs. But resistance, too, had already appeared.

---

*Though protected by steel hulls and decks, the ships lacked the heavy side armor given later battleships and armored cruisers and were consequently known as protected cruisers.

The recommendations of the two advisory boards and the character of the resulting shipbuilding programs met immediate and sustained opposition within the navy. Calling attention to changed conditions, and like Lieutenant Jacob W. Miller describing the "ideal navy" as "a fighting machine," naval officers who wished to rebuild the American fleet on a war basis attacked at every point the arguments for maintaining a peace navy.[11]

That attack proceeded along three general lines, the first of which challenged both the peacetime usefulness and the wartime effectiveness of a peace navy. The United States, wrote the staff officers constituting the minority of the first Naval Advisory Board, had little use for unarmored cruisers. Because the country had neither "colonies to protect" nor a compelling need to maintain "difficult commercial relations . . . with barbarous and half-civilized nations," those officers urged the navy to disband its far-flung squadrons of small, lightly armed cruisers, which then-Captain George Dewey claimed only "went from port to port to meet . . . wives . . . and to get letters from sweethearts." Other line officers agreed and pressed the government to make future construction of cruising vessels dependent upon a prior revival of the national merchant marine, which the advocates of a war navy regarded as a wartime auxiliary to the battle fleet rather than the navy's raison d'être. The speed of both modern communications and the new steam-powered vessels also convinced the war navy's proponents that the United States could keep its cruisers in home waters until a foreign disturbance arose to justify the dispatch of a ship or perhaps an entire squadron to the threatened point.[12]

In the event of war, claimed the minority report, the United States needed powerful cruisers, "first-rate of their type and . . . larger and more efficient vessels . . . [than] corresponding types in foreign navies." Having cruisers with "speed and guns enough to enable us to hold our own against any power in the world," wrote Admiral Porter, the United States could hope to defeat any enemy raiders preying on American commerce. The lightly armored, sail-and-steam-powered cruisers recommended by the two advisory boards lacked that capacity, and denied access to coal when neutrals closed their ports to belligerent ships, American cruisers proceeding home under sail would become easy victims of an enemy fleet. Lieutenant Francis M. Barber, otherwise an advocate of a cruiser navy, consequently urged the United States Navy, in the event of war, to advise the captains of its cruisers on foreign station: "*Stay in port*, . . . dismantle ships and send crew and officers home." If by some chance, however, American cruisers could keep the seas in a future conflict, proponents of a war navy nevertheless doubted the effectiveness of commerce raiding; surely an enemy's merchant vessels would quickly shift their registry and thereby gain the protection of a neutral flag.[13]

The second line of attack on the concept of a peace navy stressed the value of a fleet of armored ships, which alone could keep foreign naval vessels away from American ports and drive an enemy's blockading squadrons from American coastal waters. Because foreign (and in a war, neutral) merchant ships already carried the majority of America's overseas trade, a battle fleet that kept the nation's ports open to neutral commerce provided a more effective means of keeping that trade flowing than a fleet of cruisers. Only a battle fleet, moreover, could both intercept enemy convoys bringing men and war materials to the Western Hemisphere and close the offshore bases in, for example, Bermuda and the Caribbean from which an enemy would support a naval blockade or expeditionary army.[14]

Advocates of a battleship fleet suggested one other advantage of such a force: It would strengthen America's foreign policy. In that regard, naval officers most often had in mind defense of the Monroe Doctrine. But a battleship navy might also secure a future isthmian canal, guard America's neutral rights in the event of war between third parties, and defend American national honor, which as matters stood could even be challenged by the superior armored ships possessed by the navies of the larger South American powers. In the 1880s such a challenge was not impossible, and Passed Assistant Engineer N. B. Clark speculated that in a war with Chile the navy's antiquated monitors, then its only armored ships, "could not get to the seat of war, while the unarmored fleet could not fight with any chance of success after having done so."[15]

Proponents of a war navy lastly rejected the recommendations of the advisory boards because of the method by which the latter had determined the navy's proper size. Those boards had suggested a building program appropriate for "what is required in peace," which Rear Admiral Edward Simpson and Lieutenant Theodorus B. M. Mason described as "absurd," a "farce," and likely to lead to disaster. War being the "ultimate object of any armed force," wrote Lieutenant Roy C. Smith, the United States must build a navy suitable for war purposes, which must also determine the size of the national fleet. And during peace, the navy must organize and train its forces for their principal wartime duty—defense of the coasts. Armored battleships, not unarmored cruisers, were consequently the navy's "indispensable part," and in the opinion of Admiral Porter deserving "the first consideration."[16]

Within a decade after the appointment of that first Naval Advisory Board in 1881, the war-navy approach to policy began to dominate military thought. The proposals of a new naval secretary, the report of a new advisory body, and the influence of seapower as revealed in a new examination of naval history all indicated the extent of that domination.

Although Congress had authorized a single seagoing* battleship in 1886, the 1889 annual report of Secretary of the Navy Benjamin F. Tracy gave the best official indication of the triumph of those reformers advocating construction of a war navy.[17] America's present navy, Tracy explained to Congress, ranked below those of Europe's nine principal powers as well as the navies of both Turkey and China. The United States must consequently stop building "small, slow-going steamers, that are unnecessary in peace and useless in war." If the United States wished to protect its coasts, the navy must build enough seagoing armored ships to guard its ports, prevent blockade, and, by possessing the capability to threaten an opponent's own coasts, force an enemy to retain most of its ships in its home waters. Moreover, because future naval wars would be "short and sharp" and "fought out to the end with the force available at the beginning," the United States must abandon plans "to improvise a [battle] force in time of war." In Tracy's opinion, continuation of peace-navy policies constituted a "fatal mistake," and the "necessities of our vulnerable position . . . demand[ed] the immediate creation of two fleets of battle-ships." In addition to a fleet of twenty monitors for harbor defense, Tracy proposed an equal force of seagoing battleships, twelve of which he would use to guard the Atlantic and Gulf coasts while the remaining eight secured the Pacific.[18]

Asking Congress to refrain from voting any new unarmored cruisers, which he described as mere "adjuncts of an armored fleet," or any new gunboats, which he "condemned," Tracy recommended instead immediate appropriations for eight seagoing battleships. Totally reversing

*That designation distinguished recognizably modern battleships from the armored monitors like those of Civil War fame, which lacked the speed, freeboard, and coal capacity to operate effectively outside of harbors or other protected waters.

the priorities of the peace-navy advocates, the secretary also declared that commerce raiders might be improvised after the start of a war, and to ensure an adequate supply of fast merchant ships for such conversion, Tracy suggested a government subsidy to promote rehabilitation of the national mercantile fleet.[19]

While the ships that Tracy recommended provided the navy with an offensive capacity, the secretary denied that the United States had any "policy of military aggrandizement," which he characterized as "totally repugnant to American institutions."[20] Nor was Tracy necessarily mouthing platitudes. Too much has sometimes been made of the imagined passive or defensive qualities of the old navy as compared to the supposedly aggressive character of battleships. Even in time of peace, that old cruiser navy constantly engaged in operations that were offensive in their use of violence or intimidation vis-à-vis nonindustrialized peoples. In time of war, that same navy, now used as a commerce-raiding force, waged war on an enemy's citizens and their property, surely an offensive strategy despite its avoidance of direct assaults on the opponent's battle fleet. Whether America possessed a fleet of armored battleships or several squadrons of unarmored cruisers, the very existence of either force posed a threat of offensive action against other states; the naval reformers simply sought to make that threat more credible.

In a report submitted in January 1890, the Policy Board that Secretary Tracy had appointed the preceding July gave similar support to construction of a battleship navy. The board also carried Tracy's analysis to its logical conclusion and recommended thirty-five seagoing battleships instead of Tracy's mix of battleships and harborbound monitors. In addition, the board specifically eschewed pursuit of parity with European powers, asking only for a fleet sufficient to counter the largest force any European navy, restrained by continental and imperial responsibilities, might detach for service in the Western Hemisphere.[21]

While the Policy Board's report essentially followed the path already blazed by Tracy, one of its more revealing passages called attention to the dangers posed by America's growing export trade and the eventual construction of an isthmian canal. Because the United States was isolated, the board wrote, owned no colonies, had no "apparent desire to acquire them," possessed but a small carrying trade, and lacked significant commercial rivals, America's interests presently conflicted "with the interests of other nations to the least possible extent." The board found, however, no lack of "indications that this comparative isolation will soon cease to exist." A new canal, for example, would reverse world trade patterns, drawing Europeans into the New World in a scramble to control routes to the isthmus. The future would also undoubtedly bring ''sharp commercial competition with others in every part of the world.'' Though the board considered such dangers still years away, it reminded Congress of the time required to build a navy. The United States must therefore immediately begin adapting its naval policies to anticipated future conditions.[22]

The manner in which completion of an isthmian canal might threaten American interests and prompt construction of a battleship fleet also formed part of the argument developed in Captain Alfred Thayer Mahan's study of *The Influence of Sea Power upon History, 1660-1783*.[23] The analysis presented in the book that made him famous failed, however, to point unambiguously toward the need for an American naval resurgence or the creation of a battleship fleet.

In a general survey of the origins of seapower, Mahan identified two sets of circumstances that had historically caused nations to seek command of the sea. On the one hand, the growth of productive capacity within a nation desirous of exchanging goods abroad for items unattainable at home usually induced the construction of a commercial marine. Because many foreign ports had previously offered neither a safe haven nor a ready supply of the desired goods, commercial nations had frequently resorted to force to gain control of ports for the security of traders and resident agents alike. Such actions, Mahan claimed, led eventually to the creation of overseas colonies. Because piratical lawlessness had once threatened the routes between home ports and the colony, mercantile nations had also built navies and established overseas naval bases from which to guard their ships in transit. Three things then—production, shipping, and colonies—had encouraged some nations to create navies. In contrasting circumstances, even nations lacking those three elements had sometimes built armed fleets ''as a branch of the military establishment,'' usually with some aggressive purpose in mind.[24]

In Mahan's view, neither set of circumstances yet required the United States to maintain a strong navy. With neither a merchant marine and colonies to protect nor an aggressive purpose to pursue, ''the dwindling of . . . [America's] armed fleet and [the] general lack of interest in it are strictly logical consequences.''[25] True, America did have a large productive capacity, but the country could also live comfortably in its own ''little corner.'' Foreign ships already carried its overseas trade in peace, and neutrals might continue to do so in war—so long as America's navy could prevent a blockade. Because the United States had so little apparent need for seapower, Mahan rhetorically asked why "her people should desire that which, if possessed, must be defended at great cost?"[26]

His analysis also answered that question, noting the one development that might require a stronger navy: completion of an interoceanic canal through Central America. Like the Policy Board, Mahan concluded that a canal, whoever built it, would alter world trade patterns and change the Caribbean from a terminus to a strategically important defile. The trade routes eventually passing through that defile would draw Europeans to the New World, making it impossible for the United States to remain aloof from world affairs and giving it a position from which to control the flow of international trade. To meet that challenge and to take advantage of that opportunity, as well as to protect its coasts against wartime blockade, the United States needed a small fleet of battleships plus some Caribbean naval bases, and it must acquire both well before any threat of war appeared on the horizon.[27]

If the United States failed to do so, the canal would expose the nation's defenseless Pacific frontier to foreign attack, just as the Atlantic and Gulf were already vulnerable. With a fleet and bases, however, Mahan thought that the United States could keep its ports open and its coasts clear of blockade, thus ensuring that "the conditions of trade and commerce . . . remain, as far as possible, unaffected by external war."[28] Like Secretary Tracy and the Policy Board, Mahan proposed construction of seagoing battleships as the best means to defend America's coasts, keep open its ports even during hostilities, and guard American interests against Europeans seeking to strengthen their strategic position in the New World.

Differences among army officers lacked the clarity and depth of the issues that for a time divided the naval service. Nor did army thought experience a comparably dramatic transition during the eighties or nineties. Unlike plans for a new navy, which required a clear choice between competing shipbuilding programs, proposals for modernization of the army, such as construction of new coastal fortifications or reorganization and concentration of the infantry and cavalry, seemed more complementary than conflicting. Army differences were also more easily compromised. Because land forces possessed a high degree of flexibility, a single army reform often contributed to the accomplishment of several missions, thus taking the edge off debate and encouraging officers with quite different purposes to support a common program. In the same manner, the division of the army's combat forces into several arms permitted each branch of the service to follow its own agenda, even when the plans for reform derived from quite different assumptions. Army differences accordingly tended to be matters of degree and emphasis rather than clearly contrasting points of view.

Differences did, however, exist, and army officers convinced of their service's uncertain future debated the proper lines along which to pursue modernization of the land forces. With the paths that opened before the army leading to quite different points, army officers made many small choices whose cumulative effect established important trends and determined the future of the United States Army.

One of those paths would have shifted the army to a new locale from which to continue its old role as a federal constabulary. The military police force that for over a century had restrained the Indians on the frontier might in the future, some officers believed, find employment suppressing labor violence in the cities. Keeping in mind such workers' riots as those of the Molly Maguires in the early seventies and the railroad general strike of 1877, and sensitive to the growing unrest that a decade later precipitated the notorious Haymarket Massacre, one of the army's essayists, Captain James Chester, suggested doubling the size of the land forces to sixty thousand. With half that number he would continue the army's work on the maritime and demographic frontiers, and with the other he proposed to police strikers and disperse riots, "the new and equally important duties near our great cities."[29] In the 1880s, when controlling Indians had a limited future as the basis for maintaining an army, officers who minimized the chances of war and invasion apparently thought to win public support for their service by calling the army's possible usefulness in the cities to the attention of conservative citizens.

The pages of the army's professional journals indicate that service interest in riot duty increased sharply during labor troubles in the mid-nineties. And in 1894, the army's senior officer, Major General John M. Schofield, used his annual report to urge a slight increase in the ground forces, citing as his reason the need to quell domestic violence. Schofield's successor as commander in the East, Major General Oliver O. Howard, went even further. Because of the recent labor violence in his region, Howard "strongly recommend[ed] an increase of the Army to at least double the size of our present force."[30]

That swell of interest quickly subsided, however, and judging from the articles appearing in the army journals, officers never found strike duty very appealing. The editor of the *Army and Navy Journal* attributed that lack of appeal to the fact that officers found no task "so distasteful . . . as riot duty," a conclusion supported by General William T. Sherman's claim that controlling strikers fell "beneath a soldier's vocation." Younger officers agreed; one of the army's young intellectuals, for example, described that use of his service as a "pernicious policy."[31]

Lieutenant General John M. Schofield's annual reports suggest another reason for the transient interest in riot duty. When he argued, in 1894, that growing domestic violence justified an increase in the army, he merely used a new and topical argument to advocate the same increase in strength that he had long sought on the basis of the threat to America's coasts. When popular concern about domestic violence declined, so did the usefulness of the argument.[32]

Even military writing that called attention to the need to perform riot duty quite uniformly gave it a lower priority than other army missions, a status stemming in part from the fact that preparing the army to accomplish what officers regarded as its principal tasks simultaneously readied the service to deploy to the cities.[33] One of those more important tasks was aiding the states' militia, a mission requiring the army to become a school for war.

Those army officers who proposed to reform their service by making it a school often had in mind quite disparate groups of pupils. Some, including many who emphasized the links between the army and society, sought to direct the regular army's educational efforts toward improving the quality of the states' militia. Others hoped to disseminate military skills among all male citizens of military age. Still others, thinking of a smaller group of students, urged better training for the service's own corps of officers.

Many of the officers who like General William T. Sherman considered the army a "School of Instruction" described its principal educational responsibility as training the states' organized militia. Because the state forces were usually the first to be called in the event of domestic disorder, aiding the militia seemed compatible with both the army's role as a constabulary and its performance of more obviously military functions.[34]

The regular forces sought to fulfill that training responsibility in several ways. During his tenure as commanding general, Sherman temporarily detailed regular officers to attend the annual military encampments, where they assisted the instruction of state forces. To extend and regularize that practice, one of his successors, John M. Schofield, proposed that Congress authorize the assignment of regular officers to four-year periods of duty with the militia.[35] Sherman also widened the contacts between federal and state forces by allowing the latters' artillery batteries to encamp alongside regular garrisons so that the militia might become "practiced in the use of heavy Sea Coast Guns &c." That cooperation between regular and militia units later extended inland as federal infantry and cavalry units participated with state organizations in periodic joint maneuvers designed to prepare the latter for modern warfare.[36] In the late nineteenth century, regular officers also supported the new National Guard Association's efforts to reform the antiquated Militia Act of 1792. Army Adjutant General John C. Kelton, for instance, worked closely with state officers who sought to win federal recognition for the growing number of National Guard units and end such anachronisms as the requirement that militiamen provide themselves with shot pouches and powder horns.[37]

The second way in which some officers thought the army might become a school was by tasking it to help educate the citizenry, thus aiding both regular and militia forces. Used in that way, General Nelson A. Miles, who commanded the army between 1894 and 1903, thought his service might become the "one great school of patriotism in which the young men of the country . . . [are] so benefited as to enable them to return to civil life better citizens."[38]

The army made its first efforts at such general military education when it began assigning regular officers as instructors of military science at public and private colleges.[39] Other officers, however, wanted to make the training more nearly universal. In 1888, for example, Colonel August V. Kautz proposed five-year enlistments in which young men, drawn pro rata from each Congressional district, would receive a military, academic, and vocational education at government expense. At the end of five years, those veterans would return to their home districts with both a civilian skill and the ability to drill the militia in peace and to command volunteers in war. In a later version of his plan, Kautz called attention to other benefits the country—and the army—might derive from such training. Now that the Indians, he wrote, were "no longer a pretext for maintaining an army," using that service to train the general public "would be the best of reasons for its continuance." If, moreover, the training helped foster a proper military spirit among the citizenry, public support for the regulars might rise yet higher.[40] Finally, the enforced military education would facilitate the army's maintenance of domestic order because veterans of army service would presumably learn both patriotism and respect for the law, thus reducing the incidence of domestic violence.[41]

Most of those military, social, and self-interested arguments favoring a system of general military training reappeared with greater vigor in the twentieth century. In the last quarter of the nineteenth, however, they had little effect. So long as American officers had no fear of a major invasion and saw no need for large expeditionary forces, they had only a slight interest in educational programs aimed at the rapid creation of a mass army. Instead, the most significant of the army's educational programs had in view one of the few groups over which the army had much control—its own officer corps.

There again, William Tecumseh Sherman played a decisive role. As the army's commanding general from 1869 to 1883, he sustained the 1868 revival of the Artillery School at Fort Monroe, encouraged the metamorphosis of the 1866 Essayons Club into the Engineering School of Application at Willett's Point, and founded the 1881 School of Application for Infantry and Cavalry at Fort Leavenworth. Two younger officers who grasped Sherman's intent, Eben Swift and Arthur L. Wagner, guided the evolution of the latter as it made a two-decade transformation from an elementary school of tactics for company-grade officers to a true staff college training future field officers in the analysis of past campaigns, the conduct of war games to test new plans and concepts, and the preparation of combat orders—skills officers would use throughout their careers as they assumed direction of larger units, even those comprising several arms of the service. At the turn of the century, two others of Sherman's followers, Tasker H. Bliss and William H. Carter, assisted the 1901 establishment of the Army War College, the capstone of the service's educational system and preparatory school for the high-level planners of the future general staff. Sherman's influence also extended to the navy. Rear Admiral Stephen B. Luce, founder of the Naval War College, wrote that his own mind had been opened to the need for advanced naval education by Civil War service on Sherman's staff. Later taking his direction from both Sherman and Major General

Emory Upton, another army intellectual, Luce modeled the navy's own college "somewhat after the fashion of the Artillery School at Fort Monroe & the Cavalry School at Fort Leavenworth."[42]

Education was more, however, than useful peacetime employment for an officer corps soon to obtain release from the burdens of active campaigning against the Plains Indians. Between 1870 and 1920, many civilian occupational groups emphasized the importance of specialized education in asserting their claims to the prestige, autonomy, and authority associated with status as a profession. Despite the features differentiating the officer corps from other professions, army and navy leaders used education to the same end.

In many respects, members of the military officer corps constituted a unique group. In contrast to the autonomy of the nineteenth century's largely self-employed doctors and lawyers, who provided direct personal services upon the consumer's request, military officers served as salaried members of a hierarchic bureaucracy that both limited their independence and mediated between the consumer and the military specialist. In contrast even to other salaried groups, like the older teaching and emerging engineering professionals, military officers experienced the greater limitation of having in effect but one prospective employer: the government. Although governmental employment exacerbated the bureaucratic threat to the autonomy of the military professions, federal service did provide what other groups initially lacked: a long-standing national focus—upon which to build a group consciousness—and an institutional framework for intragroup cooperation. As a consequence, the late-nineteenth-century shift of markets from local to national levels, which required a similar change in the orientation of civilian professional groups, found the military professions already partially organized at the national level and focused on national elites.[43]

Despite those differences, the crisis facing army and navy officers paralleled in many ways the nineteenth-century disruptions shaping other professions. Both civil and military change resulted in part from new applications of science and technology, which also stimulated the creation of new social organizations. Epitomized but not limited to the large-scale industrial corporation, the new structures tried to reestablish order in American life by organizing individuals into highly coordinated and regimented work forces that sought to control the many variables shaping the organization's environment. That degree of control required the creation of managerial structures capable of studying that environment, devising plans for its domination, and coordinating the organization's efforts to impose order. Unavoidably involved in a larger world, the members of the new class of managers came to recognize the deficiencies of the old, localistic order and used the emerging organizations to disseminate new cosmopolitan values. Those same managerial bureaucracies, whether directing public or private organizations, provided yet other opportunities to the new specialists and professionals. As control migrated upward, the managers increasingly dominated their own organizations, and as they sensed their ties to others engaged in similar work, they fostered new functional organizations designed to promote their specialized interests, usually through demands that their group be accorded professional status.[44]

To win the approval of both the public and the governing elite for the specialists' autonomous control of the new organizations, professionals maintained that their special duties required technical education and systematic training in the skills of the profession. That same education, as a prerequisite for achieving professional status, also served to exclude "unqualified" competitors and to unify the group internally, as did the creation of professional associations of nationwide scope that gave status to their members, sought to assure the public of their qualifications, and provided agencies for both controlling membership and pursuing group interests. In return the professionals promised to place their skills at the service of the public, serving its needs rather than seeking personal gain.[45]

Late in the nineteenth century, the military professions commenced a similar evolution. As technology transformed both society and warfare, army and navy officers argued that they too possessed a body of specialized knowledge acquired only from preprofessional education and many years of training. Modern war, the regulars claimed, had become a science so complicated that only those having a special education and engaged in constant study of warfare could hope to achieve success in combat. The regulars consequently sought to control entry into the officer corps, criticizing especially the traditional American practice of awarding high wartime rank to individuals with no better recommendation than good political connections and local social leadership. In the early twentieth century, the regulars similarly sought to bring the states' militia under federal control, thus ensuring the regulars' monopoly of military expertise.[46] In return for the government's reliance upon a single source of military advice, armed forces officers implicitly pledged to use their expertise only in the public's interest. In addition, they would eschew partisan political activity and adhere strictly to the principles of civil supremacy. They would also ensure, primarily through education and study but also by elimination of the unfit through merit promotion, that they possessed the claimed military expertise. They would keep alive, wrote General Sherman, "the knowledge and habits, the tone and spirit, the particular devotion and patriotism of the soldier."[47]

Like other functional groups, military officers also created professional societies dedicated, in the words of Major General John M. Schofield, to the "preservation of the vital military germ from which . . . [the] country expects great armies to spring in time of public danger." The navy led the way in 1873, when its officers created the still extant United States Naval Institute. In 1878, army officers followed with the establishment of the Military Service Institution of the United States, which served as a model for the United States Cavalry Association (1887) and the Infantry Society (1893), which in 1904 became the United States Infantry Association. To promote the spread of military knowledge and increase professional consciousness, each of those societies published its own journal, as did the artillerymen stationed at the United States Artillery School.[48]

Those officers who regarded the army as a school for war had taken, however, but a partial step beyond the earlier emphasis on the army's traditional domestic uses and toward peacetime preparation for conflict with a great power. Advocates of military education like General Sherman and the editors of the *Army and Navy Journal* had asserted that "the chief object of every army is *war*," and they had recognized that military duty was "performed in time of peace, not for its own sake, but as a means of instruction for war." Yet, their program of military reform, while aiming at increasing the nation's war potential through education, had still delayed significant mobilization of American strength until the very eve of battle. Discounting the chances of invasion and with little attention to the precise circumstances in which the United States might become involved in war, those officers elected to run the risk of both early setbacks and annoying raids on coastal cities.[49]

Some officers who shared the widespread interest in education and professionalism nevertheless did refuse to discount the possibility of a foreign assault on the United States. In their opinion, it was not enough that their service preserve military knowledge or disseminate martial skills among the general public; the army must also achieve a state of peacetime readiness sufficient to accomplish its initial wartime tasks, even in the face of sudden assault. Those views derived from several sources, each linked either to technological developments or to the evolution of international politics but all pointing toward maintenance of an army whose principal peacetime duty was preparation to counter a foreign attack.

Technological development of course had many facets, and some officers confined themselves to the general observation that modern wars arose suddenly and rapidly reached their decisive phase. Because only previously trained and equipped forces might therefore contribute to the war's outcome, a prudent nation commenced preparations long before the development of a significant probability of conflict. Such preparations had an added advantage: They might even deter the attack.[50]

Those general observations provided little indication of the precise character of needed military reform, however, and the federal government consequently took the first steps toward creation of adequate forces-in-being in response to the more specific appeals from artillery, engineer, and ordnance officers who called attention to America's obsolete coastal defenses and the possibly disastrous consequences of even minor coastal raids—loss of life, destruction of property, and suspension of trade. The joint army-navy Board on Fortifications or Other Defenses, which Congress established in March 1885, under the chairmanship of war secretary William C. Endicott, gave official confirmation to the officers' analysis of the dangerous vulnerability of the American coast and consequently recommended the appropriation, over the next twelve to fifteen years, of $127 million for the fortification of the nation's principal ports and several strategic points along the Canadian border.[51] When Congress ended fifteen years of parsimony and began to appropriate money for coastal defense in 1890, even senior officers of the infantry and cavalry expressed satisfaction with the nation's soon-to-be-realized capacity to meet war's most immediate threat. The Congressional appropriations, wrote Commanding General John M. Schofield, have settled the "important question of national defense" and the country would soon be "in condition to resist any attack from a foreign country."[52]

Concern for defense of the coasts was not, however, limited to the technical branches and senior officers of the army's line. Many junior spokesmen for the infantry and cavalry began to turn their attention from the interior to argue for the army's deployment near the coasts and to assert that the Divisions of the Atlantic and Pacific had replaced the Division of the Missouri as the army's most important command.[53]

A loss of confidence in America's freedom from invasion, occasioned in part by the Sino-Japanese War of 1894–95, seems to have contributed to that change in emphasis. Although superficially a result of Korean factional strife, that war in fact grew out of Chinese efforts, initiated as early as 1880, to tighten control over its Korean tributary and counter nascent Japanese imperialism, which arose with the latter nation's 1868 emergence from several centuries of isolation. Despite the pro-Chinese orientation of early-twentieth-century United States policy, in 1894 American sympathies lay with Japan, which for some time had given a friendly reception to American trade and missionaries, had sought American advice in the modernization of its educational, agricultural, and financial systems, and was regarded in the United States, claimed one observer, as "almost . . . a ward in the world of international affairs." China, in contrast, had resisted America's own efforts to open Korea to trade and had become the scene of both a renewal of domestic antiforeign outbursts and increased diplomatic tension over American hostility to the further immigration of Chinese labor. The United States consequently lent its moral support to Japan, initially by opposing European plans to intervene in the conflict with the object of placing Korea under international control and later by helping Japan moderate its peace treaty with China in the face of threatening pressure from Russia, France, and Germany.[54]

Despite that war's convincing demonstration of China's weakness, making it the victim of a new surge of imperialism, and of tiny Japan's military strength and growing expansionism, few Americans took much notice of the conflict, which developed almost simultaneously with the more exciting debate over the Hawaiian treaty of annexation and concluded during the dispute with Great Britain over the Venezuelan boundary. American army and navy officers, however, gave the war considerable thought. On the one hand, they shared General Schofield's conclusion that Japan's successful invasion revealed that technology had changed oceans from barriers to highways and rendered the Atlantic "little more serious an obstacle to the navies and transports of Europe than are the Japan and Yellow seas to those of Japan." On the other hand, officers also drew alarming analogies between the position and

policies of China and those of the United States. Geographically isolated and possessed of a large population, China too had maintained
only third-rate military forces and paid little attention to the art of war.
When tiny but militarily advanced Japan transported its army across the
Yellow and Japanese seas, successfully invaded China, and threatened
its capital, some officers interpreted China's defeat as a warning to the
United States. To Major General Nelson A. Miles, Schofield's successor
as commanding general, the war demonstrated that "the richest and
most populous nations" could be "humiliated and subjugated" by
powers "one-tenth" their size if "the smaller nation had paid more attention to the modern appliances of war" while the larger had relied
upon "vastly superior numbers" but made no peacetime preparations
to develop its potential.[55]

The significance of technological change, as highlighted by the
Sino-Japanese War, was but one development forcing the conclusion
that America must create a war army. As officers looked abroad, they
also observed the increasing aggressiveness and expansionist tendencies
of the world's major powers, and army writers soon added France, Germany, and Japan to Spain and England on the list of powers with which
the United States might become entangled in political disputes likely to
lead to war. To validate that prediction, officers referred to recent policy
disputes between the United States and those nations and expressed fear
of European imperialism, a future struggle for control of an isthmian
canal, and commercial rivalries that might lead to a challenge to the
Monroe Doctrine.[56]

General Schofield's writings well illustrate the evolution of military
thought. Although as early as 1890 he had declared that the time had
"now come when the future possible or probable military necessities of
the country should dictate military policy," he had then recommended
only modest federal support for the militia, some redeployment of the
regular forces, and better preparations for defense of the seacoast. The
first two proposals derived from the army's role as a school for war, and
only the latter preparations suggested the need to create stronger forces-
in-being, which Schofield hoped to augment by five thousand men in
order to bring artillery and infantry units to authorized strength. He
then made no suggestion that the United States should attempt to
match the growing European armies. Four years later his views had
changed, and Schofield warned Congress that the United States could
not "hope to maintain itself among the great nations of the earth, un-

less its military strength . . . [was] made by development to bear a reasonable proportion to that maintained by other great nations." When
in 1897 Schofield published his autobiography, he added the warning
that unless Americans were

> willing to prepare in advance for putting into the field at a moment's notice a very
> large and effective army, as well as to fortify all important seaports, they may as
> well make up their minds to submit, at least for a time, to whatever indignity any
> considerable naval power may see fit to inflict upon them.[57]

The late-nineteenth-century debate over military missions thus paralleled developments in civil life. Like other Americans who observed
their institutions collapse in the face of disruptive change, army and
navy officers recognized that the armed forces too faced a crisis. And
military officers, like their fellow citizens, initially displayed little capacity to agree upon an appropriate response. Some officers for a time
looked to the past and tried to preserve the old ways and the old values;
that group emphasized the domestic and commercial uses of a peacetime military force. Others rejected the old missions and sought to
reform the armed forces; those officers would transcend the past, disseminate new values, and prepare the army and navy for a still dimly
perceived future. During a quarter century of such discussion, the members of the officer corps resolved their differences as the advocates of war
forces convinced their colleagues, and later most of the nation's governing elite, that the proper peacetime duty of the army and navy was
preparation for war. The parallels do not rest there, however; the debate
gave military officers a national, perhaps even international perspective,
and while becoming increasingly conscious of their special expertise and
mutual interests, they also struggled to achieve professional recognition. The crisis the services faced and the response their officers devised
revealed both the military officers' awareness of the forces reshaping
America and the extent to which army and navy reformers shared the
values of the new class seeking to reimpose order on national life.

CHAPTER 3

The Reform Impulse

THUS BY THE 1890s readiness for war had become the goal that military reformers believed should shape the rehabilitation of America's decrepit armed forces and determine their peacetime employment. To convince the officer corps, the service secretaries, and the Congress that such preparedness should guide the funding of new ships, new forts, and new guns, the reformers had described their proposals as prudent adaptations to a range of new developments that, taken together, diminished the importance of the armed forces' traditional peacetime missions, rendered obsolete most of their arms and equipment, and exacerbated the dangers of delaying war preparations until hostilities had become imminent. As part of the effort to win others to the concept of a war army and navy, service reformers of the century's last quarter also engaged in two other, related sets of tasks. They sought to demonstrate that the United States, despite its great military potential and inherent security, might become victim of a punitive attack by a great power, and they resolved a host of minor issues in ways that enhanced the services' war readiness, thereby emphasizing the preeminence of that goal.

The reformers' fears of a great-power war were particularly significant. While reflecting the dwindling importance of the services' traditional peacetime work and enhanced concern for their growing technological obsolescence, such fears also gave focus and direction to the

41

reform movement. In the opinion of an increasing number of army
and navy officers, international developments had begun to carry the
United States, whatever its preferences, into a new era in which long-
standing national policies would inevitably collide with the ambitions
of other states. War with another great power, while not a certain result
of such collisions, seemed a likely consequence—at least so long as the
United States did nothing by way of military preparation to deter that
outcome.

Military officers placed foremost among threatening developments
the "new imperialism" that dominated European international politics
in the nineteenth century's last quarter. While generally denying that
the United States had any reason to join in the scramble for colonies, reformers speculated that European imperial ambitions might lead to the
creation of new dependencies in Latin America and force the United
States to choose between abandonment of the Monroe Doctrine and its
vigorous support, a diplomatic posture likely to lead to war.[1]

Military officers also anticipated that America's own economic
growth and expanding foreign trade, which they assumed the government had an obligation to support, might involve the United States in
an armed confrontation. Army captain George F. Price, for example,
feared that the nation's growing export trade would soon threaten "the
commercial and political interests of foreign powers," who would respond by absorbing the contested markets within their empires. Should
the United States too vigorously protest the subsequent exclusion of its
commerce from a new colony, the imperial power might counter by
threatening an attack on America's exposed coastal cities.[2] Speaking of
American trade and investment in Mexico, Lieutenant Commander
Henry H. Gorringe added to Price's fears the possibility that commercial ties, which he claimed sowed "the seed of discord that may ripen
into war," might lead to conflict even with industrially undeveloped
nations if America's "bosses" sent in the army and navy to secure financial interests against the inevitable local interference.[3] Only stronger
armed forces, the reformers reasoned, could both deter European expansionism and ensure respect for American interests.

The work of a presidential commission appointed by Ulysses Grant
in the 1870s and the initative of Ferdinand de Lesseps, supported by the
French Société de Géographie, brought to the attention of military officers another potentially war-producing development: the construction
of a Central American interoceanic canal. If that canal were built by a
French company, as seemed probable after the 1879 meeting of the

Congrès International d'Études du Canal Interocéanique lent support to de Lesseps's plans, the resulting expansion of French influence in the Western Hemisphere would challenge the Monroe Doctrine and threaten America's strategic isolation. Even if the United States eventually built the canal, military writers expected the new waterway to alter world trade routes and tempt European powers into the Caribbean and Central America in search of bases from which to guard the movement of their commerce. In either event, European efforts to dominate use of the canal would threaten to extend to the New World the competitive militarism characteristic of the Old. Unless the United States became sufficiently powerful to frustrate the initial attempts at such expansion, the reformers predicted that European military power would quickly establish itself in the Western Hemisphere, thereby forcing the United States to maintain an even larger standing army and navy, forces comparable to those found abroad.[4]

The course of American foreign relations in the late nineteenth century also helped convince military officers that a new era of increased international tension had arrived. During that period, the United States engaged in almost constant controversy with Great Britain over fisheries, pelagic sealing, revision of the Clayton-Bulwer treaty, the Venezuelan boundary, and the Pacific island groups of Samoa and Hawaii— which also troubled American relations with Germany and Japan. The 1891 murder of Italian citizens in New Orleans and of American sailors in Valparaiso even raised the possibility of conflict with Italy and Chile, and Spain's inability to prevent periodic insurrection in Cuba vexed relations with yet another European power.[5] Military officers did not expect each of those differences to lead to war. Indeed, rather than advocate an aggressive American response to such issues, military officers consistently criticized the irrationality of the country's jingoistic diplomacy. "In talking war without making proper preparation for war, or, in fact, any preparation whatever," complained the *Army and Navy Journal*, "we are simply making a display of ourselves which excites the derision of the instructed the world over."[6]

While the reformers' analysis of the international situation gave direction to the reform movement, their views on the peacetime work appropriate to the armed forces further demonstrated their commitment to the goal of war readiness. On the one hand, the reformers' pursuit of readiness inspired proposals for inexpensive intramural reforms of mi-

nor interest to the general public. On the other, the reformers advocated costly war-oriented rearmament programs to which the public often responded with hostility. And they persisted in supporting such
programs even when peace-oriented alternatives seemed more certain to
win popular approval as well as to provide secure governmental employment for excess officers.

Had the government, for example, completed the peace-navy program described in the preceding chapter, the United States Navy would
have comprised several squadrons of small, modern cruisers deployed to
promote overseas trade, thus continuing that service's traditional commercial orientation and possibly winning for naval rehabilitation the
support of a generally antimilitary public.[7] For defense of the coasts, the
peace-navy oriented advisory boards had looked to the construction of
new torpedo boats and the renovation of old monitors, which would
have created billets providing challenging work for junior officers, who
according to the *Army and Navy Journal* would "gain more in personal
development by commanding a torpedo boat than by holding some
subordinate position in a battle ship."[8] The reformers nevertheless consistently rejected such naval reconstruction, whatever its merits in terms
of winning popular support or leading to the advancement of younger
officers, because it failed to achieve adequate readiness for war.

That same concern for war readiness shaped the reaction of naval reformers to other programs designed to make their service more useful in
the eyes of the public as well as to create interesting new jobs for naval
officers rendered excess by the decay of wooden ships. Throughout the
eighties, for instance, the service secretaries and the *Army and Navy
Journal* repeatedly proposed that the navy absorb the Revenue Marine
(the future Coast Guard), the Light-House Establishment, the Life-
Saving Service, and the Coast and Geodetic Survey.[9] In addition, the
Journal advanced a scheme to improve the State Department's consular
service by filling new vacancies with naval officers rather than the bene-
ficiaries of political patronage.[10] Most naval officers, however, expressed
consistent opposition to such employment, whose nonmilitary character
they believed had no place in a modern navy. Moreover, even the advocates of such programs justified them primarily as a means to preserve a
larger corps of officers for emergency wartime service.[11]

In refusing finally either to reorganize or to justify the army for its
usefulness in quelling urban unrest or as a school for the militia, that
service's reformers also abandoned missions that might have disarmed
those Congressional critics of military spending who doubted the likelihood of foreign war. Insisting upon war readiness as the army's proper

peacetime mission, advocates of a war army instead risked the loss of public support for service rehabilitation and advanced proposals for a modest five-to-ten-thousand-man increase in the regular forces, sufficient men to bring existing units to authorized enlisted strength but not enough to boost officer promotion.[12]

Although expenditures on the construction of new ships, the fabrication of better guns and forts and the enlistment of more soldiers constituted the major programs leading to war readiness, officers also displayed their commitment to that goal by advocating a variety of ancillary reforms. In the eighties, for example, army reformers began with little success to urge the concentration of the Indian-fighting army's scattered fragments at regimental garrisons where companies could learn to function in the larger formations appropriate to conflicts with fellow Occidentals.[13] Naval reformers similarly sought to unite far-flung cruising vessels into tactical units, and in 1889 the Navy Department authorized formation of a "Squadron of Evolution" to develop and test modern fleet tactics. Five years later that department again yielded to the reformers' demands by reorganizing all the old cruising squadrons and directing each to assemble periodically for tactical exercises.[14]

Concurrent with efforts to reorganize and concentrate the combat forces, reformers in both services also sought to increase the military efficiency of units by advocating the study of gunnery and increased target practice.[15]

Maneuvers—major exercises in which the forces participated in mock battles—served a similar purpose and became a common aim of the reformers, who saw in such exercises a means to provide both simulated combat training for enlisted men and valuable staff experience for senior officers and their aides. Large-scale exercises also forced senior commanders to think in terms of divisions or fleets rather than single regiments or ships.[16]

In the late nineteenth century, officers in both services and at a variety of posts consequently began to experiment with mock combat. For Sherman's 1881 School of Application at Fort Leavenworth, Colonel Arthur L. Wagner claimed the honor of its being the "birth-place of systematic field exercises in the United States Army." Although the conduct of such exercises as part of a school curriculum soon spread to Fort Riley's course for cavalry and field artillerymen, neither school ever sponsored an exercise involving more than a regiment* of infantry rein-

---

* An army regiment comprised 1,000 to 1,200 men; a brigade, three regiments plus supporting arms (4,000 to 5,000 men); a division, three brigades (about 18,000); and a corps, several divisions (40,000 plus).

forced by cavalry and field artillery. Unrelated to any army academic program, Major General Nelson A. Miles in 1888, in Arizona, and 1889, in California, held similar small-scale exercises using the troops under his command. But there is reason to doubt the significance of Miles's efforts. During the 1889 exercise, for example, while Miles and his staff lodged at the Monterey Peninsula's Hotel del Monte and his surgeon, Captain Leonard Wood, courted the latter's future wife at the nightly soirees, the troops dubbed the unaccustomed field work "the monkey war of Jack Rabbit Flat."[17]

Major General Hugh L. Scott thus seems correct in assigning to Wesley Merritt's 1889 exercise at Chilocco in the Indian Territory (Oklahoma) credit for "the first real maneuvers the army had ever conducted." For that exercise Merritt gathered two regiments of cavalry, fourteen companies of infantry, and two batteries of field artillery, which he organized as a partly fictitious division of infantry reinforced with a brigade of cavalry. During the three-week program, Merritt provided for instruction in a new form of drill thought more compatible with modern infantry weapons and "civilized" warfare, and he conducted a variety of mock combats associated with patrolling, marches, retreats, and attacks—all resisted by one of the cavalry units in the role of an "enemy" force. Though irreverently christened the "Bloody War of 1889," one observer claimed that the maneuver drew from even the enlisted men "a lively interest in the work of instruction" because the "practical drills . . . really seemed to mean training for the battlefield." From officer participants and observers the maneuver won near universal praise, and Scott recalled that it "had the salutary effect of awakening a good many of us to the fact that the day of Indian wars was over and that we must fit ourselves for war with civilized peoples." Another young officer, Captain James W. Pope, found manifested among officers participating in Merritt's maneuver a greater interest "than in many a real campaign. . . . In fact, every proof was seen of the greatest interest excited in the minds of the whole command."[18]

According to Major William R. Livermore, though, the "far more needful and far more interesting" maneuvers were those conducted jointly with the navy and the states' militia and designed to test the adequacy of America's coastal defenses. In 1887, for instance, Rear Admiral Stephen B. Luce's North Atlantic Squadron and troops under the command of Major General John M. Schofield conducted a joint trial of the fortifications on Narragansett Bay, and they made plans for a much larger exercise the next year—until the Navy Department took all but two of Luce's ships and ordered him to charge the army for coal used ferrying the troops to the maneuver site. Despite that disappointment, planning for subsequent years resumed, and according to Major Livermore:

> The officers and men of the Army and Navy throughout the country were enthusiastic at the prospect of witnessing or participating in these combined maneuvers. . . . Nor was the enthusiasm confined to the Regular Service, for the Militia of the neighboring States expressed their desire to be included, and the owners and crews of vessels look forward to this opportunity of practicing the duties of a Naval Reserve.

Such enthusiasm apparently stemmed from the novelty, realism, and utility of the exercises, in which—under the supervision and scoring of umpires—the naval forces attempted either to "reduce" the forts by direct assault, perhaps assisted by landing parties, or to run under their guns at night, and the army's artillerymen sought to "sink" the invading naval force while its infantry blocked any amphibious landing.[19]

The zeal for modernization also drew the reformers' attention to the services' headquarters staffs. Concerned about the possibility of conflict with a great power, the navy in 1882 and the army in 1885 created intelligence bureaus charged with gathering data on the armed forces and military strength of foreign powers and on their capacity to deploy troops, ships, and war matériel to the Western Hemisphere. That innovation led in turn to the assignment of military attachés in each of America's principal embassies.[20]

The reformers found other improvements in the headquarters staffs less easy to make, as illustrated by the long struggle to supersede the services' powerful bureaus with some form of general staff. Under the bureau system, semiautonomous agencies purchased, stored, transported, issued, or repaired each separate category of the services' supplies and equipment or filled their administrative, medical, or legal needs. While capable of managing the services' day-to-day peacetime activities, the bureaus lacked the capacity—short of active supervision by the usually inexperienced and often indifferent civilian secretary—to coordinate unanticipated demands, to plan against the possibility of war, to direct both the peacetime training and the wartime employment of tactical units, or to ensure the proper subordination of the bureaus to the needs of the combat forces. Although Rear Admiral George E. Belknap spoke only of his own service, he clearly explained why the reformers in both sought such subordination when he told students at the Naval War College that the Navy Department was created for war and "it can never divest itself of that quality. . . . [W]hatever it does, the possibilities and contingencies of war are, and must ever be, its prime concern; . . . the work of peace is but preparation for war in its every phase." Because the bureaus seemed to have neglected that orientation, reformers in both services sought the creation of a general staff that would not.[21]

Improvements in the services' educational systems also displayed the reformers' commitment to war readiness. The "prime object" of the Naval War College, emphasized its founder, Stephen B. Luce, was to teach "officers the science of their own profession—the Science of War." Each naval captain must become "a strategist as well as a tactician" and thus acquire skills beyond those needed for the peacetime promotion of commerce. Naval reformers also hoped to use their new college as an embryonic general staff where students would prepare and test plans for the defense of the American coast against the attack of modern warships.[22] Army educators had comparable goals. Their service's schools would keep officers abreast of the latest developments in military science and, because the army would undoubtedly increase manifold in the event of war, prepare junior leaders for the wartime command of regiments and field officers for the direction of newly created brigades and divisions.[23]

Although predicated on the evolution of technology, national needs, or international events, the military reform impulse received additional encouragement from a variety of unrelated stimuli: personal embarrassment stemming from the services' antiquated equipment; the officers' prolonged physical isolation from civil society; and the boredom associated with military routine, much of it due to promotion stagnation. Lieutenant Arthur L. Wagner, for instance, only partly concealed his personal mortification when he wrote that the army's equipment exposed the United States to both "disaster and disgrace," and Admiral George Dewey suggested similar humiliation when he recalled that the decrepit condition of the late-nineteenth-century navy made it "the laughing-stock of the nations."[24] Whether at sea or on the frontier, moreover, America's military leaders often passed long periods in the company of fewer than a dozen educated men, their fellow officers. Embarrassed by obsolete equipment and physically isolated from both civil society and the larger military community, many officers also found the daily routine of service life stultifying, leading to a sense of frustration that the slow rate of promotion only exacerbated. By 1890, for example, the senior lieutenant of artillery had more than twenty-eight years of army service, all but five at his present rank, and the senior subalterns of infantry and cavalry had nineteen and fifteen respectively. The most senior naval officer of equivalent rank had fifteen years' service, the last seven at his current grade. Fast approaching middle age, many of the services' junior officers had long ago learned a lieutenant's duties; yet they still seemed years away from positions of significant responsibility.[25]

Officers responded to that situation in quite different ways. Some, wrote Admiral Dewey, found that the easy thing was "to drift along in . . . grade, losing interest and remaining in the navy only because too old to change occupation." For army officers, cards, alcohol, or sport often eased a life of comparable aimlessness. As reported by William H. Carter, however, some late-nineteenth-century army officers found an outlet in the study of their craft, there being no "period of American military history when so much attention and study was given to improvements in arms, drill, etc." In "compensation for the quiet that pervade[d]" service life, wrote Ensign Charles C. Marsh in the same vein, he had turned to the study of naval gunnery, which left him "happy" and "contented." That combination of disappointing circumstances and fascination with the changes in weaponry and the art of war could also produce frustration, wrote Admiral Dewey, whenever the "earnest . . . effort of an officer to keep up with progress" only made him "more sensitive to [his handicaps]."[26]

Some observers have cited that undeniable evidence of the frustrations of military life as the real explanation for the entire reform impulse. Army historian William Ganoe, for example, argued that the boredom of life at tiny frontier posts, the neglect and hostility of the public, and the resentment caused by the army's involuntary backwardness and lack of training made officers "restless for something better" and created a "stir of honest ambition" that led to that service's renaissance. Others have given Ganoe's argument a clearly pejorative twist, characterizing the reformers as Young Turks whose professed concern for the nation's defense was in fact little more than a public relations device for winning popular support. Confusing national security with both institutional interests and career advancement, young officers, in that interpretation, sought to enlarge and modernize the army and navy as a means to end the logjam in promotions and wrest control of the services from an older, conservative generation of officers.[27]

Such analyses rest, of course, on the questionable assumptions that institutions are adaptive organizations that reflexively seek new roles whenever their usefulness is questioned and that personal ambition constantly generates a desire for change among a hierarchical institution's junior members, who see in reform the path to their own advancement.

Although institutional survival undoubtedly did contribute to the impetus behind reform, excessive emphasis on that factor both ignores the services' rejection of available alternatives that would have guaranteed survival and fails altogether to account for the specific aims of the reform movement. A peace navy, for example, however unsuitable in the eyes of the reformers, would have ensured that service's existence, as would the proposed absorption of such nonmilitary maritime activities as the Revenue Marine or the assignment of naval officers to consular duties. Converting the army to an urban antilabor constabulary or merging it with the militia offered that service, too, a sort of institutional second life. In light of the era's industrial expansion and the nation's traditional antimilitarism, such peace-oriented programs with obvious civic value had a potential for winning wide public support. Military officers, nevertheless, vigorously opposed such programs, even while advocating possibly less popular, war-focused reforms whose rejection in Congress might have doomed the armed forces.

That opposition is best understood in terms of the military officers' expectation, correct as it turned out, that the United States would soon become involved in great-power war. Only that focus, for instance, explains the services' insistence upon a war-oriented reform movement, whatever supporting role institutional survival and personal ambition may have played in the movement's generation. In addition, the services' common interest in tactical reorganization, periodic maneuvers, educational reform, and staff modernization, all of clear utility to forces seeking to prepare against the possibility of war, did little to win public support for the reform movement and seem irrelevant to an institution bent only on its own survival.

The attempt to explain service reform in terms of a clash between junior and senior officers is yet less satisfactory. Although junior officers, those below the ranks of lieutenant commander and major, produced about half the writing on military reform appearing between 1880 and 1898, they made up between 70 (navy) and 90 (army) percent of the services' officer corps. Those who attribute military reform to the efforts of ambitious Young Turks must explain both why junior officers wrote on that subject less frequently than statistically predictable and why senior officers made so significant a literary contribution to the cause of military modernization.[28]

In the debates over military policy, moreover, officers of every rank took opposite sides on the issues without clear division along lines of seniority. Young advocates of a war navy, like Wainwright, Fiske, Goodrich, Soley, and Chambers, and junior proponents of a war army, like Wagner, Greene, Sanger, Carter, and Bliss, opposed for a time the navy's equally youthful Kelley, Barber, and Very and verbally dueled with Chester and Regan from the army's junior ranks, all of whom promoted nonmilitary reforms. The same issues divided older officers. The navy's John Rodgers and Robert Shufeldt proposed a course of reform quite different from that of Luce, Mahan, Dewey, and Sampson. Senior army men, like Schofield, Abbot, and Newton, became early advocates of a war army, while the navy's Porter and the army's Sherman, Sheridan, Miles, and Kautz held somewhat ambivalent positions—supporting certain forms of war readiness and displaying indifference to others. By the nineties, when a consensus began to develop, many of the former advocates of a peace army or navy started urging readiness for war, apparently convinced, whatever their rank, by the arguments of their former opponents. In fact, the evidence of a sharp clash between junior and senior officers is confined almost solely to reform of the promotion system—where interests did differ according to rank.[29]

However much boredom, stagnation in promotion, and fears for the services' futures may have contributed to the impetus behind military reform, only the armed services officers' concern for national security and their belief in the likelihood of great-power war adequately explain the nature and direction of military modernization. Had officers sought only more rapid promotion or a more secure future, other reforms offered equally bright prospects. The officers' interest, instead, in a variety of reforms that brought no obvious career benefits but contributed to the services' preparation for great-power conflict strongly suggests that the reformers' commitment to peacetime readiness was far more than the simple pursuit of personal or institutional interests.

According to a second critical interpretation, the military reformers' possibly sincere but allegedly misguided concern for national security reflected a gross misunderstanding of America's strategic situation. Claiming that events in Europe were "none of our business" and asserting that an invasion of the United States was "technically much less possible at that time [1880s] than it had been in 1775," one advocate of that interpretation found not "even [a] distant threat of war . . . visible on the horizon." He consequently concluded that the military reformers had advanced a doctrine "of 'adequate' preparedness beforehand to meet all the imponderables and unpredictables of war and policy" at the very time when "no vital national interest was even remotely imperiled" by America's military weakness. While admitting the "profoundly defensive . . . inspiration'' of military reform, he nevertheless characterized as "megalomania" such proposals as those of the 1890 Policy Board. In the same vein, a more recent criticism claimed that the Endicott board "dispensed bloodcurdling fantasies" about "rationally [in]-conceivable" coastal attacks.[30]

That line of criticism contains three flaws. It overlooks the officer corps' own appreciation of the very great national assets upon which those critics based their conclusions—demographic strength, industrial power, geopolitical isolation, and freedom from continental rivals. The interpretation also ignores the course of late-nineteenth-century international politics, which also alarmed many civilians, and it implicitly confuses a lack of armed conflict with evidence of war's improbability.

Commanding General William T. Sherman's 1880 dismissal of the idea of invasion as "simply preposterous" provides but one indication that army and navy officers of the century's last quarter had a realistic understanding of the circumstances that guarded the United States against foreign occupation. Brigadier General John Gibbons, commander of forces in the Pacific Northwest, explained the bases of Sherman's assertion. America's great population and the power derived from its railroads, manufactures, and agriculture, wrote Gibbons, discredited "the idea that *any* force from abroad—even the largest that the available transportation of the world could bring—could ever succeed in obtaining possession of or permanently hold[ing] any considerable portion of our widely extended country." Captain Francis V. Greene, one of the army's younger reformers, observed that "no nation which has a great army has the mercantile marine for transporting it across the ocean." Invasion fears were therefore "chimerical," and any "attempt to carry on war across three thousand miles of ocean . . . would be the act of a madman." Naval officers reached similar conclusions, Captain William T. Sampson arguing for example that the "probability of an invasion from any nation is very remote."[31]

Officers also recognized that continental rivalries restrained the overseas ambitions of European nations and that military power diminished in proportion to its distance from the home base. In 1890 Captain Alfred T. Mahan wrote that such political and military facts had become "undeniable and just elements" in both "the calculations of the statesmen" and plans for continental defense. Speaking for army officers, Major General William H. Carter looked back on the nation's military situation in the eighties to recall that America's "isolation and the rivalries of European nations . . . served . . . to guard us from the usual result of neglect of military policies."[32] Only after the Sino-Japanese War of

1894–95 seemingly demonstrated that physical isolation alone failed to provide invulnerability to invasion did the reformers consistently offer plans for significantly larger land forces, which even then would usually have brought their total to less than one hundred thousand men.[33]

Rather than demonstrating megalomaniacal fears of invasion, military reform proposals of the eighties and early nineties sought simply to protect the nation's coasts against the blockades, raids, and bombardments that clearly lay within the capability of America's potential enemies. Against such assaults, isolation and the elements of potential but as yet undeveloped military strength offered no certain safeguard. Although army and navy officers recognized that political rivalries for the moment restrained any likely European enemy, they also knew that coastal fortifications and a modern navy would take at least a decade to build. In the meantime, an unpredicted change in the European political climate would have found the United States years away from an effective defense. Reform advocates could hardly therefore have accepted the analysis of those critics who in hindsight have argued that the rational approach required delaying preparation until war had become "visible on the horizon."[34]

The extent to which responsible civil leaders shared the military reformers' strategic analysis also lays open to question interpretations casting doubt on the latter's rationality. Both the service secretaries and the presidents who appointed them, for example, supported programs of military reform in language quite similar to that used by armed services officers.[35] In 1881 and again in 1884 President Chester A. Arthur called the attention of Congress to the sad state of America's coastal defenses and stated his "conviction that every consideration of national safety, economy, and honor imperatively demands a thorough rehabilitation of our navy." The "teachings of history," he claimed, also suggested the wisdom of adequate preparation "to enforce any policy . . . we think wise to adopt." Like Arthur, who feared that a "long peace" had lulled Americans into a "sense of fancied security," President Grover Cleveland maintained that any "nation that cannot resist aggression is constantly exposed to it."[36] In words that any military officer might have used, former Democratic presidential candidate Samuel Tilden too warned that "the recent scramble of the European powers for the acquisition of colonies" might lead to a challenge to the Monroe Doctrine and assaults on coastal cities.[37]

Similar observations came from members of Congress. Representative William McAdoo of New Jersey, like military officers acknowledging the improbability of invasion, nevertheless urged reasonable preparation for war. And Pennsylvania congressman Andrew G. Curtin argued that the pitiful state of America's defenses and the "perfect preparations of the nations of Europe" enabled any of them to "bring to the harbor of New York a naval force which would pass the guns stationed in the fortifications there and lay under tribute that metropolitan city."[38]

The probability of war and the condition of both the navy's ships and the army's forts also became the fare of such leading civilian journals as *Scribner's Magazine*, the *Atlantic Monthly*, *Forum*, *Harper's Monthly*, *Century Magazine*, and the *North American Review*, whose editor claimed that Ferdinand de Lesseps's plans for a canal had made the European threat to the Monroe Doctrine "the theme of politicians and the press."[39] Whatever the cause, civilian monthlies treated military subjects much as did service publications. Reviewing Lieutenant Kelley's *The Question of Ships* in 1884, the *Atlantic Monthly* claimed to find no subject "of greater or more pressing public importance to this country than the immediate construction of a powerful and efficient fleet." Like many military officers, John Kasson, a popular historian and American minister to Austria-Hungary, warned readers of the *North American Review* about the threat to the Monroe Doctrine posed by European imperialism, commercial rivalry, and construction of an isthmian canal.[40]

The similarity of military and some official as well as popular analyses of the world scene reveals that civilian fears of the possibly dire consequences of continued American defenselessness oftentimes matched the concerns of army and navy officers. If in hindsight some critics concluded that the description of danger was overdrawn, they must at least extend their critique to a significant portion of civil society as well. Moreover, the period's history of frequent diplomatic controversy stopping just short of war, the military officers' recognition of the elements of strength in America's international position, and the modest nature of their reforms suggest that the services had a quite realistic comprehension of the age, an understanding shared by many thoughtful and perceptive contemporaries.[41]

The motives of America's military reformers have recently received yet a third challenge, one often only implicit in a fresh reexamination of the forces shaping the history of modern America. Nineteenth-century industrial developments, runs that new analysis, provided the United

States with more capital and productive capacity than its society, as then structured, could absorb. That surplus caused extreme economic fluctuations characterized by extravagant booms followed by deep and prolonged depressions accompanied by severe unemployment, social unrest, and, most important, demands for political reform. Fearing one of the latter periods might produce a revolution in the social order, some American leaders, the interpretation suggests, sought to dispose of the excess abroad and thereby moderate the extremes of the business cycle and eliminate the attendant unrest. To guarantee continued access to the requisite overseas markets, those leaders supposedly advocated the establishment of an American insular empire from which strengthened armed forces could guard the nation's foreign trade and investment.

That socioeconomic interpretation of American turn-of-the-century expansionism implies that military reformers concealed behind their rhetoric about possible assaults on the continental United States a desire to create an imperial army and navy capable of establishing an American overseas empire. Nor does the challenge to the reformers' stated motives always remain implicit. One study of nineteenth-century military reform charges, for example, that naval officers abandoned their traditional opposition to imperialism when their long-standing belief in a vigorous commerce as the basis of ''America's economic and social vitality . . . metamorphosed into a rationale for overseas territorial expansion.'' Another account, resting largely on the work of Admiral Mahan, has supplied the reasons for that claimed metamorphosis. Naval officers at least, the study asserted, saw the route to national greatness in a large manufacturing output, overseas colonial markets, a numerous merchant fleet, and a powerful navy to secure the whole. At the same time, concluded the study, officers feared that a large manufacturing output would outstrip home consumption and produce unemployment and social upheaval, thus threatening national greatness unless the United States seized an insular empire from which a strengthened army and navy could guarantee access to the Asian and Latin American markets for the nation's industrial surplus.[42]

Superficially, much can be said for that analysis. Many late-nineteenth-century army and navy officers were clearly disposed to support imperial policies. For more than a century the armed services had been promoting territorial and economic expansion—the navy as it opened new overseas markets and protected the merchants' access to old ones, and the army as it conquered and fostered development of the American West. Creation of an overseas empire would in a sense merely allow

the services to continue their old roles in new theaters. Experience had
also accustomed military officers to the use of force in imposing American domination and American values on populations that the *Army
and Navy Journal* described as "semicivilized people who look upon
magnanimity and fair dealing as pusillanimity and cowardice."[43] And
officers of both services did comment on the rapid expansion of America's export trade, using possible European resistance to American commercial expansion as an argument for military preparedness. In regard
to Hawaii at least, the *Army and Navy Journal* claimed that "Army and
Navy officers have urged upon various administrations the necessity of
the United States taking possession . . . or securing control."[44] A few
(mostly naval) officers also seemed explicitly and unreservedly imperial
in their hopes for America's future. The eighties, Commodore Robert
W. Shufeldt told his daughter, were "America's opportunity—with
Europe discontented and hungry, Monarchs threatened & the Masses
threatening, we could . . . rise to the dignity of the first nation on
Earth." Shufeldt even felt certain that he could " 'annex' the whole
'Orient' under our starry banner." In the same vein, a young reformer,
Commander Henry C. Taylor, claimed that American control of an interoceanic canal in Nicaragua meant one thing: *"Empire."*[45] Military
officers seemed therefore predisposed to accept arguments favoring creation of an insular empire, especially if such expansion seemed likely to
promote the national welfare.

Whether that predisposition became inspiration is another matter;
in fact the socioeconomic interpretation of American history gives rise
to a misleading analysis of the origins of military reform. That the
United States eventually used its strengthened army and navy to establish the rudiments of an island empire offers no certain indication that
such was the reformers' intention. More important, a closer examination of the evidence used in the study linking Admiral Mahan and the
military reformers to a socioeconomically motivated imperialism reveals
little support for the notion that military officers were familiar with, let
alone responded to, the idea that an insular empire would keep American society "ongoing without the problems of underemployment and
resulting social upheavals." That popular study's conclusion rests largely upon a misleading juxtaposition of statements drawn from two of
Mahan's essays. "A Twentieth Century Outlook," published in 1897,
included the claim that "the increase of home consumption . . . [could]
not keep up with the increase of forth-putting and the faculty of distribution afforded by steam." Joined with the prediction, found in an

1890 essay, "The United States Looking Outward," that "whether they will or no, Americans must now begin to look outward" because the "growing production of the country demands it," Mahan seemingly revealed an awareness of overproduction, its social implications, and an imperial means for its relief, while advocating a program of naval increase and territorial expansion that led to the 1898 war with Spain and the establishment of America's insular empire.[46]

That juxtaposition, however, conceals Mahan's meaning. The first statement refers not to the United States but to a mid-nineteenth-century European condition that Mahan believed was passing as he wrote. Mahan expected, moreover, that "increased ease of living, increased wealth, increased population," and "great resources only partially developed" would provide the United States an alternative to overseas commercial expansion and absorb its energies for years to come. Later in the same essay, published with the possibility of war with Spain clearly on the horizon, Mahan specifically denied that the United States had "yet felt the outward impulse that now markedly characterizes European peoples."[47] In sum, as the admiral's most recent biographer has correctly noted, "Mahan was not in the vanguard of those imperialists in 1898 who . . . saw in a victorious war with Spain for Cuba Libre an opportunity to annex the distant Philippines." As late as July of that year, Mahan, who even left on a European holiday as war threatened, confessed his inability to adjust "to the new point of view opened . . . by Dewey's victory at Manila." Until that time ignorant of the asserted relation between events in Cuba and the acquisition of the Philippines as a base from which to exploit Oriental markets, Mahan confessed that Dewey's triumph had "opened a vista of possibilities which were not by me in the least foreseen."[48]

The perplexed Mahan had earlier rested his case for a very modest acquisition of overseas bases upon arguments of a strategic and racial rather than commercial character. As Europeans exported their surplus production to the Orient, he wrote, the Eastern states appropriated "the material progress of Europe unfettered by Christian traditions." That appropriation reduced the relative military advantage of the West, exposing it to attack by nations that lacked "the principles which powerfully modify, though they cannot yet control wholly even now, the merely natural impulses of Western peoples." The world in Mahan's view consequently stood "at the opening of a period when the question is to be settled decisively . . . whether Eastern or Western civilization is to dominate throughout the earth and to control its future." Until the

West fulfilled its mission "to receive into its own bosom and raise to its own ideals" the peoples of the East, it must compensate for the material advantage lost through trade by strengthening its armed forces and seizing the outposts of its civilization. Along those outposts, the West must prepare to fight to "insure that it shall not go down till it has leavened the character of the world."[49]

Speaking of one such strategic point, whose possession he and other officers had long advocated, Mahan wrote:

> It is a question for the whole civilized world, and not for the United States only, whether the Sandwich [Hawaiian] Islands, with their geographic and military importance unrivaled by that of any other position in the North Pacific, shall in the future be an outpost of European civilization or of the comparative barbarism of China. . . . [M]any military men abroad . . . look with apprehension toward the day when the vast mass of China—now inert—may yield to one of those impulses which have in past ages buried civilization under a wave of barbaric invasion.

The "insular empire" proposed by Mahan before 1898 in fact extended only to Hawaii and the Caribbean, and it sought not a route for commercial expansion, which naval officers thought required no special aid unless hindered by antagonistic Europeans, but a part of that outpost line along which the United States in company with the European powers would defend their common culture.[50]

Military attitudes toward expansion also reflected an amalgam of other ideas, most of them originating in the eighteenth century and only remotely related to the socioeconomic interpretation of American expansionism. Rather than a form of exploitation or a means to secure the social order, military officers believed that foreign trade brought economic benefits to both parties and that commerce required the support of armed force only to remove the unnatural impediments to its growth. By promoting foreign trade, wrote Lieutenant Commander Robert M. G. Brown, the navy sought to destroy "the barriers between the last exclusive empires of the Orient and the civilization and progress of the more enlightened West." Speaking of the army's comparable role, the *Army and Navy Journal* claimed that soldiers had "opened the path of civilization across the Continent, and substituted the domestic virtues and productive industries of a peace loving and progressive people for the savage freedom and wasteful, destructive vices of barbarism." Because commerce spread civilization and ultimately promoted creation of a peaceful world of federated republican states, military officers felt justified in their occasional use of force to open new areas to trade's beneficial effects. If allowed to move freely, explained the *Journal*, trade became the "Hand-Maid of Peace," and the "idealist dreams of peace" would be realized when the "area of free commercial intercourse" had achieved global dimensions and stimulated the creation of a voluntary federation of republican states.[51]

Although such attitudes toward trade and Western civilization are clearly arrogant, ethnocentric, and potentially imperialistic, their character differs sharply from the socioeconomic conception. Before 1898, moreover, the American military made little effort to exploit the imperialistic potential of such attitudes, and officers in fact expressed grave doubts about the usefulness of a far-flung insular empire. Thoughtful naval men, recognizing that the United States Navy could accomplish its peacetime mission without overseas bases, argued that the small American fleet must in war look to the defense of the nation's coasts. Any island empire would only weaken America's defenses as it diverted ships to guard isolated outposts. "It would be a real misfortune," warned naval reformer William S. Sims, "for us to acquire any territory in this direction [the China coast], for we could not possibly hold it unless our fleet were as strong at least as the first power that wanted to take it away from us."[52] So long as the army and navy could keep open American ports to neutral shipping, the reformers maintained, the nation's commerce could find its way to overseas markets. That task required the United States to keep its armed forces at home—the army manning the coastal fortifications and preventing small amphibious landings, and the navy using a small fleet of limited-range battleships to disrupt any invasion force, counter naval raids, and preclude that dispersal of enemy forces necessary to conduct a close blockade of American ports.

Because the reformers' demands for a military revival antedated significant recognition of the socioeconomic argument that insular expansion would promote American trade and thereby ensure domestic stability, the very timing of the military reform movement undercuts that interpretation. Naval officers who wrote about trade in the eighties, for instance, sought not the acquisition of empire but a revival of the merchant marine, whose growth lagged far behind the increase in American overseas commerce. Those same naval officers failed, moreover, to exploit even the island coaling privileges the navy had already established, and reformers like Admiral David D. Porter recommended the retention of sails on American steam cruisers, thus relieving them of depend-

ence upon island coaling stations.[53] During the same period, army officers showed little interest in the creation of expeditionary forces of the
type required to seize and hold an island base, and they revealed a general indifference, even hostility, to territorial expansion. "We want no
more territory," wrote General William T. Sherman, who opposed annexation of both Canada and bases in the West Indies.[54]

Neither the approach of war with Spain nor growing civilian support
for insular expansion significantly changed those attitudes, especially
regarding expansion along the Asian coast and near the markets supposedly coveted by American imperialists. Lieutenant Sims's opposition
and Admiral Mahan's lack of prevision, already noted, paralleled the
views of Commodore George Dewey and the officers of the squadron
soon to seize Manila Bay. As late as the spring of 1898 they doubted
there would be war with Spain, a conflict they hoped to avoid, and
Dewey later recalled that it had never occurred to him "that we should
be taking Manila Bay permanently."[55]

As war approached, army officers criticized civilian jingoism and,
according to one historian, were "by no means in the forefront of the
call for an aggressive policy toward Spain." The army's commanding
general, Nelson A. Miles, hoped that the differences would be peacefully resolved, perhaps by arbitration, and young Captain Tasker H.
Bliss, enroute to Spain as America's army attaché, took a similar stand.
He told Ambassador Stewart L. Woodford that "army officers generally" doubted the differences with Spain were "worth a war under any
circumstances . . . ; it was infinitely better for us to . . . [leave Cuba] under Spanish control, than to force an issue merely for seizing the
island." A future army chief of staff, Captain Hugh L. Scott, then on
duty in Washington, claimed that the war with Spain had come "without the soldiers exerting the slightest influence toward that end."[56]

If, as the socioeconomic interpretation of American history implies,
military reform sprang from a program of commercially motivated insular expansion aimed at preserving America's social order, army and
navy reformers unaccountably sought to throw away the unique opportunity presented by the Cuban problem.

In the nineteenth century's last quarter armed forces officers engaged
in an intramural debate over the direction of military reform, a debate
that ended in wide support for an army and navy equipped and trained

in peace to defend America against great-power attack. Military officers buttressed the consensus that emerged within the services by calling attention to developments that exacerbated international tensions and increased the likelihood of a conflict along the American coasts, which according to West Point's Professor Peter S. Michie were "bound to be the theatre of immediate and active operations in case of war."[57] While thus justifying programs designed to prepare the services for war rather than a continuation of traditional but no longer needed peace-oriented commercial and constabulary duties, military reformers also began to propose concentration of the combat forces, improved officer education, and periodic maneuvers—all of which would enhance the services' readiness for war. Working from the top down as well, the reformers supported creation of military intelligence agencies and advocated the establishment within each departmental headquarters of a general staff that could coordinate the work of the administrative and logistical bureaus and ensure adequate planning against the possibility of war.

Although latter-day critics have challenged the stated purposes of service reform, denying that readiness was ever the reformers' chief motive, the criticisms derive whatever force they possess from a selective examination of the available evidence. The interpretations charging reformers with the pursuit of institutional rather than national interests fail, for instance, to explain why reformers rejected potentially popular peace-oriented reforms that too would have fulfilled institutional needs. The critics who describe service reform as the result of a conflict between junior and senior officers—a conflict actually present only in regard to changes in the promotion system—not only ignore the lack of any clear rank-based divisions among officers in the debate over war- versus peace-oriented forces but also overlook the consensus that emerged among most officers in the nineties. Those writers stressing an alleged military megalomania have similarly slighted an important fact: the invariably modest character of reforms advanced by service personnel, who thoroughly understood the great military advantages inherent in America's strategic and political position. Military officers, moreover, described the international situation much as did important segments of the nation's civilian leadership, whose rationality the critics failed to question. In regard to the more recent suggestion of a socioeconomic motive for military reform, the evidence reveals that military officers were generally unfamiliar with that argument for American imperialism. Prior to 1898, in fact, military officers usually opposed Ori-

ental territorial expansion, and those who advocated limited insular an-
nexations closer to home did so for strategic and defensive reasons rather
than out of a desire to promote American trade in order to preserve the
domestic social order.[58] Indeed, only an acceptance of the reformers'
claims that they sought to prepare the army and navy for a new era of increasing international tension provides an explanation for both the impetus and the focus of the movement for military reform.

PART II

The Imperial Experience

The war with Spain . . . procured us a prominent place among the nations, . . . [and] although we abstain from proclaiming ourselves as such, we are virtually one of the Great Powers and one of the greatest of them. With our new position there has descended on our shoulders the heavy burden resting on all Great Powers, of assisting in the regulating and shaping of human affairs. From the moral and intellectual point of view no nation is better qualified for such a task.

Captain Carl Reichmann, USA
"In Pace Para Bellum," *Inf. J.*,
II (January 1906), 5

CHAPTER 4

The Response to Imperialism

AMERICA'S UNPRECEDENTED DEPLOYMENT of its armed forces overseas in 1898 generated a broad reassessment of national military policy that engaged the attention of the officer corps throughout the following decade and produced a strong current of optimism that characterized military thought until the close of the Roosevelt administration. While a minority of officers, including some who shared the anti-imperialists' objections to an expansive foreign policy, continued to focus on the problems of coastal defense, many others looked outward, either eagerly embracing or reluctantly accepting America's new obligations as the inevitable accompaniment of great-power status. Unlike the fundamental issues that had divided military officers in the eighties, a degree of consensus quickly characterized the new review. While groups sometimes differed in their conclusions, none looked backward as they all accepted that the armed forces must seek adaptation to changing national circumstances. Even more noticeable, army and navy officers almost without exception expressed exuberant satisfaction with America's new place in world affairs and great confidence in the armed forces' postwar rehabilitation.

By any measure the services' strength increased dramatically during the new century's first decade, a circumstance contributing markedly to

65

the confidence and optimism pervading America's military leadership. In 1899 Congress voted an almost threefold expansion of the prewar regular army and simultaneously approved an increment of twenty-eight-month volunteers sufficient to bring the total force to four times pre-1898 levels. When those volunteer enlistments approached their expiration, the nation's legislators created an expansible regular force that the president, at his discretion, might raise to one hundred thousand men. For the first time in several decades a commanding general could report that the United States had "a military force . . . commensurate with its requirements, magnitude, and institutions."[1]

As Congress also more than doubled the naval building program of the previous decade, authorizing between 1898 and 1907 the construction of nineteen battleships and ten armored cruisers, the navy's growth gave comparable encouragement to that service's officers. Naval strength grew in another way when the new battleships reached almost twice the displacement of prewar models, which had carried only four rather than eight or ten of the largest caliber guns. America's navy consequently rose from sixth to second rank, the *Army and Navy Journal* confidently predicting that the United States could now "mobilize in home waters a fleet sufficiently powerful to provide adequate protection for our coasts and take the offensive against an enemy disposed to attack them."[2]

The postwar improvement in America's coastal fortifications, which at last approximated the program advanced by the 1885 Endicott board, also encouraged confidence in the armed forces' capacity to secure the continental United States, and the *Journal* described the "magnificent" new forts and guns as "the strongest chain of sea coast defenses in the world," one placing the United States "almost beyond the possibility of successful assault by any enemy, no matter how powerful."[3]

Congress and the Roosevelt administration also enhanced satisfaction with the nation's military policy by educational and organizational reforms that strengthened the services in less material ways. In 1901 Secretary of War Elihu Root fulfilled one of the reformers' hopes with a redesigned educational system capped by an army war college that, like its older naval counterpart, would prepare officers to meet the wartime demands of the highest command and staff positions as well as devise plans for the organization, training, and employment of the land forces. As a planning agency that might coordinate the actions of the combat forces with the work of the Washington bureaus, the college was but the forerunner of a general staff, whose approval Root steered through Congress only two years later. The secretary sought in effect to vest direction of both the field army and the administrative staff in the hands of a single agency responsible to the war secretary and devoted to the reformers' concept that preparation against the possibility of war had become an army's essential peacetime activity. Within three years that new general staff, according to the *Army and Navy Journal*, "demonstrated . . . [its] practical value" while directing the 1906 reoccupation of Cuba with a smooth efficiency contrasting sharply with the chaos and scandalous mismanagement that in 1898 had left three quarters of General Shafter's Fifth Corps ridden with malaria, put unneeded volunteer troops in filthy, unsanitary camps where disease, most often the rampant typhoid fever, killed six men in every thousand, jammed a thousand freight cars of desperately needed equipment into Tampa rail yards capable of unloading but three a day, and led to charges by the army's commanding general that his troops were being fed embalmed and maggot-filled beef.[4]

Naval reformers advocating a general staff for their service as well had to settle in 1900 for an ad hoc planning and advisory body known as the General Board, which lacked both legislative sanction and legal authority over the navy's bureau chiefs. Determined eventually to succeed, Rear Admiral Henry C. Taylor, a reformer who subsequently served on the new board, concluded that "these things work slowly and must be reformed slowly—or else reform is transitory." But not too slowly, for Taylor hoped that the "long weary tapping" needed to "break through the crust of custom" might result, during Roosevelt's second term, in the creation of a modern naval staff.[5]

Ironically, the naval reformers' failure may have resulted from their service's success, its spectacular victories in the Spanish-American War offering no obvious evidence of the need for reform. Lack of support from Secretary of the Navy John D. Long also certainly contributed, hampering the reformers' ability to overcome both Congressional suspicion of a staff system with monarchial associations and bureau opposition to any control except that of the secretary—resistance that Root had surmounted for the army. In the meantime, the navy's war college and intelligence office might perform some of the planning duties assigned to the army's general staff.[6]

Less tangible developments also contributed to the military officers' optimism and their greater confidence in the services' joint capacity to defend American interests. Army captain Carl Reichmann put the first of those developments into words when he typically noted how America's stunning defeat of Spain gave the United States "a prominent place among nations" as "one of the greatest" of the great powers. That victory, wrote the editor of the *Army and Navy Journal*, had "given the world a demonstration of national strength" and "gained the increased respect of other powers." Because the "nation that is most thoroughly prepared to fight is least likely to have to fight," America's new status and the modest postwar improvements in the regular forces had, in the view of the editor and many military officers, reduced the chances of an assault.[7]

Military confidence also reflected the officers' belief that the recent war had awakened both the public and the administration to the need for stronger forces-in-being. The United States, wrote the *Journal*'s editor, had surely "relearned the old lesson—let us hope never to forget it—that the Army is one of the vital institutions of the Republic." In President Roosevelt, moreover, "both services have a steadfast friend in the White House. He discusses their needs with knowledge and sympathy, and his utterances show that he is vitally concerned in the development of the national defenses."[8]

The enhanced rewards of military life may too have contributed to the optimism that characterized army and navy officers in the decade after 1898. The services' formerly deadening routine gave way to a life of "hurrah, hurry, bustle, and unusualness," wrote Captain Robert L. Bullard, who would command the United States Second Army in World War I.[9] New duties, such as the military government of Cuba and the Philippines, the pacification of the latter islands, and participation in international peacekeeping ventures like the China Relief Expedition also boosted military prestige, thus easing many of the humiliations and frustrations of the preceding quarter century, as did more rapid promotion in the enlarged armed forces and the study of techniques for use of the services' new ships and guns.

The military officers' sense of confidence might have been complete but for their uncertainty concerning the exact nature of America's future role in world affairs. As the services' leaders eventually looked beyond their strengthened services and began to discuss the possible future duties of the army and navy, their agreement faltered, and military thought came to reflect many of the differences dividing the civilian community at the turn of the century. Officers who believed the United States should enter the struggle for international commercial supremacy employed arguments for military reform very like those of the civilian advocates of territorial expansion and armed intervention overseas. Of-

ficers who believed that American policy should continue along traditional lines revealed an awareness of the military and political dangers
associated with the assumption of colonial responsibilities, a common
theme of those civilians who attacked recent American policy. Between
those two limits, other military officers seemed both attracted and re-
pelled by the imperial vision, describing such responsibilities as both
the inevitable burden and ultimate glory of great-power status. Those
officers joined the many civilians who considered imperial expansion an
unpleasant duty that Americans neither could nor should avoid. An examination of those three lines of thought and the military proposals designed to facilitate each illustrates the influences on army and navy officers of both international events and civilian opinion.

From the civilian apologists for America's conquest of the Philippines and continued control of Cuba, expansion-minded military officers borrowed an entire array of arguments, the least sophisticated of
which built upon the late-nineteenth-century Anglo-Saxonism popular-
ized in the United States by John Fiske, John Burgess, and Josiah
Strong. History, heredity, and a fortunate geography, according to their
argument, had endowed Americans, and other Anglo-Saxon or Teutonic peoples, with advanced economies, superior moral qualities, and
peerless political skills. America's imperial expansion consequently afforded the United States an opportunity, in cooperation with the other
"civilized" powers, to bring order and progress to the world by displac-
ing inferior peoples or educating them in Anglo-Saxon ways.[10] Aug-
menting that argument in the aftermath of the war with Spain and the
prolonged depression of the nineties, Strong maintained that bearing
the white man's burden also meant an increased export of manufactures
that would assist both the United States and the underdeveloped world.
The latter would receive with its goods the benefits of civilization, and
the former could dispose of its excess production and thereby maintain
high levels of employment and forestall domestic unrest.[11]

The socioeconomic aspect of Strong's argument received more profound attention from Charles A. Conant, an economist and government financial consultant. Possessing savings in excess of the opportunities for remunerative domestic investment, Conant argued, Americans
had built factories that produced goods that found no buyers. When
those factories consequently closed, unemployment and social unrest
followed. Because the United States could neither significantly increase

home consumption (at best a short-run solution) nor eliminate the excess savings by turning to socialism (a philosophy Americans then abhorred), only one policy promised relief from periodic economic hardship and political unrest. The United States must adopt imperialism, which Conant defined as the maintenance of free access to foreign markets for investment and consumer goods.[12]

If America's potential overseas customers refused to purchase its goods or its industrialized competitors resisted American encroachment in their markets, commercial expansion might lead to armed intervention. Faced with that possibility, both Conant and Strong equivocated. Criticizing recent American foreign policy for its intimidation of weaker nations and describing empire and a powerful military establishment as an economic drain, Conant hoped to win commercial supremacy by urging America to lower its tariff, expand its banking facilities, and improve its marketing techniques. More tolerant of territorial expansion, if it could be accomplished righteously, Strong nevertheless opposed the large standing army possibly required to carry out his proposals for constructing an isthmian canal, absorbing the Caribbean, and blocking Russian efforts to dominate the Orient.

Other civilian expansionists, however, refused to hedge. Brooks Adams, a member of the influential circle joining Theodore Roosevelt, Henry Cabot Lodge, John Hay, and Alfred Thayer Mahan, fully endorsed the use of armed force to forestall his earlier gloomy predictions of America's imminent decline. In a work antedating the conflict with Spain, *The Law of Civilization and Decay*, Adams had hypothesized that nature endowed human societies with varying levels of energy, which they converted into goods to satisfy basic needs or stored as wealth. Militant societies, by converting energy into goods through the conquest of wealthy neighbors or the seizure of strategic points from which to tax their trade, quickly reached the limits of their growth as they exhausted themselves in constant combat. Advanced, economic societies, of which America was one, expanded their store of wealth virtually without limit because they achieved it through efficiency in production and trade. That very efficiency, however, led to decline, accompanied—as increasing productivity must be—by the growth of a class of bankers who sought to create additional wealth by reducing their fellow citizens to income levels sufficient only to sustain peasants and laborers, whom Adams regarded as a distinct hereditary group within each society. The imaginative and militant types, who had built the society and protected it from rapacious neighbors, perished on so meager a diet, leaving the resulting nation of bankers and proletarians to stagnate while awaiting internal disintegration or external destruction by more virile aliens.[13]

Following the war with Spain, a more hopeful Adams wrote that the United States might postpone its inevitable collapse by altering its educational and organizational systems in the interests of greater productivity and reducing its transportation costs with a secure network of worldwide communications based upon an isthmian canal and control of Central America. Operating behind the dual protection of overseas bases, like the Philippines, and a powerful army and navy, the United States might aggressively exploit the markets and resources of the East and seize from London the scepter of world commercial supremacy. America could, Adams predicted, "outweigh any single empire, if not all empires combined. The whole world will pay her tribute." A failure to meet the challenge, however, would mean a transfer of England's former supremacy to a continental nexus of France, Germany, and especially Russia, which would dominate the world.[14]

Similar fears of a Slavic threat to Western civilization and appeals for commercial and territorial conquests also found their way into the work of those early-twentieth-century military officers who advocated an expansionist foreign policy. In 1901 for example, the Naval War College grouped the principal powers according to their perceived interests in China and commenced study of a hypothetical Far Eastern war in which the United States, Great Britain, and Japan jointly resisted the efforts of Russia, aided by France and Germany, to absorb the fading Celestial Empire. Regarding Japan as the principal barrier to Slavic expansion, military leaders initially supported the 1902 Anglo-Japanese alliance, to which the *Army and Navy Journal* gave its "unqualified approval" because the treaty served as "a full expression of the American policy respecting China's territorial status."[15]

Assuming the public's willingness to support that policy, forcibly if necessary, some army and navy officers joined civilian expansionists in urging the acquisition of a base in northern China. Members of the navy's General Board, for instance, suggested the annexation of a port in northern or central China after the 1900 China Relief Expedition demonstrated the Philippines' inadequacies as a base for operations in those areas of China most threatened by Russia.[16] Army officers participating in the expedition reacted in a similar manner. Immediately following relief of the legations, Major General Adna R. Chaffee, commander of the American contingent and later the army's chief of staff, recommended the prompt withdrawal of all foreign troops, including his own. Otherwise, he advised the adjutant general, China's lack of food and housing would make Peking the scene of mass civilian starvation and death. When the administration apparently rejected his advice—for "political reasons not apparent to [him]"—Chaffee cautioned Adjutant General Henry C. Corbin that if the United States wished to "secure its purpose, viz[.] preservation of the Empire of the Chinese," it must recognize the need to be more "forceful" in defending American interests there. And when Chaffee became convinced that the other powers had "doomed [China] to disruption," he yielded to the apparently inevitable and urged creation of an American sphere of influence in Chili Province, the "fairest field remaining uninfluenced by other powers."[17]

For a time after 1898, imperially minded military officers also considered further territorial expansion in the Caribbean. Some, like Rear Admiral George W. Melville, one of his service's Washington bureau chiefs, recommended the purchase of all European holdings in the West Indies, while Admiral George Dewey pressed Secretary Long to buy the Danish-owned islands, asserting: "The further east the acquisition [of a naval base in the Caribbean], the greater the value as against aggression from European bases; the further south the acquisition, the greater the value for aggressive action on our part against localities in South America." Though army officers generally showed less interest in Caribbean acquisitions, some, like Major William A. Glassford, a frequent contributor to army journals, urged the establishment of a "few fortified stations . . . with a view to facilitate naval operations," and Brigadier General Leonard Wood, soon Cuba's military governor, some of his staff, and at least one other departmental commander hoped that Cuba would one day petition the United States for annexation.[18]

Less formal means of control also drew the attention of what the Naval Institute's president, Rear Admiral Caspar Goodrich, described as "a large and enthusiastic body of officers" who argued for a much strengthened navy, one comprising perhaps a hundred battleships. While recognizing that America's existing navy could "very easily" protect the nation's trade and citizens in all those countries where they seemed most "liable to get unfair treatment," Commander Bradley A. Fiske, the holder of sixty patents for his inventive solutions to naval problems, asserted that "we need a navy even larger than Great Britain's . . . because our policy is more provocative of war than hers." The United States Navy, wrote the institute's 1904 prize essayist, Lieutenant

Simon P. Fullinwider, must become "such a power as the world has never seen." So strengthened, the country could follow the advice of another young navalist, Richmond P. Hobson, who won promotion to captain for his 1898 derring-do outside Santiago Harbor and later left the navy to pursue a Congressional career. The United States, he wrote, "should extend the Monroe Doctrine to cover the Empire of China . . . [and] into an American Doctrine . . . to [cover] all the less happy peoples of the earth, . . . all the yellow and black peoples." It was the "will of God" that America build a "dominating navy," one that could "dictate peace to the world and . . . hasten the reign of beneficence in world politics."[19]

As another possible alternative to annexation, turn-of-the-century army officers showed a marked interest in expeditionary operations to police the Caribbean, and they frequently predicted that future great-power conflicts would occur, not along the borders of those states but in areas overseas, far from the contestants' home territories. Reflecting that assumption, the army staff began to prepare plans for Caribbean expeditionary forces capable of maintaining order and defending American interests in that region.[20]

In addition to the strategic justification for Oriental or Caribbean expansion, army and navy officers made use of the commercial arguments found in the work of Adams, Strong, and Conant. Addressing its military readers, the *Army and Navy Journal* claimed that

> the tremendous forces which have until recently been devoted to the development of our internal resources, and which have placed the country upon its present high level of prosperity, have been partially diverted to the sea in quest of new outlets for the products of American industry. In spite of the great absorptive capacity of the home markets, the productive enterprises of the United States must look beyond our own coasts for consumers for at least fifty per cent. of their output. And in this fact, together with [t]he changes of commercial policy which it incidentally involves, is to be found the genesis of the American policy of expansion.

With similar concerns seemingly in mind, naval officers like Commander Charles H. Stockton and Rear Admiral Stephen B. Luce, both former presidents of the Naval War College, urged upon Senator Henry Cabot Lodge the need for island "stepping stones" across the Pacific. And an army officer soon sent to observe Japan's operations in Manchuria, Captain Henry T. Allen, described the United States as "destined to be the dominant factor in the Oriental market" and therefore advised Secretary of War William H. Taft to obtain a coaling station in north China to aid "the proper development of our Oriental interests within the coming generation or two.'' During that same period, the army's first chief of staff, Major General Samuel B. M. Young, and the navy's senior officer, Admiral George Dewey, publicly defended acquisition of the Philippines on the grounds that they facilitated both access to the Chinese market and defense of America's Far Eastern interests.[21]

The military officers' arguments favoring commercial expansion generally lacked, however, one element figuring prominently in the analysis advanced by Charles Conant. Rather than advocate foreign trade for its supposed contribution to domestic stability, and use that relationship to justify a large military establishment, army and navy officers continued to stress older themes by emphasizing the potential of international trade to provoke conflict. Taking note of the country's expanding export trade, armed forces officers expected war to result less from America's imperialism than from foreign efforts to exclude its goods from the remaining open markets. War would come as the United States protested European imperialism and exclusiveness, protests that carried the risk of war. In that sense trade expansion had become a more important but not unforeseen element in America's strategic situation, bringing dangers against which the services' leaders had long urged the country to prepare. Trade, moreover, remained but one factor that might involve the United States in war. In the opinion of military officers, America's vigorous defense of the Monroe Doctrine and its increasing participation in great-power politics seemed equally provocative. To Commander Bradley A. Fiske, a future member of the General Board and aid to the naval secretary, each nation's rise to great-power status had required it to wage prolonged warfare. ''Shall not we? . . . [T]here is not a single reason to give, or to imagine, why the American people should not go through the same series of wars that all other nations have gone through.''[22]

Whereas officers like Fiske gloried in America's turn-of-the-century imperialism, others became its vigorous critics. The army's commanding general, Nelson A. Miles, even while making plans for the dispatch of an expeditionary army to the Philippines, wanted it clearly understood that the ''force ordered at this time is not expected to carry on a war to conquer an extensive territory.'' According to Miles's biographer, the general sought only to relieve Dewey, regarding a ''policy of expansionism, especially in the Philippines, . . . [as] a violation of the principles of the founding fathers.'' Nor did time soften Miles's opposition. Following retirement he sounded a theme common to many civilian anti-imperialists when condemning the Second Cuban Intervention as a war of conquest that could threaten "an end of the republic." For at least a decade after that Sunday in May 1898 when he privately accused President McKinley of waging a "political war," Miles opposed the acquisition of "territory against the will of the people thereof." Becoming the "police of the world" was, for a self-governing society, simply "too big a job."[23]

Unlike the outspoken Miles, most officers seemingly obeyed the earlier admonition of his predecessor, Lieutenant General John M. Schofield, who exemplified the late-nineteenth-century military tradition when he explained that officers must neither "judge what ought to be the public policy of the government . . . nor lay down general rules of policy for the future." Political constraints permitted officers to do no more than "explain fully and without reservation . . . the indispensable means for carrying out the national policy."[24]

Although that tradition, which service regulations reinforced, created no obstacle for those favoring expansionist policies, it probably silenced potential critics. However wise such constraints, they make it difficult to learn how many officers may have shared Miles's views or otherwise supported the civilian anti-imperialists. Nor can the relative paucity of open military opposition to expansion therefore serve as conclusive evidence that the course of American policy after 1898 left officers untroubled.

The meager evidence that has survived suggests to the contrary that many officers, especially those senior or retired service members whose ambitions no longer restrained their voices, had grave reservations. Rear Admiral Daniel Ammen, who in retirement served the government on a variety of isthmian canal commissions, in May 1898 warned then-Commodore George Dewey that holding the Philippines "would entail a very great . . . responsibility and under our form of government a very doubtful means of meeting it." For a time Dewey shared that view, believing, according to Frederick Palmer, that the American government was "not fitted for the rule of colonies." While those two naval officers doubted the wisdom of American policy, an army general who died fighting the Filipino insurrectionists, Henry W. Lawton, questioned the justice of what he described as an "unholy" war. Commenting publicly only after the rebellion's collapse, Major General John P. Story

asserted that the "United States . . . have ruthlessly suppressed in the
Philippines an insurrection better justified than was our Revolution of
glorious memory." In the same vein, Major General James Parker recorded in his memoirs the belief that annexation of the Philippines had
placed a stain on the nation's escutcheon without bringing any of the
promised economic advantages.[25]

The numerous oblique references to the Philippines in military writing, even by younger officers during the period of open conflict, suggest
a more widespread opposition to expansionist policies. The *Army and
Navy Journal*, which was free to speak on behalf of military opinion, almost invariably referred to the Philippines as a "burden" and selected
such editorial titles as "Those Horrid Philippines" for its labored attempts to put the best possible face on the course the government had
chosen and that military officers must support, whatever their personal
views.[26] Those views were often quietly hostile, claimed one young infantry officer, Major Robert L. Bullard, who kicked up a controversy
when he wrote:

> It is the recent experience of many of us to have seen officers of the United States
> Army who had been years in the service, by opinion and conduct, nullify over wide
> regions and render ineffective the settled and well-considered policy of their gov-
> ernment, because they were not, in their words, "in sympathy with the govern-
> ment's policy in keeping these islands."

To Bullard's claim, "Candor" replied that such officers constituted a
"small fraction" of the corps, while "Critic" maintained that it was
"no crime" to express opposition "to the acquisition and retention of
the Philippines," and a "policy of our Government . . . not in accord
with our ideas of justice." Naval commander Charles S. Sperry also
hinted at extensive malaise in the Philippines when he wrote to Mrs.
William S. Cowles, wife of another naval officer and sister to Theodore
Roosevelt, that he knew of no "expansionists or imperialists out
here."[27]

America's civilian anti-imperialists, while making a far more extensive case for the political dangers of colonialism than anything found in
military writing, similarly attacked the wisdom and justice of the government's policy. Colonialism, which they described as governing other
peoples against their will, violated the American Constitution, sub-
verted the national political tradition, and endangered the republic,
which, claimed quadrennial presidential aspirant William Jennings Bryan, "can have no subjects. A subject is possible only in a government

resting upon force; he is unknown in a government deriving its just powers from the consent of the governed.'' The United States could not therefore make Filipinos subjects "without endangering our form of government.'' Americans should devote their energies, wrote Carl Schurz, another leading opponent of imperialism, to solving the "great problem of democratic government, based upon equal rights and universal suffrage.'' Participation in European-style colonialism distracted Americans from that problem and threatened to block fulfillment of their "greatest responsibility.'' As David Starr Jordan, Stanford's president, told the university's graduates on May 25, 1898, the issue before the United States was "not what we shall do with Cuba, Porto [*sic*] Rico and the Philippines. It is what these prizes will do to us.'' Colonialism, being "un-American,'' would lead to centralized government, a disciplined population, and abandonment of the republican social order necessary for each individual's full development—in short to the destruction of American democracy.[28]

Civilian anti-imperialists also challenged the economic argument for expansion. No less eager for an increase in exports than the imperialists, Carl Schurz argued that the United States was "very extensively enlarging its foreign fields without big fleets and without colonies'' because America produced "more things that other nations wanted, and we could offer them at prices with which other nations could not compete.'' Military officers sometimes made the same point. Major John H. Parker and Lieutenant Commander Edward L. Beach, for instance, told their military readers that the United States could gain access to the Chinese market and benefit from the trade of the Philippines without retaining possession of the latter.[29] That both imperialists and their opponents were equally interested in a growing export trade also suggests that the statements of those other army and navy officers who vigorously argued in favor of commercial expansion provide no certain evidence that they favored territorial conquest.[30]

Some military officers also echoed the civilian anti-imperialists' claim that territorial expansion weakened rather than enhanced American security. Major Parker, for example, wrote that colonial possessions such as the Philippines, which were "not especially desirable from the standpoint of domestic policy, either in peace or in war, . . . may indeed prove an element of national weakness in time of war.'' Considered from "a military point of view,'' wrote Lieutenant Commander Beach, those islands were "decidedly a weakness.'' Such views paralleled those of civilian anti-imperialists like Schurz who thought that by holding the

Philippines the United States became "at once entangled in the jealousies and quarrels of European powers, of which colonial acquisition in that part of the world is the principal object."[31]

Despite their sympathy for elements of the anti-imperialists' critique, military officers found one feature of civilian opposition to imperialism exceedingly repugnant: its profound antimilitarism, which may have precluded military support for the civilian opponents of the large policy. Equating preparedness with militarism, civilian critics of expansion often sought to rouse public fears of a standing army and navy, describing such forces as a threat to civil liberty and democratic government—an assessment that military officers rejected. Because colonialism required a larger military establishment, whose very existence supposedly invited further expansion and imperial war, that policy would, the civilian anti-imperialists claimed, only add to the inequitable tax burdens of the workingman and increase the danger of militarism. Should the American government, warned Schurz, "become faithless to its origins, or fall out of accord with the public opinion of the time, the army, as an organized force subject to its will, may be used by it for ends and purposes adverse to the interests or will of the people."[32]

If Schurz feared political misuse of the army by a tyrannical government, David Starr Jordan described the dangers of colonialism, war, and a large regular force in terms of the racial and cultural theories prevalent in America at the turn of the century. Democracy, wrote Jordan, did not rest upon constitutions and elections. The United States government had become and remained democratic because the nation's superior racial stock would tolerate no other political system. "It is a free stock which creates a free nation," explained Jordan. "Our republic shall endure as long as the human harvest is good, so long as the movement of history . . . leaves for the future not the worst but the best of each generation." Standing armies and navies, and the policies that required them, however, caused racial degeneracy and therefore tyranny because the armed forces took the community's best young men for military service, forcing them to postpone fatherhood and exposing them to death, injury, and venereal disease. The best men consequently produced fewer children, and the unfit, those who avoided military service, reproduced their own kind, shaping the character of future generations and preparing the citizenry for political servitude.[33]

Though military officers shared the assumption of Anglo-Saxon racial and cultural superiority that underlay Jordan's eugenic opposition to expansion, few shared his antimilitary conclusions. Rather, military officers proceeded from that same assumption in quite a different direction. Like many civilians, they asserted that the political incapacity of supposedly inferior peoples imposed upon the United States, in its capacity as a great power, the obligation to practice colonialism and pursue interventionist policies. One historian has discovered one of the roots of that assertion in imperialism's appeal for America's civilian progressives, whose paternalistic attitude toward America's own lower class predisposed them to believe that the United States had a responsibility to shape the destinies of "less advanced" peoples. The periodic visit of an American warship or the presence of the United States Army was "a good thing for them," wrote President Roosevelt; it "tends to promote sobriety."[34]

The similar racism and ethnocentrism of American military officers—in part a reflection of the Social Darwinism and Anglo-Saxonism pervading the late-nineteenth-century American ethos—became clearly evident soon after their first close contact with the Cubans and Filipinos. Although Lieutenant Henry T. Allen, for example, regarded the Cubans' suffering as "heart rending," he told his wife in July 1898 that he had already "seen enough of the Cuban character to know that the Island can never be turned over to them." From halfway round the world, another officer wrote much the same thing about the Filipinos to the editor of the *Army and Navy Journal*: They were, he claimed, "utterly incapable of self-government."[35]

Subsequent contacts with the islanders only confirmed first impressions. Taking self-government to mean more than simple national independence under native political leadership (and military officers had in mind representative democracy on the American model and an orderly conduct of public affairs in accordance with Western norms), most army and navy officers became convinced that both peoples lacked the capacity to govern themselves. To the Filipinos, wrote Commander Charles S. Sperry, self-government "as we understand it is a merry jest excepting when it is a ghastly tragedy." Speaking of the Cubans, Lieutenant Colonel Robert L. Bullard claimed that the "principle of 'the greatest good to the greatest number' means nothing." A Cuban politician "views a majority vote against him with a deep sense of personal injustice."[36]

Faced with such political incompetence, military officers also considered their nation and its armed services the appropriate agents for its correction. By virtue of having intervened in the islanders' affairs as a consequence of the war with Spain, military officers believed that the United States had assumed an obligation to tutor the islands in good government until their inhabitants could assume control of their own affairs. Since the American flag, according to future army chief of staff Brigadier General Tasker H. Bliss, represented "all that there is of human liberty," it had become a national duty "to preach and spread wide the gospel that under its folds alone can the ideals of the people of this [Moro] province be realized." Like civilian progressives who sought, in John Gates's words, to "alleviate the ills of society and afford greater economic, political, and social justice," military officers valued discipline and order and abhorred the anarchy, spoliation, and misery they discovered in the islands. For a time, those officers also believed with Major Hugh L. Scott, another future chief of staff, that a "military government is the only kind fit to cope with such conditions . . . [and] the only government capable of safeguarding life and property and able to satisfy the aspirations of the American people." In time, claimed Major Adna R. Chaffee, the army's second staff chief, America would bring to the Philippines "the blessings of a thoroughly organized and beneficent civilized government." Another future chief of staff revealed the profound emotions stirred by that self-imposed obligation when Brigadier General J. Franklin Bell confessed: "Bettering the social and political conditions of these people is a thing so near my heart that when I get to talking about it at all, I am liable to forget that people must know these things themselves."[37]

Though officers like Commander Washington I. Chambers and Rear Admiral George Melville regarded bearing the "white man's burden" as "a thankless job," most were prepared to fulfill what Major General Leonard Wood described as America's responsibility to "develop individualism among these peoples and, little by little, teach them to stand on their own feet." The burden, wrote the *Army and Navy Journal*, must now "be borne in patience and with constant endeavor to make it lighter." To abandon the islands would be wrong because "the withdrawal of American control would plunge the territory into anarchy, savagery and desolation" while failing to ensure even a troubled independence. "Germany will probably deal for a part or the whole of what we leave, and we would have an arrogant and presuming neighbor, who would quickly teach us the measure of our mistake." Or, Spain might attempt a reconquest, which would initiate a long and bloody war and subject to cruel reprisals all those who had aided Dewey. Nor was a protectorate the answer; that involved simply lending the Filipinos "our Army to maintain such a government as they may choose to establish." In peace, moreover, an irresponsible and unstable government would require a large American army to guard against foreign intervention, and during war, an enemy would undoubtedly regard the islands as American territory, forcing the United States to defend the nominally independent state as though it formed part of the national domain.[38]

Annexation also had a brighter side; American shipping companies might establish lines to the islands, expanding the merchant marine to the benefit of both the army and the navy. Equally important, colonial obligations, hoped the *Army and Navy Journal*, would draw American energies away from "playing politics" and provide more "elevated topics for discussion" than "the question of sixteen to one, or the melancholy contemplation of the horrors of canned roast beef"—two issues that had enlivened the politics of the late nineties. In addition, military officers almost invariably assumed that the Philippines would ultimately achieve independence and put an end to an unwanted burden. In the meantime, the army would receive "war training on foreign soil," a possibly valuable "school of practice for . . . the defense of the flag against an enemy far more formidable than any we find in the tropics."[39]

Good government in the Philippines and the Caribbean meant more to military officers, however, than simply fulfilling a moral obligation. In the Caribbean, for example, unregenerate local political leaders created conditions that encouraged European imperialism, considered a threat to American policy and security. Dictatorial governments sparked revolutions whose violence might, officers thought, threaten European interests and provide a pretext for intervention. The Cuban, wrote Lieutenant Colonel Bullard, "is intolerant of tyranny, but let him once obtain power and authority, and he is autocratic, dictatorial, inconsiderate, and without any quality of toleration or compromise." The inability of that nation's politicians to "abstain from squeezing" their fellow citizens seemed to provide the conditions for a continual round of revolutions, which according to the navy's Sperry were "nothing more nor less than struggles between different crews of bandits for the possession of the customs houses—and the loot." If local violence failed to bring in the Europeans, naval captain Asa Walker feared that unpaid debts or a "trumped-up claim unsatisfied [could] be made the pretext for an armed occupancy." Such claims, according to Captain Sperry, were usually nothing more nor anything less than conspiracies "between some official of the state, and the foreign claimant, to rob the state and divide the swag." Foreign intervention, however motivated, might nevertheless become the prelude to seizure of a naval base from which to threaten the continental United States or its naval supremacy in the Caribbean.[40]

Intervention that led to the establishment of foreign bases created obvious security problems for the United States, and army and navy officers firmly believed that but for its willingness and capacity to defend the Monroe Doctrine the nation would already have witnessed European expansion. As Captain Sperry explained, every one of the Latin American "states would have been sold to the highest bidder long ago by the gang in control had not our attitude cast a cloud on their title." The United States could not, however, follow a dog-in-the-manger policy. If America limited the Europeans' undoubted right to insist upon the payment of just debts and prohibited them from acting to end disorder in Latin America, then the United States must assume those responsibilities. The *Army and Navy Journal* had encouraged just that policy, soon known as the Roosevelt Corollary to the Monroe Doctrine, for over a decade, and when affairs in the Dominican Republic reached a climax in 1904, the *Journal* claimed that the American government had been "repeatedly, explicitly and emphatically informed by more than one of the great powers that it ought either to try to evolve some order out of the financial chaos . . . or permit them to do so under the protection of their warships." American intervention consequently became, explained Sperry, "a mere military necessity" because "we *can not* safely allow European powers to acquire new holdings in the north coast of S. America, or increase old ones either there or in Central America."[41]

Military officers nevertheless regarded chronic American intervention, if it brought no fundamental improvement in the social and political conditions that necessitated it, as no better than a temporary expedient. Any American intervention should, they thought, endure sufficiently long to implant American political institutions and attitudes and to make some lasting improvement in the quality of Latin American life.[42] As an alternative to such intervention, military officers looked with favor upon schemes that might eliminate what the *Army and Navy Journal* described as the "deplorable" conditions that put the Latin republics "at the mercy of political adventurers and marplots whose policy is rule or ruin." A Central American court of justice or a political union might, for example, entirely wipe out the "monthly crop of petty wars and revolutions" in the region adjacent to the Panama Canal, or, reflected Rear Admiral Charles S. Sperry, one of America's delegates to the second peace conference at The Hague, the new convention on the collection of debts might delay the use of force until such time as arbitration achieved payment, thus discouraging the "many shady contracts" between "corrupt" local officials and "foreign adventurers" that ultimately led to armed intervention. Though "more elevated aims . . . [were] mouthed" in a "play to the Peace Gallery," Sperry attributed the United States' support for the convention to its elimination of "opportunities for foreign interference in South America to the peril of our Monroe Doctrine."[43]

For a time the military officers' prewar concern for the defense of the continental United States had partially yielded to a confidence born of new strength and a sometimes enthusiastic involvement in the execution of a more vigorous foreign policy. That growing sense of security also soon disrupted the emerging unity of military thought as army and navy officers displayed the same divisive response to imperialism characteristic of the civil community. While some officers joined imperially minded civilians in seeking further territorial expansion, others shared the civilian anti-imperialists' fears of colonialism's possibly harmful results. The largest group of officers, however, simply accepted America's new policies as the burden falling to any great power. That group consequently set about bringing the benefits of Western civilization to the peoples falling within the American sphere.

Military policy never entirely lost, however, the defensive orientation of the preceding quarter century, a persistence demonstrated in the services' concern over the possibility of European intervention in the politically unstable Caribbean. Soon reinforced by perceived new threats from Germany and Japan, as discussed in the next chapter, that concern for America's physical security began to undermine both the military officers' confidence in American strength and their interest in the overseas projection of the nation's power. Concurrent with the development of those new fears, army and navy officers also discovered the difficulties and dangers of an aggressive use of military power abroad, further eroding their enthusiasm for bearing the white man's burden. Military analyses of the nation's strategic needs remained grounded, as before, in the services' estimates of the international situation, their understanding of the aims of American policy, and their appraisal of the strength of the nation's armed forces.

CHAPTER 5

The Burdens of Empire

Despite the confidence with which military officers had faced the future in the decade after 1898 and the enthusiasm with which many had first shouldered the burdens of empire, the *Infantry Journal* soon reported that "house-cleaning among other peoples" was teaching the army "the grave difficulties to be encountered . . . and the serious consequences to itself." Imperialism, it seemed, involved officers in unwanted duties without "either important honor or material reward," a view apparently shared by at least one discontented naval lieutenant serving in the Far East. "I . . . can see no light in the future," wrote William S. Sims, "except to spend more than half of my life out here."[1] Facing long tours overseas, exposed to increased risks of death and disease, and frustrated by an inability to train for modern war, military officers soon found that imperialism had lost its former appeal.

A similar shift occurred within the civil community. In a study of America's *Imperial Years*, Foster Rhea Dulles found that popular enthusiasm for territorial expansion and an active involvement in world politics failed to outlast the Roosevelt administration. By 1909 Americans had seemingly grown weary of governing newly acquired territory, waging wars to pacify unruly populations, and intervening abroad in support of American policy or commerce. That loss of interest, concluded Dulles, was in part due to the president, who had misleadingly justified Republican foreign policy as a continuation of the national tradition and thereby enabled his countrymen to avoid confronting the implications of America's new place in the world community. Thus shielded from international realities, Americans began turning inward under the influence of a resurrected peace movement and a renewed interest in domestic reform.[2]

Although army and navy officers certainly did not share the peace advocates' conviction that war among civilized states had become an anachronism, military men too began to give increasing attention to reform—initially the unfinished business of the services' nineteenth-century program. In addition, the officer corps gradually abandoned its euphoric outlook, and planning for territorial expansion and the overseas projection of American power soon gave way to renewed concern for coastal defense—now extended to guarding the new insular possessions.

That shift in focus was particularly striking in regard to commercially motivated territorial expansion. Despite, for instance, the officer corps' post-1898 infatuation with the prospects of the China trade, the *Army and Navy Journal* soon began to raise crucial reservations. If capturing the Chinese market included "the task of governing 350,000,000 Asiatics, or even taking any considerable part in doing so, even Yankee thrift and enterprise will decline the venture." Similar reasoning led the officer corps to oppose the acquisition of new territory elsewhere. In regard to the Caribbean, two war college studies in 1911 and a General Board report the next year described additional bases as "neither necessary nor desirable." In the same period, the army's new General Staff spoke out against further American military intervention in China, and two successive army attachés extended the recommendation by asserting that China would also be "better off without any foreign money." Recognizing that such a policy might cause the United States to miss "great commercial chances," Major Albert J. Bowley nevertheless felt that America had better suffer the economic loss than become "involved in the political fight that is bound to occur [t]here."[3]

So quickly did military officers lose their interest in territorial expansion that after 1909, according to Richard D. Challener, the impetus behind the search for new bases came more often from the State Department than from either military headquarters. In the Caribbean, army and navy attitudes became largely preclusive, and the services relied upon diplomacy and the Monroe Doctrine, backed by American strength, rather than long-term physical possession to support the na-

tion's strategic needs and to block further European expansion. Only
the outbreak of war might necessitate the temporary seizure of those islands essential for military operations. For the Far East, the army and
navy began to advocate a doctrine of strategic defense, a form of deterrence requiring completion of the Panama Canal and construction of a
fortified base in Hawaii or Guam. Thus strengthened, the American
fleet and an adequate expeditionary force could deter any military challenge to United States interests and seize new territory only if deterrence
failed. While the State Department may have valued territorial expansion for the resulting increase in political influence, military officers saw
the permanent acquisition of new bases as leading to a dispersion of
America's armed forces and a consequent lessening of the services' ability to concentrate their strength for decisive action at any threatened
point.[4]

For a time, during the decade before World War I, the United
States avoided any such permanent dispersal of its forces to new colonies
by the expedient of temporary, if sometimes lengthy, interventions into
the affairs of its hemispheric neighbors. On ethical as well as practical
grounds, however, many officers soon began to object to that alternative to further territorial expansion. Naval captain Charles S. Sperry, for
example, expressed his distaste at the navy's involvement in "situations
tainted with fraud." In a similar tone, the *Army and Navy Journal* condemned American military support for Caribbean "repudiators" and
"swindlers." In an early public challenge to the president, an act that
we shall see became less rare during the prewar debate over preparedness, Major Cassius Gillette denied Wilson's "moral right" to intervene
in Mexico, it being "none of our business" if "she wishes or finds it un-
avoidable to change rulers by force." In the same vein, the editor of the
Infantry Journal asserted that the "fact that property of foreigners is destroyed and that investments cease to pay, no more warrants interference in the affairs of Mexico than they did in those of the United States
during the Civil War."[5] Questioning as well the effectiveness of intervention, army and navy leaders began to charge that it only encouraged
the degeneration of Latin American politics and united local factions in
an anti-Yankee opposition.[6] Concerned, too, about the way intervention disrupted planned training exercises and maneuvers, military officers like Rear Admiral Bradley A. Fiske, the naval secretary's aid for operations, warned against wearing "away the efficiency of the navy . . .
backing up comparatively unimportant policies in places like Haiti and
Mex[ico]."[7]

Even during the period of general preoccupation with the projection of America's power abroad, some officers of both services had continued the study of coastal defense and, implicitly, preparation for great-power conflict. As doubts about imperialism grew so did interest in such conflict, and annual maneuvers, concentration of fleets and armies, and an adequate reserve became, as in the late nineteenth century, principal topics of military thought.

Interest in maneuvers, as described in chapter 3, dates from the eighties, when Forts Leavenworth and Riley, both in Kansas, began to sponsor annual field exercises, usually of regimental size, and Brigadier General Wesley Merritt, later army commander in the Philippines, conducted a brigade-sized maneuver in the Indian Territory (Oklahoma). In 1902 those officers who maintained the nineteenth-century focus on preparing the army for modern war reinstituted the Riley maneuvers, expanding them to what Colonel Arthur L. Wagner, one of the founding fathers of the army school system, described as "the first attempt in the United States to carry out a course of tactical field exercises with a large command [in fact an understrength provisional division] and to approximate . . . the autumn maneuvers which have been universal in Europe."[8]

In the years that followed, the army sponsored division-sized exercises at a variety of locations, and navy planners joined their army counterparts to resurrect the joint maneuvers introduced in the late nineteenth century to test the adequacy of the coastal defenses. Repeated first along Long Island Sound in 1902, the services subsequently conducted similar interservice exercises at a variety of points on the Atlantic and Pacific coasts. The army assigned great importance to those exercises, so much so that when budget restraints required the cancellation of joint militia-regular field training in 1905, Secretary of War William Howard Taft hastened to remind the legislators that such maneuvers helped erase "the most radical defect in our present system of military training." Without them, "the general officers have no opportunity to handle armies, divisions, or brigades in the field." Congress was generally sympathetic, though the chairman of the House Military Affairs Committee did complain that the maneuvers as conducted worked the militiamen "too hard" and left them "completely exhausted."[9]

Because an army division remained a "fiction," wrote Captain Alfred Bjornstad, "until its regiments have camped together, marched together and maneuvered together under the intelligent direction of a division commander on a horse," the army staff also began once more to petition Congress to fund concentration of the regular forces at several large posts near rail centers that had ready access to the coasts. Still scattered throughout the West, the army remained too far from threatened points, and the tiny frontier garrisons—Fort Leavenworth with its single regiment being the largest in 1906—held too few troops for effective field training. With most posts comprising but a few hundred troops, the army could give its soldiers only "elementary instruction" in small-unit tactics. While that might suit a colonial army expected to fight a primitive foe in scattered formations, such dispersion impeded the training of a force suited to modern warfare.[10]

Modern wars had also made it an "illusion," Major General J. Franklin Bell advised Congress in 1907, to think that "a brave but untrained, unorganized, people can grapple successfully with another nation better trained and organized." America's economic and demographic transformation having dried up its former pool of skilled frontier marksmen inured to life in the field, army officers argued that the United States could no longer form effective military units after only minimal formal training. The close of the Roosevelt administration consequently found army officers maintaining that the regulars could hold America's frontiers against a major foe only if augmented by a previously trained reserve.[11]

During Roosevelt's second term, regular officers also renewed their interest in the coastal fortifications, which had temporarily benefited from the invasion fears accompanying the outbreak of war with Spain. As late as 1904, Secretary of War Taft had deprecated Corps of Engineer and Coast Artillery appeals for further improvements, referring to them as but the "natural, commendable, and useful enthusiasm of those . . . whose whole interest is centered on having defenses of the highest modern perfection." He reinforced his claim with the observation that the army staff as a whole believed "that with the present fortifications effective defense can be made whenever exigency may arise." For reasons soon to be made evident, events of the next year produced a change in army views, and 1905 found Taft supporting appointment of a new body, known as the National Coast Defense Board but also bearing his name, commissioned to update the work of the 1885 Endicott board. When the Taft board's report went to Congress in 1906, the new emphasis on coastal defense appeared in a letter of transmittal written by President Roosevelt, who warned Congress that the "necessity for a complete and adequate system of coast defense is greater to-day than twenty-years ago."[12]

Improvement of the coastal defenses also assumed a new dimension early in the twentieth century. The army's artillerymen had previously emphasized either expanding the coastal artillery organizations or providing them with more and better forts, guns, mines, and auxiliary equipment. By 1909, however, Chief of Artillery Arthur Murray had begun to call not only for new field fortifications but also for a "mobile army" of infantry and cavalry to guard the landward approaches to the coastal forts. In that year a newly created National Land Defense Board initiated a study of that proposal. Over the course of the next three years, the board examined each strategically important point along the American seacoast, indicating the troops and equipment required to secure the existing fortifications against an amphibious assault seeking to seize them from the rear.[13]

Just as the army's enthusiasm for imposing America's will on nonindustrialized peoples faded, the navy's leaders began to express some disgust, in the words of Naval Institute president Caspar Goodrich, at hearing from some of its officers "for the hundredth time the cry of more ships without explaining why more ships are needed." Like Admiral Goodrich, many naval officers had never allowed the extreme forms of turn-of-the-century navalism and fantasies about an American navy second to none to blind them to the modest force needed to forestall a great-power assault on the Western Hemisphere. Between 1899 and 1904, for example, the Naval War College and the General Board studied three hypothetical great-power wars for control of the West Indies, making defense of that region, not participation in a global struggle for empire, the measure of America's naval needs.[14] Both the *Army and Navy Journal* and *United Service* supported that defensive orientation, observing in 1904 that the "time seems opportune for a mature consideration as to the ultimate limits of the naval power of the United States." Having been "brought up to contemplate war only as a defence against aggression," wrote the institute's secretary-treasurer, Naval Academy professor Philip R. Alger, naval officers saw a need for a huge fleet only if the United States determined to maintain the Monroe Doctrine "in its extreme form."[15]

Opponents of an imperial navy based their position on national sentiment, adherence to the late-nineteenth-century naval consensus, and sound strategic thought. Even in 1899, when imperialism, both civil and military, appeared in full bloom, the institute's president, Rear Admiral William T. Sampson, fresh from his controversial victory at

Santiago, claimed that "the sentiment of our country would not permit
. . . wars of foreign conquest." Describing American policy as "*utterly*
opposed to conquest of any territory beyond the seas," the institute's
honorable mention essayist repeated the same theme a decade later and
thus demonstrated his awareness of his countrymen's declining enthusiasm for imperialism.[16]

Accepting the constraints of national sentiment, many naval officers
saw no need for so large a navy as the one advocated by the service's expansionists. As Captain Charles H. Stockton, American naval attaché in
London from 1903 to 1907, explained, the United States needed a navy
sufficient only to protect its coasts, dominate the Caribbean, secure the
new island possessions, and sustain the Monroe Doctrine "as definitely
established." While those tasks required a modest expansion of the
fleet, they imposed no obligation to match the navies of Great Britain
or the European powers. So long as the United States continued its defensive posture, wrote that former president of the Naval War College,
the "distances from the home ports" of a European power would cause
"a filtering and reduction of available force for offensive purposes to a
size which we should be able to readily meet." Stockton also recognized
that American diplomacy "should . . . assure for us at least one strong
naval friend . . . in Europe," and thus "permit . . . only a portion of
any European navy being used against us." For countering only that
portion need the United States Navy prepare, a standard that realistic
naval officers soon made the measure of America's naval sufficiency.[17]

Naval intellectuals like Lieutenant Commander Richard Wainwright, former executive officer of the unfortunate U.S.S. *Maine* and
soon the Naval Academy superintendent, also developed the European
concept of a fleet-in-being to further define the appropriate size of
America's battle fleet. The United States Navy, Wainwright claimed,
required a fleet sufficient only to stalk any larger force entering American waters. By threatening both to attack the latter's exposed landing
craft and troop ships—if it attempted to land ground forces—and to
bring on a general naval engagement—if it reduced its own strength by
detaching large elements for such independent operations as a blockade—that inferior American fleet-in-being could defend the coast while
otherwise avoiding defeat by refusing battle. In addition to deterring
European naval intervention in the Western Hemisphere, such a fleet
could challenge the small detachments that any European power might
deploy in East Asia.[18]

The General Board accepted reasoning like that of Stockton and
Wainwright in 1903 when it adopted the policy that governed its rec-

ommendations through World War I. That seventeen-year program aimed at creating an American navy of forty-eight battleships—while admittedly a large number, still less than half the force advocated by the imperially minded. That number, the board reasoned, would not suffice to match England or to challenge the powers of Europe, but it would guarantee the Western Hemisphere against an attack from Imperial Germany—as explained later in this chapter, America's most probable European assailant.[19]

Concern for such a clash also drew naval attention to many of the same organizational, training, and reserve matters that engaged army officers readying their service for modern war. Naval officers, too, urged concentration of their service's combat units into a few large formations. And in 1902 the General Board initiated the first of a series of annual fleet maneuvers, drawing ships from the European, South Atlantic, and home squadrons for exercises designed to test plans for defense of the western Atlantic, the Gulf, and the Caribbean. After naval officers also urged the Navy Department to adopt what Rear Admiral George Converse called a "policy of concentration"—putting the mobilized ships permanently into combat formations—because fleet organization gave "scope for tactical work, and the consequent instruction of flag and commanding officers," the navy assigned seven tenths of its battleships to the Atlantic, leaving the balance and the larger armored cruisers to form its principal battle force in the Pacific. Concurrently, the Atlantic and, later, the Pacific fleets were formed, further facilitating the frequent conduct of large-scale maneuvers and the daily training of commanders and staffs in the control of large naval formations.[20]

With the wartime personnel needs of such formations in mind, a few naval officers began to urge creation of a federal naval reserve comprising men with previous regular navy experience or wartime service, because like the *Army and Navy Journal* they believed that the war with Spain had demonstrated that the United States had too few merchant seamen to obtain experienced deep-water sailors from that source. Officers like Lieutenant William H. H. Southerland, then on duty with the naval staff as chief of the Militia Office, also described as the "consensus of opinion" within his service the belief that the imperfectly trained officers and men of the country's present naval militia could do little more in a war than man the smaller defense vessels operating in coastal waters. Southerland consequently called upon the Navy Department to obtain authority to "train and guide" the state militia units in their coastal-defense role and to create, pay, and periodically call to active duty a federal reserve of men qualified to serve on board the navy's principal warships.[21]

Preoccupation with the white man's burden also received a rude shock from the Russo-Japanese War of 1904–5, which according to Richard Challener acted as a "watershed" and became the "decisive influence upon military thinking about Far Eastern politics and strategy."[22] At the same time the war focused added attention upon the possibility of great-power war, as Japan replaced Russia as the principal threat to the independence of China.

Although suspicion of Japan had not arisen suddenly with the war's outbreak in 1904, military officers like Captain Peyton C. March, just returned from observing the Japanese army in Manchuria, confessed that the conflict had caused them "with reluctance" to abandon their belief in Japan's "alleged friendship for the United States." The Japanese, March stated in an official report to the General Staff and confidential addresses at the Military Academy and Army War College, hated "*all* white races" and would be satisfied with "nothing less than predominance in the Pacific." In the same vein, Captain William H. Beehler, former American naval attaché in Berlin, Rome, and Vienna, warned the members of the Naval Institute of "a distinct peril now menacing us. . . . The appearance of this formidable naval power in the Far East necessarily disturbs the world's balance of power, and it is no longer possible for the United States to ignore these conditions with the new power, our next-door neighbor in the Pacific." Major General Leonard Wood, commander of the Philippine Division and like March a future army chief of staff, seemed to speak for officers of both services when in 1905 he wrote President Roosevelt from the Philippines that "[v]ery few people who have lived in the East for any length of time take any stock in the idea that we shall be left free to work our will here." To his close friend since their days in the Rough Riders, Wood confided "Japan is very anxious to be the new England, or England, of the East."[23] While military officers doubted the imminence of war with Japan—even at the peak of the 1906–7 confrontation over California's mistreatment of Japanese schoolchildren—they generally agreed with Chief of Staff J. Franklin Bell that "it is our duty to be prepared—in case of such a contingency."[24]

The Russo-Japanese War's military, as opposed to political, result, claimed Captain March, was to render the Philippines more than ever a "strategic weakness." So long as America's potential Far Eastern opponents had been European states, that is Russia, France, Germany, and, to a much lesser extent, England, an adequately equipped Philippine naval base protected by seacoast guns and a small garrison seemed to offer a point from which to guard the islands and secure a naval base from which to contest control of the western Pacific. Military debate had consequently centered on which of two places—Manila or Subic bay—should be defended.[25] Japan, however, fighting virtually in its home waters, could bring almost its entire naval strength to bear on the Philippines, while the United States Navy would suffer the inevitable "filtering and reduction" of power associated with operating at a great distance from home ports.[26]

Military officers also drew two alarming observations from the Russo-Japanese War, during which Japan had transported its army to Manchuria, reduced the Russian fortifications by attacking from landward, and conducted sustained overseas operations against a major power. Large expeditionary forces, it now seemed, could complete long sea voyages and immediately commence extended operations against the land forces of even a "civilized" power. Moreover, any power possessing both a superior army and at least temporary naval superiority could use a land attack to overcome harbor fortifications theretofore considered invulnerable. In the initial phases of any Far Eastern war with the United States, Japan would possess such military superiority, making the Philippines, wrote Colonel Charles J. Crane, "hostages to fortune, and pledges of good conduct on our part." How to reinforce the Philippines' defenders and how far east to withdraw America's principal military base in the Pacific henceforth replaced possible intervention in China and the acquisition of new bases as the major issues of America's Far Eastern strategy.[27]

Technological, political, and strategic developments associated with the Russo-Japanese War, or occurring soon thereafter, also contributed to the end of military speculation about future expansion in China. Concerning a base for anti-Russian operations in northern China, the General Board had advised the secretary of the navy in 1903: "If Japan were an ally, no such station would be necessary; and if not, no such station would be tenable." By temporarily disposing of the Russian threat to China and by raising Japan to the status of a probable enemy, the Russo-Japanese War led logically to the conclusion that such a station was no longer defensible. Interest in a base in northern China consequently lingered only in civilian circles.[28]

Technology provided another reason for the navy's declining interest in far-flung bases. The development of colliers capable of refueling a
fleet at sea reduced dependence upon overseas coaling stations, and
when in 1907 President Roosevelt ordered America's Great White Fleet
to circumnavigate the globe, naval officers learned of the ability of battleships to complete long sea voyages and arrive ready to fight, thus lessening the need for local repair facilities like those in the Philippines.
Such new capabilities meant that the navy could await the commencement of hostilities before seizing, with the aid of standby expeditionary
forces, whatever advance bases the conflict might require. A fleet based
at Hawaii or even in California, rather than at Subic or Manila, might
consequently provide for the Philippines' strategic defense, an early
deterrence concept based upon America's capacity eventually to seize
command of the western Pacific and to establish advanced bases for subsequent operations against any potential enemy. Despite America's tactical vulnerability in the Orient, the services' planners anticipated that
the probability of its ultimate victory would restrain even Japan—provided the United States maintained both a powerful fleet and an adequate land force on the Pacific coast.[29]

In the Atlantic and Caribbean a similar combination of circumstances drew military attention away from an aggressive search for new
island bases, swinging it initially toward the goal of precluding future
European expansion in Latin America and ultimately stirring new fears
for America's own territorial vulnerability. During that swing Germany
replaced England as America's most probable European enemy and the
power most likely to challenge the Monroe Doctrine.

Military suspicion of Germany had grown slowly since the late-nineteenth-century friction over control of Samoa, and the reputedly threatening behavior of the German squadron at Manila in 1898 further
roused distrust of Teutonic intentions.[30] Nevertheless, as late as 1902,
when Germany in concert with Britain and Italy blockaded Venezuelan
ports because of dictator Cipriano Castro's refusal to pay that nation's
debts, army and navy officers accepted the view expressed by the *Army
and Navy Journal*: "It would be a brutal perversion of the Monroe Doctrine to interpose it as a bar to prevent the collection of honest debts
from delinquent governments." Whatever the significance of President

Roosevelt's eventual use of the American fleet's presence in the Caribbean to pressure Germany into an early withdrawal, the navy had neither concentrated for that purpose nor pressed the administration to protest the European intrusion. Instead, naval officers felt dismay at the manner in which the administration's use of the fleet during the crisis disrupted the summer's planned drills and maneuvers.[31]

Germany's subsequent behavior, however, soon converted ripening suspicion into outright hostility. Germany's 1902 decision to form squadrons for the Atlantic and Pacific coasts of North and South America, for example, prompted the *Army and Navy Journal* to reconsider and to declare that a "German naval squadron in American waters means ultimately a German naval station on the American continent. . . . [T]hen what?" Excessively aggressive behavior in the later phases of the Venezuelan blockade and subsequent high-handedness elsewhere in the Caribbean convinced the *Journal* that "everything points to the acquisition of territory on the South American continent" as Germany's goal. Military officers later saw Germany's hand in Denmark's rejection of a treaty for the sale of the Virgin Islands to the United States and in the efforts of a German-controlled Danish steamship company to acquire a Caribbean coaling facility capable of conversion into a military base.[32]

The services also correctly suspected that Germany had prepared plans for a war with the United States in the event that the former's achievement of naval parity did not force Americans to acquiesce in German expansion in the Caribbean and Brazil—believed to be the ultimate target of German imperialism because of that South American republic's large German-born population. Initiated rather casually in 1899, by the following year the German admiralty's contingency planning for war against the United States became at the kaiser's direction a joint army-navy effort involving both Admiral Alfred von Tirpitz and the army chief of staff, Count Alfred von Schlieffen.[33]

Paralleling the identification of a new foe, military officers reassessed the value of new Caribbean bases and came to question their usefulness for the same technological and strategic reasons that changed interservice views about the Pacific. Politics, too, played a role. Because the European powers realized that expansion in the Caribbean was for the United States a *casus belli*, they would, military officers reasoned, hesitate to seek new territory there so long as America possessed a strong army and navy. In the event that such deterrence failed, a strong and concentrated fleet, supported from a few well-guarded harbors, would have a better chance of overcoming any European invasion than a force that had been dispersed to defend a host of unessential bases.[34]

Similar reasoning applied to the defense of the Panama Canal. Because the army could guard a fortified canal against minor naval raids and small expeditionary forces (the kind that might be carried on a few warships) and the American fleet (based upon the fortified bases in Cuba and Culebra) could intercept and attempt to defeat any larger force before it entered the Caribbean, the United States could defend the canal by concentrating its forces at a few bases. A strategy of precluding, both in peace and war, any new European footholds in the Caribbean would therefore, military officers believed, better secure the Western Hemisphere than an American scramble for more territory.[35]

Army planning for war in the Atlantic, however, involved more than support for a strategy of preclusion—seen as an essentially naval responsibility. The military lessons of the Russo-Japanese War rekindled the army's interest in continental defense. The Japanese had, after all, demonstrated that a nation possessing both a first-rate navy and a powerful army could execute a successful overseas invasion of the home territory of another major power. Because Germany had both—as well as plans for their use against the United States—army officers began to study how to counter that threat. Their concern contributed to the establishment of the previously discussed Taft and Land Defense boards, the advancement of proposals for improvements in the organization and training of the mobile army, and recommendations for creation of an adequate peacetime reserve, all of which would strengthen the service for a conflict with either Germany or Japan.[36]

Seeking to keep ''the American people alive to their interests in the grave problems which will be raised in the Far East by the future development of China and Japan,'' Herbert Croly, considered the philosopher of progressivism, became one of the few civilian intellectuals struggling to keep Americans from turning their backs on world affairs. The herald of Roosevelt's ''New Nationalism'' even risked rousing the civilian community's ''pious horror'' by suggesting that only ''a policy of irresponsibility and unwisdom'' would refuse to contemplate the ''notion of American intervention in a European conflict.'' If the United States ''wants peace,'' Croly warned in 1909, ''it must be spiritually and physically prepared to fight for it.''[37]

While Americans generally refused to heed Croly's advice, they often shared his alarm (and that of the officer corps) at the increasing aggressiveness of both Japan and Germany. In the nineteenth century, Americans had regarded both nations sympathetically, admiring Germany for its culture, respecting Japan for its rapid Westernization, and showing an appreciative understanding of each nation's aspirations. Early in the next century, however, America's civilians, like its military elite, generally came to suspect that Germany intended to challenge the Monroe Doctrine with a policy of Latin American colonization and that Japan had resolved to set aside the Open Door in China and supplant the United States in the Philippines.[38] Yet Americans perversely rejected the response to that threat advocated by military officers and those intellectuals like Croly who urged their countrymen to overcome their exclusive preoccupation with domestic affairs and recognize the implications of a changing world order.[39] An examination of Croly's classic *The Promise of American Life* reveals, however, some of the close intellectual links between military opinion and the thinking of an influential segment of the civilian community.

Like most American military officers, Croly recognized the way in which the "growth of modern seapower and the vast sweep of modern national political interests" had diminished America's security by multiplying "the possible sources of contact between American and European interests" and thus invalidating the assumptions of the nation's isolationist tradition. "No matter how peacefully the United States is inclined, and no matter how advantageously it is situated, the American nation is none the less constantly threatened by political warfare, and constantly engaged in industrial warfare." And while war had become more likely, Croly concluded, modern warfare had rendered more perilous America's traditional lack of military preparation. If the United States wanted to maintain the peace, he argued, it must not only be willing to intervene in the affairs of Europe, it must also do as the peace-loving nations of that continent had done—prepare to fight. Peace, he claimed, resulted from a "righteous use of superior force," and unprepared nations go "down with a crash, . . . as France did in 1870, or as Russia has just [1905] done."[40]

Croly similarly challenged the basis of United States policy in Latin America and drew out the implications of the nation's position in the Pacific. Contrary to the situation when President Monroe issued his 1823 doctrine, Croly wrote in 1909, Europe no longer threatened the Western Hemisphere with the establishment of a "monarchial and aristocratic political system . . . inimical in spirit and in effect to the American democratic state." Nor could the United States object to an expansion of Europe's commercial interests, which Croly regarded as both legitimate and essential to Latin America's economic development. Because of the region's "treacherous and unstable political conditions," which gave "European or Asiatic Powers a justifiable right . . . to interfere," however, Latin America threatened either to "embroil the United States . . . in continual trouble" or to force it "to become a predominately military power, armed to the teeth . . . [and] a part of the European political system with a vengeance." Faced with a choice between interventionism and militarism, Croly anticipated more recent American policy by recommending creation of a "stable and peaceful" regional political system policed by the United States in cooperation with the mature Latin powers, who would forcibly pacify the "centers of disorder" and intervene to eliminate the "legitimate excuses for revolutionary protest."[41]

In regard to the Far East, Croly shared the military officers' distrust of Japan and their description of the Philippines as "a source of weakness and danger." If the United States wished to secure those islands and maintain its access to markets in China, he wrote, Americans must willingly support a "considerable . . . concentration of naval strength in the Pacific" and prepare for "a great deal of diplomacy and more or less of fighting."[42]

While Croly's book represented the progressive outlook and the optimistic belief that the righteous use of governmental power could rectify domestic and international ills and achieve both order and justice, a curious work, *The Valor of Ignorance*, by a now little-known figure employed some of the previous century's determinism to justify a similar policy of national discipline and military preparation. The book's author, "General" Homer Lea, had fulfilled his ambition to follow a military career by joining the "army" of the imprisoned Chinese emperor Kuang-hsü. Despite a crippling illness that earned him the childhood nickname "Little Scrunchneck" and his Anglo-Saxon ancestry and American citizenship, Lea received a lieutenant general's commission from the emperor in 1899, served as Dr. Sun Yat-sen's chief of staff following the Boxer Rebellion, and later commanded one of the revolutionary doctor's divisions. Upon returning to the United States in 1905, Lea prepared the first draft of his principal work, which appeared in 1909, made a triumphal tour of Europe, where he conferred with the kaiser and British field marshal Lord Roberts, and then hastened back to

China in 1911 to lead an army in the Republicans' final assault on the Imperial government.[43]

According to Charles D. Tarlton, Lea's literary output exemplified the "deterministic internationalism" typical of Alfred Thayer Mahan, Henry Cabot Lodge, Albert J. Beveridge, Theodore Roosevelt, and Brooks Adams, who also thought of war as the result of immutable laws by which militant peoples created nations and built mighty empires at the expense of weak peoples or declining states. The United States and China, Lea said of the countries he knew best, only appeared to be exceptions to that rule. Like all states "born out of the womb of war," those two had grown "at the expense of aboriginal tribes or petty kingdoms." With such weak opponents, however, China and the United States had failed to develop the military spirit now essential to their survival in an age when improved global communications and modern instruments of warfare robbed them of the advantages of their geographic isolation and vast size. If the United States wished to continue its independent existence, and China to throw off foreign domination, Lea claimed, each must cultivate its military vigor.[44]

Although Lea regarded industrial strength as a prerequisite to national greatness, he feared that America's economic growth had led to "gratification of individual avarice" and made the United States "a glutton among nations, vulgar, swinish, arrogant." In a blatantly nativist and elitist passage, Lea also asserted that "the ambitions of the heterogeneous masses that now riot and revel" in the United States regarded the nation as little more than "a land to batten on and grow big in," as a place "to satisfy the[ir] larval greed." Because America's "opulence and unmartial qualities . . . stand in inverse ratio to the poverty and the military prowess" of states like Japan and Germany, which threaten the "inviolability of the Western Continents," he wrote, the United States had entered a period of special peril, and its failure to achieve self-discipline and rouse its martial spirit increased the risk of defeat in the inevitable clash.[45]

After making that dismal forecast in the first portion of *The Valor of Ignorance*, Lea used a hypothetical war with Japan to make his point that the United States must abandon the illusion that its isolation provided either freedom from conflict or time to prepare, that great wealth could match developed military resources, and that untrained volunteers and militia could overcome regular troops, which Americans wrongly regarded as a menace to peace and democratic government. In that war, which later seemed to bear too close a parallel to events after

December 7, 1941, Japan quickly stripped a somnolent America of its Far Eastern possessions, attacked the Hawaiian Islands, and successfully invaded the poorly defended Pacific coast, whose nearby mountain barriers enabled the Japanese army to secure itself indefinitely against any successful counterattack.[46]

Coming three decades too soon, Lea's lurid prophecies failed to hold America's attention, and like Croly's more sober urgings, they failed in 1909 to convince Americans of the need for greater military preparation—a goal achieved only under the spur of world conflict. The work of the two authors nevertheless reveals the thinking of that minority of Americans who, like the members of the officer corps, anticipated great-power conflict and sought to strengthen the nation's defenses.

Military thought in the early twentieth century kept rather singular pace with the shifts in American civilian attitudes. At the peak of civilian enthusiasm for picking up the white man's burden and taking a hand in international affairs, military officers responded by advancing programs that both enhanced the services' ability to carry the new burden and their readiness to meet the demands of an imperial exercise of American power. Confident of the nation's strength and anticipating future military cooperation with at least some of the major "civilized" powers, army and navy officers for a time gave relatively little attention to continental defense.

Before the end of the new century's first decade, however, growing military disenchantment with America's efforts to bring civilization to the backward and peace to the unruly swelled the ranks of those officers who either opposed imperialism or remained primarily concerned with territorial defense. A similar disenchantment with imperialism combined with a growing interest in domestic reform, led many civilians to respond to threatening international developments by seeking security either through isolation or from one of the panaceas offered by the period's many peace societies. While sharing that distaste for future imperial adventures, military officers continued to keep close watch on world events. Alarmed by German aggressiveness in the Caribbean, suspicious of Japanese intentions in the Far East, and aware of the political, strategic, and technological implications of the latter's victory over Russia, army and navy officers turned from thoughts of further territorial expansion and periodic intervention and gave renewed attention to the defense of America's coasts and overseas possessions. Those officers had not turned inward to attend solely to an incomplete program of military reform; they had instead turned homeward as they contemplated the costs of a too active globalism and considered the vulnerability of the nation's exposed coasts and overseas possessions.

Though military thought had much in common with that minority of civilians who shared the reveries of Lea or the pragmatism of Croly, few military officers allowed their concern for Germany or Japan to carry them to the same extremes. Army and navy officers simply accepted that the United States had unavoidably become a part of the international community, and they prepared to deal with the world on its own terms. That required no more than modest increases in the armed forces—reforms sufficient to enhance the strength derived from America's special geography and Europe's divisive rivalries. However much military officers sympathized with Lea's warning, few described the nation's security needs in terms of an interminable Darwinian struggle against alien civilizations or an inevitable national decline. Nor did military officers advocate the degree of armed intervention in the affairs of Europe, Asia, and Latin America inherent in Croly's proposals. Army and navy officers, aware of the costs of an overactive internationalism and of the dangers of a disarmed isolationism, advocated a middle road requiring only modest efforts to strengthen America's bastion in the New World and to guard the Philippines, now considered an enervating extension onto the periphery of East Asia.

PART III

The Military Progressives

It has long been known that the most important part of the "business" of the Department has to do with WAR, or preparation for war. Those in authority realize that that part of the "business" has been quite overlooked.

Rear Admiral Stephen B. Luce, USN
"Memorandum on Naval Administration," March 27, 1905, Luce Papers

CHAPTER 6

The Quest for Efficiency

THE ARMY GENERAL STAFF'S 1915 "Statement of a Proper Military Policy for the United States" illustrated the extent to which the language and methods of progressivism had supplanted Social Darwinism as an intellectual justification for military reform. Twentieth-century technology, wrote the General Staff that year, required a new "scheme of defense," one unfettered by national military traditions that had too often produced "a startling picture of faulty leadership, needless waste of lives and property, costly overhead charges . . . , undue prolongations of . . . [war], and . . . reckless expenditure of public funds." The assumptions of the past and unsatisfactory policies derived in a haphazard, unprofessional manner must yield to expert study of the nation's strategic situation, to rational and coordinated solutions for its military problems, and to efficient, orderly preparation of the armed services for the accomplishment of their primary tasks. As Brigadier General Robert K. Evans told the readers of *Infantry Journal* in 1911, the nation's military forces must become more "businesslike."[1]

The values and methods of progressivism had, of course, begun to influence military thought more than a decade before that General Staff report. Although military officers had described their work in Cuba and the Philippines as bearing the burden that Social Darwinism assigned to the Anglo-Saxon race, they nevertheless held beliefs and employed methods similar to those with which civilian progressives were soon to confront America's domestic problems. Military governors, their staffs, and many of their subordinates, for example, expressed disdain for the traditional compromises of politics and the tendency of local governments especially to fall into corrupt relations with businessmen. In America's dependencies, those military progressives also executed educational, public health, and regulatory programs characterized by expert investigation, scientific decisions, and implementation under the close supervision of strong leaders who saw the need for active government and centralized direction. Army and navy officers at colonial posts seemed thus to share the assumption that Samuel P. Hays attributed to civilian progressives, that only "a highly organized, technical, and centrally planned and directed social organization could meet a complex world with efficiency and purpose." Recent students of American colonial administration have verified that impression; whether engaged in promoting public health and morals, regulating public utilities and business practices, or tutoring Cubans and Filipinos on social justice and disciplined democracy, military officers overseas, in the words of John M. Gates, "acted like reformers, shared many characteristics with them, . . . held many of the same ideals . . . [and] were, in fact, a leading force for reform in many of the same areas as progressives in America."[2]

Late in the Roosevelt administration, as military officers turned their attention away from colonial affairs under the pressure of a new appreciation for both the burden of colonialism and the military vulnerability of the Western Hemisphere, they simply repatriated their progressivism and used it to address a different range of problems.

No issue better illustrates that military use of the language of progressives than the army's handling of its manpower problems. That service's interest in the creation of an orderly system for passing its small regular establishment from a peace to a war footing had not, of course, arisen only with the progressive era. Prior to the Russo-Japanese War, however, a new navy and improved coastal fortifications had seemed to provide adequate protection against the devastatingly sudden attacks characteristic of modern warfare. So long as the regular army received proper training, Congressional approval of organizational changes, and enough men to garrison those forts and execute minor expeditionary tasks, any extensive mobilization of the nation's manpower might proceed at a leisurely pace. By 1905, though, military technology and an apparently more threatening international environment had begun to raise doubts about both the adequacy of that protection and the wisdom of relying upon a small regular army that lacked a large, well-trained reserve. Fearing that the United States Army might have to counter a major attack with a massive and rapid expansion of its regular forces, professional organs like the *Infantry Journal* were soon describing a well-trained reserve as "beyond all doubt a necessity of modern military efficiency." Referring to the lack of such a reserve as the "paramount evil" of America's military policy because it meant that any emergency would require the regulars to suffer a last-minute infusion of raw recruits, Lieutenant Colonel Daniel H. Boughton, who served on the General Staff as he wrote, decried the army's "inability . . . to pass from a peace to a war footing without practically destroying, for a time, the efficiency of the whole fighting machine."[3]

Such conclusions received official backing and a fuller explanation, still somewhat reminiscent of the earlier Darwinism, in a 1912 General Staff study based upon the assertion that "[p]olitical conditions affecting our country have changed very materially in the past 20 years. . . . [P]ractically the whole earth is now divided up among the principal nations." The resulting close contact "between great nations and races" and the "increase of population and national needs" has created a global "competition, commercial, national, and racial, whose ultimate seriousness current events already enable us to gauge." The United States had consequently "been drawn from [its] state of isolation and . . . [become] inevitably involved in this competition."[4] In a hardly veiled reference to Germany and Japan, the General Staff three years later pointed to the existence of "virile, capable, and progressive nations . . . imbued . . . with the belief that their vital interests demand an active aggressive policy . . . to fulfill at any cost what they conceive to be their destiny." Each of the world's major powers, excepting only England and the United States, had become moreover a "nation in arms . . . in which nearly all of the male inhabitants of suitable physique are given a minimum of two years' training with the colors in time of peace."[5]

A host of semiofficial publications similarly elaborated on the need for a larger reserve. Because, explained army lieutenant Henry J. Reilly, later a war correspondent, writer, and the army's youngest brigade commander in World War I, "complete naval supremacy is not necessary before an expedition of troops may be risked upon the sea," the United States must no longer rely upon geographic isolation to provide time to mobilize. After calculating the availability of foreign shipping, Brigadier General Tasker H. Bliss, a future chief of staff who would later represent the United States on the wartime Supreme War Council and at the postwar peace conference, claimed that the vessels found in "two or three ports of a possible enemy" could transport to the Western Hemisphere in only a "few days" an invading army of 250,000 men. In 1910 Chief of Staff J. Franklin Bell gave official credit to such claims when he advised the war secretary that "it would [currently] be easier to conduct a campaign from Europe against New York and Boston than it was for General Grant in 1864 to conduct his campaign through Northern Virginia against the city of Richmond."[6]

More than logistics were involved, however. Whereas frontier conditions had formerly bred in Americans such soldierly qualities as courage, patience, endurance to hardships, and familiarity with weapons, thus making, wrote army captain William Wallace, "nearly every citizen . . . more than half a soldier," the living conditions of an urbanized, industrialized society no longer prepared citizens for life in the field. "[A]s a nation," he concluded, "we can't hike or shoot." Also lengthening the time required to prepare a soldier was the way modern technology increased the complexity of weapons and lengthened the training required to gain skill in their use. Such changes and the ability of potential enemies rapidly to mobilize a mass army were exacerbated by both foreign aggressiveness and America's own expansionism—its advocacy of the Open Door in China, its decision to retain the Philippines, and what Major James W. McAndrew described as the nation's arrogant claim "to be alone sovereign in the Western Hemisphere." By the close of the new century's first decade, army officers had consequently concluded that the country must prepare a trained reserve, one sufficient to permit the United States, in the event of a major conflict, rapidly to create a much larger force than America's eighty-thousand-man regular establishment.[7]

Although such reasoning caused most army officers to agree with Captain Fred R. Brown that the "relative advance in preparedness for war by all other nations and the great change in the art of war" had rendered "the United States . . . less prepared for sudden war than at the outbreak of the Spanish-American War," they did not conclude that such weakness would enable an aggressor to accomplish the total military defeat of the United States—unless devastating early setbacks destroyed the nation's will to resist. To the contrary, army officers expected the nation to expel any invader—ultimately. In true progressive fashion, however, they objected to the needlessly long, wasteful, and possibly preventable war that might result, wrote Captain Charles Crawford, from America's inability "to stand up against a trained foreign army of modern size invading this country for nearly a year after it lands."[8]

To overcome that situation, army thought about the manpower problem began, in the decade before World War I, to move along one of three complementary paths. The nation might, first, substantially increase the size of its regular forces, making them sufficiently large to counter any invasion. Most officers recognized, however, that such an increase both challenged America's traditional opposition to standing armies and raised troubling questions about the peacetime recruitment of so large a force. The nation might instead, therefore, create a federally controlled reserve of trained civilians who could in an emergency reinforce the traditionally small regular forces. That approach too posed questions about recruiting, while also threatening the interests closely associated with the third choice, expanding and improving the states' militia. As the decade wore on, however, officers increasingly doubted that the militia could achieve either expansion or improvement. Perhaps recognizing the shortcomings inherent in each option, officers like Chief of Staff Bell variously supported all three choices in their pursuit of an efficient solution to the army's manpower problem.[9]

The Dick Act of 1903 marked the army's first systematic attempt to expand and improve the militia, whose organized units were known as the National Guard. In return for Federal recognition, free arms and ammunition, and authority to expend the annual federal appropriation for general military supplies, the act required militia units to hold periodic drills and an annual five-day summer encampment. To eliminate several weaknesses and ambiguities of the earlier law, a 1908 amendment removed the nine-month limit on the period a military unit might be called into federal service and made the then constitutionally questionable assertion that the Guard could be used outside the territorial limits of the United States.[10]

Though many historians have relied upon the works of Civil War hero and military intellectual Major General Emory Upton to argue otherwise, regular officers generally supported those changes. The editor of *United Service*, for instance, claimed the Dick Act had initiated an "era of good feeling" between the National Guard and the regular army, and the *Army and Navy Journal*, discovering "closer and more sympathetic relations between the officers of the Army and those of the citizen soldiery," commended regular officers for the "hearty spirit" with which they had entered into efforts to improve the militia. During the conduct of the more frequent regular-militia joint maneuvers that ensued, militiamen detected the same spirit. Captain C. C. Pierce of the West Virginia National Guard, for instance, found that regular officers were not stuck up and crusty, as expected, but rather had "agreeably surprised" the militiamen by their "patience and kindness."[11]

Even while the Guard was failing to fulfill the Dick Act's requirement to achieve the organizational standards of regular units and a strength proportionate to each state's delegation in Congress, the *Journal* described officers of the General Staff as "not only hopeful . . . but enthusiastic about the ultimate prospects of making the National Guard an adequate reserve force." In a further pledge of good faith, the War Department organized a Division of Militia Affairs, placing at its head Lieutenant Colonel Erasmus M. Weaver, a long-standing advocate of cooperation between militia and regulars, who in a letter to the *Journal*'s editor claimed that Upton's criticisms of the militia had lost their validity. With regular instructors, improved organization, and periodic joint maneuvers, the new National Guard had become an "altogether . . . different type" of force than the one condemned by Upton.[12]

For reasons to be discussed later, after 1910 the harmony between officers of the National Guard and regular army began to give way to discord, but regulars like Major General Tasker H. Bliss continued to argue that "the National Guard is composed, in the main, of the very best element that could be called on for military service." The militiamen, he claimed, "are handicapped only by their system. . . . If we could only change the system and at the same time keep the personnel we could not do better."[13]

By late 1916, however, President Wilson's response to the deterioration in Mexican-American relations had taken a turn that gave even the Guard's most ardent supporters little cause to rejoice. In 1911 a liberal Mexican government, led by Francisco Madero, had overthrown the regime of dictator Porfirio Diaz, a change supported by the Taft administration despite losses to American businessmen. Madero's assassination in February 1913 by agents of General Victoriano Huerta resulted first in the reestablishment of a reactionary government, which neither Taft nor the recently elected Wilson would support, and then in further revolutionary upheaval as a variety of Mexican presidential hopefuls united in opposition to Huerta. In an effort to isolate the new dictator and support his more liberal opponents, headed by Venustiano Carranza, Wilson sent naval units to block Huerta's receipt of arms from Europe. That intervention led in April 1914 to the temporary arrest at Tampico of sailors from the U.S.S. *Dolphin*, to the subsequent American occupation of Vera Cruz, and, to Wilson's chagrin, to the unification of Mexican opinion behind Huerta, who broke relations with the United States and brought the two countries close to war. Subsequent mediation by Argentina, Brazil, and Chile and the withdrawal of American forces from Vera Cruz in October 1915, however, assisted the transfer of the Mexican presidency to the liberal Carranza, whom Wilson supported.

That might have resolved the crisis in Mexican-American relations had not several of the other presidential aspirants, each with a regional power base, not soon thereafter initiated revolutionary resistance to the new Carranza government. Even that would have created no major problems had not Pancho Villa, the regional chieftain in northern Mexico, begun to raid the border towns of Texas and New Mexico. Originally tolerant of such attacks, Wilson lost his patience after the March 1916 assault on Columbus, New Mexico, left seventeen Americans dead. Under pressure from Congress, the frustrated president dispatched Brigadier General John J. Pershing and a force of regulars in pursuit of Villa. Carranza had given but reluctant consent to Pershing's expedition, which risked once again the unification of all the Mexican factions in opposition to the United States—and the Mexican leader. To secure the Southwest against the possible anti-American coalition and the predictable border raids, Wilson in May 1916 called out the National Guard of the three southwestern states and reinforced it in June by mobilization of troops from the other states.

Ordered into federal service, the Guard responded almost to a man. Besides being too few in number, however, many of those men also proved physically incapable of field service. Despite a last-minute recruiting effort that had flooded the Guard with new men, many of whom could not fire a military rifle, its units fell 100,000 men short of prescribed war strength, and the mobilization further demonstrated the Guard's lack of engineers, cavalry, artillery, and other special troops needed to support its infantry units. After a month on the border, moreover, General Bliss found that most of the units had yet to begin serious tactical instruction, and he advised the adjutant general to consider as "a matter of profound gratification to the country that it was unnecessary to attempt to use them for immediate service, even for defensive purposes, at this time."[14]

Denied the glory of a combat role, separated from homes and families, out of touch with businesses or fearful of losing jobs, the guardsmen themselves, during the hot, dusty months on the border, began to

lose enthusiasm for the militia system, and many returned home receptive to the idea of universal military training and some form of conscription as the only just means of preparing a war reserve and ordering it to
active duty.[15]

Serious criticism of the Guard among regulars had begun, however,
a half dozen years before the disastrous 1916 mobilization, which in effect validated the organizational shortcomings already identified by regular officers. Regulars had strongly objected to the 1908 Congressional
decision requiring the Guard to be called into service before federal attempts to raise volunteer units, but true acrimony developed only in
1910 when the National Guard Association initiated its campaign for a
pay bill to compensate guardsmen for the time devoted to military
training. The struggle over the pay bill finally brought to fruition the
potential conflict between regular officers, who pursued military efficiency through centralization and rationalization, and those guardsmen
who retained their local orientation and laissez-faire approach to military affairs.[16]

Calling attention to the inefficiency of the militia system, Captain
George Van Horn Moseley, in an article written before the 1916 mobilization, observed that the National Guard comprised peacetime volunteers often precluded by business and family obligations from accepting
long federal service "while thousands of strong, able-bodied young
men who are fully available for service are wholly untrained and unprepared to serve." In addition to that inefficient use of the nation's military manpower, there was the matter of control. According to Major
John McAuley Palmer, one of the army's most prominent young reformers and writers and a postwar aide to General Pershing, "efficiency
demands that the *war-making* power must also be the *war-preparing
power.*" To the editor of the *Infantry Journal,* local or divided control
meant "administrative chaos and military inefficiency." No military
force "that cannot be controlled by, or used by, the national government ought . . . to be paid from the national treasury." As regular officers considered opportunity costs, they also concluded that the active army had better uses for the nine million dollars needed annually to pay
the militiamen. The pay bill, Palmer asserted, was "one means of securing a national citizen soldiery . . . , but an examination of the facts will
reveal that it is the most expensive and the least effective means of accomplishing the object in view." The federal government, the regulars
believed, could more efficiently use the money destined to be spent on
the states' militia to create either a federal militia or a paid reserve of

The Fifth Infantry's rude 1877 cantonment at the mouth of the Tongue River in the Montana Territory (above right) had been renamed Fort Keogh before Lieutenant Hunter Liggett arrived in 1879. The improved barracks of the permanent establishment only somewhat moderated the harshness of life on the frontier. William Tecumseh Sherman, USMA 1840 (above left), who in 1869 succeeded Ulysses S. Grant as the army's Commanding General, recognized the changing nature of warfare, for which he prepared the officer corps by sustaining the engineer and artillery schools at Willett's Point and Fortress Monroe, respectively, founding the School of Application for Infantry and Cavalry at Fort Leavenworth, and contributing, through his influence on Stephen B. Luce, to the creation of the Naval War College. Big-game hunting (shown below in an 1886 photograph of Lieutenant Lewis D. Green and companions from the Seventh Infantry, then stationed in Wyoming) sometimes relieved the boredom and routine of late nineteenth-century army life on the Plains. Card playing, alcohol, and private study of military science often served the same ends.

Though aboard the USS Trenton *(1874–1891), until the late eighties the U.S. Navy's finest ship, the crew of the 11-inch Dahlgren gun (above) would service it while completely exposed to an enemy's fire. In modern navies, however, breech-loading rifles had by the eighties begun to replace such cast-iron, muzzle-loading smoothbores, which had reached their ultimate development in the two decades preceding the Civil War.*

The handful of officers aboard the USS Swatara, *photographed (left) during the 1883–1886 cruise in which it maintained order in the ports of the West Indies and Central America, suggests that extended isolation at sea could limit the horizons of naval officers just as the frontier could confine the army's leaders. Young William S. Sims, with a beard third from right in the rear kept mentally alert, however, by commenting on international politics and writing for newspapers in New York and Chicago.*

Sims commenced his forty-two years of active service aboard the USS Tennessee *(1865–1886), shown below while it was flagship of the North Atlantic Squadron. The stacks for the steam engines that provided an alternate source of propulsion for the fully-rigged, wooden-hulled ship could be lowered, as had the rearmost when this picture was taken.*

A part of the Third System of American coastal fortifications built in the four decades before the Civil War, San Francisco's Fort Winfield Scott (begun in 1853 and now known as Fort Point) had three tiers of casemated cannon (two are fully visible above) to seaward and roof batteries to guard both land and sea approaches. That arrangement, attained by use of vertical masonry construction, permitted the era's smoothbore cannon to achieve high densities of fire.

Because the longer-ranged and more destructive rifles of the late nineteenth century could quickly reduce a masonry fort to rubble, they forced coastal defenders to place their own new rifled ordnance on "disappearing carriages" that provided concealment as well as protection when drawn below the concrete and earthen embankment. (Note the relative positions of the weapons pictured at Fort Armistead, Hawkins Point, Maryland, below.) The power, range, and rapid fire of the new rifles compensated for their dispersal, and the new carriages and fortifications rendered them virtually invulnerable to naval gunfire.

Cruising independently, ships like the USS Colorado *(1856–1885), shown above at Woosung, China, about 1871, helped American commerce by keeping order and seeking new markets.*

Rear Admirals John Rodgers, above left, and Robert W. Shufeldt, below left, presided over the two naval advisory boards of the early eighties, both of which recommended continuation of that policy of "squadron" cruising.

The Squadron of Evolution, in 1891 composed of the USS Yorktown, Boston, Concord, Atlanta, Newark, *and* Chicago *(far right below), all with unarmored steel hulls and decks, represented a change in that policy as the U.S. Navy increasingly emphasized fleet tactics and control of the waters along America's coasts.*

Sherman's School of Application for Infantry and Cavalry, shown above in its original Fort Leavenworth home, experienced a two-decade evolution from tactical school to Staff College, which trained general staff officers and bridged the gap between the former schools and the 1903 Army War College.

Naval War College founder Stephen B. Luce, who was commissioned in 1841, acknowledged the influence of Sherman's ideas on officer education and the scientific study of warfare and sponsored the research and teaching that led to Alfred Thayer Mahan's seminal work, The Influence of Sea Power upon History, 1660–1783.

The Naval War College, shown below as it appeared about 1884, barely survived the attacks of a naval hierarchy that doubted the value of any formal study of naval science.

AMERICAN MILITARY REFORMERS

Though separated by age, rank, and service, a common determination to prepare the armed forces for modern warfare united America's military reformers. David Dixon Porter, above right, who led the U.S. Navy from 1870 through its rehabilitation of the eighties, received his commission in 1829 but often criticized the shipbuilding programs of the advisory boards led by his contemporaries Rodgers and Shufledt. Another older officer and Civil War veteran, John M. Schofield, above left, entered the army in 1853 and became its commander in 1888, by which time he had become an advocate of staff reform, maneuvers, and improved training. William H. Carter, USMA 1873, one of the younger reformers, served as Secretary of War Elihu Root's principal advisor on creation of the Army War College and General Staff Corps and frequently wrote about army reform for both service and civilian journals.

NAVAL REFORMERS I

Above left, Robley D. Evans, USNA 1863, early advocate of armored ships and commander of the American fleet, 1907–8. Above right, Caspar F. Goodrich, USNA 1865, naval educator and publicist with ties to the academic community and president of both the NWC and Naval Institute. Below left, Richard Wainwright, USNA 1868, USNA superintendent, Chief of Naval Intelligence, and Aide for Operations. Below right, Richmond P. Hobson, USNA 1889, Spanish-American War hero who subsequently assisted naval reform as a congressman.

NAVAL REFORMERS II

Above left, George Dewey, USNA 1858, hero of Manila Bay in 1898 and subsequently president of the General Board. Above right, Henry C. Taylor, USNA 1863, early advocate of battleships, staff reform, and naval education; NWC president; member of the General Board. Below left, Charles S. Sperry, USNA 1866, NWC president, U.S. representative to the Second Hague Peace Conference, commander of the American fleet, 1908–9. Below right, Bradley A. Fiske, USNA 1874, naval inventor, critic of American naval policy and administration, and Aide for Operations.

ARMY REFORMERS

Above left, Tasker H. Bliss, USMA 1875, USMA and NWC instructor, first president of the AWC, Chief of Staff, and U.S. military representative to the Allied Supreme War Council. Above right, Henry T. Allen, USMA 1882, attaché in St. Petersburg and Berlin, observer with Japanese Army in 1904, and wartime corps commander. Below left, John McA. Palmer, USMA 1897, intellectual and literary contributor to prewar preparedness studies and postwar reform of military policy. Below right, Frank R. McCoy, USMA 1897, soldier-statesman protégé of Leonard Wood, who had extensive postwar diplomatic experience.

Turn-of-the-century imperial politics brought American infantry to Peking's Temple of Agriculture, above. Right, Troop L of the Sixth U.S. Cavalry assembles on the Avenue of Statues near China's Ming Tombs.

Though the China Relief Expedition only temporarily involved the United States in the government of overseas territories, the Philippines imposed enduring resonsibilities. Left, military governor and later army Chief of Staff, Hugh L. Scott, poses with the Sultan of Jolo, and below, an American soldier enrolls Filipino children in school, an aspect of the army's efforts to "civilize" its colonial subjects.

In 1886 Congress authorized the new navy's first two armored ships, the battleships USS Maine *and USS* Texas, *above, whose domestic construction was made possible by improvements in the American steel industry.*

Sailors, like those shown below at Vera Cruz in 1914, often went ashore — along with soldiers and marines — to enforce American policy, in this case to block German arms deliveries to a Mexican regime considered undemocratic by President Wilson.

During the 1916–17 Punitive Expedition into Mexico, the U.S. Army began its transition from the mule-drawn escort wagon at right to motor transport.

The National Guard's 1916 mobilization along the Mexican border brought little martial glory but an excellent opportunity for both field training and regular indoctrination in the shortcomings of American military policy.

To improve the training of the states' militia, regulars also used joint maneuvers, like those at Fort Riley, Kansas, in 1902, to demonstrate basic military skills such as the construction of field fortifications.

The General Board, in 1900 comprising Henry Ward, left rear, Charles Stockton, French Chadwick, Robert Milligan, Henry Taylor, Arent Crowninshield, Asa Walker, George Dewey, Charles Clark, Charles Sigsbee, and George Reed, left foreground, performed some of the navy's general staff functions until the 1916 establishment of the Office of the Chief of Naval Operations.

America's predreadnought or all big-gun battleships reached their zenith in the Connecticut-class ships, among them the USS Minnesota, *below, which William S. Sims commanded for two years after its participation in the fleet's circumnavigation of the world.*

A frontier tea party. Even on the frontier, officers' wives, as in this c. 1890 photograph from the album of Charles D. Rhodes, USMA 1889, sought to maintain the standards of their social class.

Government-business relations. The USS Kearsarge *(1862–1894), famous veteran of the Civil War, also had a claim on the sentiments of those congressmen in whose districts lay the shipyards profiting from the more than a million dollars' worth of often politically timed repairs done on the obsolete, quarter-million-dollar steam sloop.*

Hunter Liggett, shown left in France as commander of the First U.S. Army, entered an Indian-fighting army scattered throughout the American West. Four decades later he commanded soldiers equipped with: machine guns, shown above in May, 1918, engaging German planes near Villers, France; aircraft, below left in October, 1918, photograph of the French S.P.A.D. of American Ace of Aces Eddie Rickenbacker; and tanks, bottom, from Company C, 327th Tank Battalion, in action near Sercheprey, France, September, 1918.

Using ships like the SS Leviathan, *shown above at Brest, France, in May, 1918, wartime Chief of Staff Peyton C. March, USMA 1888, above right, planned and the U.S. Navy secured one of history's largest and most rapid migrations— the movement of an American army to France, and back. The large rifled guns in the turreted main batteries of the armored battleship* Tennessee *c. 1924, below, reveal how far the American navy had progressed in the nearly four decades since William S. Sims, shown below right in 1918 as the senior American naval officer in Europe, had served aboard an earlier, wooden-hulled* Tennessee *with its cast-iron, smoothbore, muzzle-loading cannon mounted broadside.*

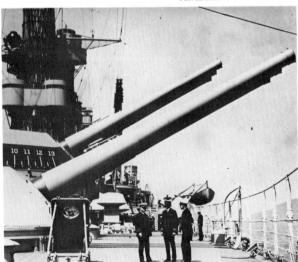

ex-soldiers capable of bringing the regular establishment to full war strength.[17]

As regular officers grew disillusioned with the militia's capacity to produce an adequate supply of trained men, the army gave increasing attention to other methods of reinforcing the regular forces. Had the choice been entirely the army's, officers might have elected to expand the regular forces to the 250,000- to 500,000-man level variously estimated as the minimum needed to repulse the first echelon of any invasion force.[18] Still, few of them proposed such an extensive increase, and as the 1912 General Staff report on "The Organization of the Land Forces of the United States" made clear, regular officers understood and respected the limits imposed by the American military tradition. "The military pedant," explained the report, "may fail by proposing adequate and economical forces under forms that are intolerable to the national genius." Eager to avoid pedantry, regular officers generally ignored military policies they considered "impracticable or foreign [to] . . . familiar institutions that have grown with the national life." Proposals for expansion of the regular force therefore remained modest in size, and even when some officers ultimately came to advocate universal military training and conscript service, they sought to place those proposals within a traditional context by equating conscript service to the universal obligation inherent in the 1792 militia law.[19]

In the meantime, army officers experimented with a third approach —attempts to reinforce America's small standing army with a federally controlled volunteer militia or a reserve of ex-servicemen. Regular officers had long debated the latter form of federally controlled reinforcement, which they had initially described as a means to fill vacancies created as units rose from peace to war strength or suffered battle casualties.[20]

One of those schemes for avoiding the inefficiencies associated with any infusion of raw recruits became official policy between 1907 and 1910 when Chief of Staff Bell sought Congressional authority to "enlist" 50,000 ex-servicemen. In return for a federal wage of twenty-four to forty-eight dollars per year, those men must agree to: participate in a short annual or biennial training camp, keep the War Department informed of their whereabouts, and respond to any wartime call for regular service. Otherwise the former soldiers remained free to pursue their civilian careers, and the army could be confident of having enough trained men to bring regular units to war strength without a significant loss of effectiveness.[21]

Bell's proposal, which Congress ignored, failed to exploit fully the possibilities inherent in the concept of a federal reserve, but his successor as chief of staff, Major General Leonard Wood, took the logical next step and asked Congress for authority to enlist not ex-soldiers but civilians. He urged upon it an enlistment option calling for six years of service—three on active duty and three in furlough status, the latter constituting the reserve. Whenever recruiting conditions were favorable, Wood also hoped to shorten the period of active service to a single year, thus making enlistment more attractive, adding men to the reserve at a greater rate, and extending their period of reserve service to five years.[22]

Many older officers opposed that plan because they doubted the army's ability to train good soldiers in a single year. Wood nevertheless had the support of the army's most progressive element and, more important, of war secretary Henry L. Stimson, who considered the reserve plan "the most important reform to be obtained for the Army." Like Wood, he seemed to sense the plan's full potential, and his annual reports clearly suggest that both men sought ultimately to give one year's military training to a vast pool of civilian volunteers. Wood, for instance, considered "short service and few re-enlistments, . . . passing through the Army and return[ing] to civil and industrial pursuits . . . as many men as possible," the key to "preparedness for war at minimum expense, and by means in accord with our ideas." And Stimson asserted that the "theory of the modern state is that it is the duty of the citizen to train himself . . . to perform his function as a soldier in case of possible war and to return as quickly as possible to his normal civil life." If so developed, the reserve concept could turn the army into a school operating under federal auspices to prepare citizen-soldiers immediately available to satisfy the military needs of both the regular army and an expanded war force.[23]

While refusing to cooperate fully, Congress did amend the 1912 appropriations act to authorize an alternative enlistment contract providing for a seven-year obligation including four years of active service, three years in the new reserve, but payment—at the rate of five dollars per month—only if the reservists were eventually called into federal service. Because the national legislature had accepted the principle of a federal reserve, Stimson considered the amendment a "beginning," and Wood called it a "very great advance." Surveying the new law's less attractive features, a young General Staff Corps officer, Major Carl Reichmann, more accurately predicted that "the present law requiring four years of service with the colors will not furnish a sufficient reserve."

Reichmann was right. At the end of the first year, the reserve comprised eight men; in the second, sixteen; and in the third, seventeen. Of over twenty-thousand enlistments between November 1912 and August 1913 only sixty-one men applied to enter the reserve.[24]

Wood consequently began to press for changes to "perfect" the law, and subsequent General Staff reports more clearly revealed the trend of army thought. Seeking to feed sufficient men into the reserve to create a force of 379,000 men, the 1915 "Statement of a Proper Military Policy for the United States" proposed an eight-year enlistment with only two years' active service. The statement also revealed a change in concept. Rather than a modest body of ex-soldiers to bring regular units to war strength and replace battle losses, the army now sought a reserve sufficient to boost America's tiny regular establishment to a field force totaling a half million trained men. The statement introduced yet another innovation by proposing a federal volunteer militia of another half million men, each of whom would receive nine months of concentrated military training but otherwise remain in civil life. In the event of emergency, the federal militiamen would receive another three months' training before being committed to combat. Designating as the Continental Army a modified version of such a militia, Secretary of War Lindley M. Garrison recommended in 1915 that Congress authorize the government to raise, in three annual increments, a 400,000-man force whose members would receive the preliminary training and return to civil life subject only to a call to service during the remainder of a three-year enlistment.[25]

The Continental Army plan drew a host of opponents. While antipreparedness forces challenged the need for any increase in military strength, the South contemplated the possibility that a federally controlled militia might quickly train to arms the region's entire black male population. And the National Guard Association rightly perceived the Continental Army as a device to relegate the states' militia to a minor role. While congressmen from rural areas were skeptical of both regular officers and their proposals for centralized control of the nation's military forces, Assistant Chief of Staff Tasker H. Bliss suspected that congressmen generally feared "any proposition for training citizen reserves under the voluntary principle." Bliss claimed the legislators secretly doubted "that citizens will volunteer in sufficient numbers, and that will bring them face to face with the issue of compulsory training." Rather than consider such implications, Bliss confided to a friend, Congress preferred to "fall back on the militia as a sop to public senti-

ment.'' Though Woodrow Wilson had by 1916 begun to advocate preparedness, and had even shown early support for Garrison's program,
the president eventually abandoned both his war secretary and the Continental Army in favor of Congressional proposals to improve the militia
act by obligating guardsmen to take a dual oath for both state and federal service, increasing the militia's total strength, and extending federal control over the Guard's training, organization, and equipment.
That compromise came too late, however, to prevent a public demonstration of the shortcomings of the militia concept during the previously
described 1916–17 mobilization on the Mexican border.[26]

In the meantime a group of vocal and energetic officers had begun
to explore yet another way of creating citizen soldiers for the army—
summer camps giving military training to college men. Narrowly conceived, such camps could do little more than provide rudimentary training to the men most likely to command the companies and battalions of
United States Volunteers—emergency organizations created to supplement both militia and regular units. But even the first camps, held at
Gettysburg and Monterey in 1913, had a wider purpose. According to
Secretary of War Garrison, the camps also served to create a ''patriotic
spirit'' in America and provide a ''training school for manly men and
good citizens.'' Spurred on by the lessons seemingly taught by the outbreak of war in Europe, army officers and their civilian allies sought to
use that patriotic spirit to build within American society a base of support for such improvements in military policy as adoption of universal
military training (UMT).[27]

By the time of America's entry into the World War, military officers
and their spokesmen had almost two decades' experience in advocacy of
UMT, a cooperation that clearly reveals the degree to which military officers both shared the values of civilian reformers and sought to use the
federal government to correct the ills of American society. In his study
of the *Citizen Soldiers*, John Clifford has found that the civilian advocates of UMT had more in mind than military defense; they also feared
for America's national unity, supposedly under attack from immigration, urbanization, and industrialization. In their view, military service
provided a means to Americanize the immigrant, to counter the physically and morally debilitating aspects of urban life, and to promote a re-
birth of democratic feeling within the military camps as men of all stations met as equals. Those civilian reformers also hoped that a period of
UMT would rouse young Americans from their pursuit of self-interest
and excess and awaken them to the responsibilities of democratic citi-

zenship. According to the progressive *New Republic,* universal training would serve as "social hygiene," a sort of "moral equivalent of war."[28]

Military officers discovered similar virtues in their plans for a federal reserve. A future West Point superintendent, Captain Merch B. Stewart, urged his fellow citizens to view the army as one of the nation's "agencies of social improvement," and the author of *An Army of the People,* Major John McAuley Palmer, hoped to make the year of obligatory service "the most valuable from an educational standpoint in the life of the American boy." Not only would the latter "learn to defend his country," he would "learn the lesson of nationalism as well as the lesson of individualism." Equally important, each American youth who served would receive "a better educated physique and a better educated character." He would also "learn to serve with his fellows in a democratic environment . . . [and] prepare . . . for a new type of democratic citizenship." Senior officers agreed. Former chief of staff Hugh L. Scott, for instance, described compulsory military training as "worthwhile for the physical and mental uplift which it would produce; worthwhile alone as a fact in increasing the Americanization and amalgamation of our foreign population; worth-while alone for the discipline enforced, with constant respect for law and the diminution of crime." In a possible appeal to businessmen, former chief of staff Wood stressed the socioeconomic advantages of military training, which he claimed would render ex-soldiers "more effective in their work" because they would have become "more respectful of authority, do things more promptly and do them exactly as they are told to do them, which makes them all around better working men." The eugenic theories then common in intellectual circles also received acknowledgment from General Scott and the editor of the *Cavalry Journal,* who claimed that military service would reverse the "physical deterioration of the race in modern times" and achieve "race improvement through [a better] environment."[29]

Military support for UMT reflected far more, of course, than close ties to the civil community and a response to the progressive trend of civilian thought. The officers' emphasis on the social value of military service seems, on the one hand, an attempt to counter the arguments of civilian antimilitarists who described armies and navies as a drain on the Treasury, a threat to democracy, and, for the individual serviceman, a path to genetic, physical, and moral decay.[30] On the other hand, and far more important, military support for UMT, and later wartime conscription, revealed the officers' previously described reassessment of international and domestic conditions. The World War, by fully demonstrating the fighting capacities of what Chief of Staff Scott described as "the highly trained and splendidly disciplined armies of our possible enemies," convincingly proved to regular officers that "the conditions of modern war do not afford time to train an army after war becomes imminent."[31] And the intermittent threat of war with Mexico, which culminated in the disastrous National Guard mobilization and ineffective Punitive Expedition of 1916–17, exposed the militia's inadequacies as a regular army reserve.[32]

In that light, progressive officers like Major Palmer, a member of the General Staff committee preparing plans for UMT, interpreted the preparedness agitation as an indication that the correct political moment had arrived for an open and vigorous advocacy of compulsory training. The "sentiment of the country is settling upon universal training," he wrote in 1916; for "the first time we have not been informed that the subject is 'taboo' politically." Imbued with both the progressive's concern for efficiency and social improvement and the soldier's analysis of the increased military dangers facing the United States, Palmer and his fellow officers hoped the country would adopt the system of universal military training he described as "the cheapest, fairest, and most democratic method of distributing the burden of military preparation."[33]

Prior to the late nineteenth century, when the navy established an Office of Naval Militia, that service had given only indifferent support to the states' naval militia and the training of citizen-sailors. Able to train seamen faster than it could build ships, the nineteenth-century navy also expected to supply its modest manpower needs by drawing skilled sailors from the nation's merchant marine.[34]

By the turn of the century, the situation had changed. Naval officers, on the one hand, shared the army's concern for the drift of American society: the threat to an imagined ethnic homogeneity posed by massive immigration from southern and eastern Europe; the undemocratic features of an increasingly industrialized, urbanized, and stratified society; and the growing disrespect for law and traditional cultural values. And naval officers too described military service as a cure for those ills. Service with the colors would Americanize the foreign born, strengthen democracy by temporarily obliterating the barriers separating men of different social classes, increase the industrial productivity of those who had served aboard ship, overcome the typical civilian's physical softness, and replace self-indulgence with a fierce national pride.[35]

On the other hand, more than social concern drew naval attention to manpower problems. In another parallel with army thought, naval officers concluded that economic and technological change had robbed their service of its traditional source of partially trained recruits. Because the United States had "practically no seagoing merchant marine today" and because "seamanship, as . . . understood by the merchantman, plays but a small role in the duties of a modern navy," wrote Lieutenant Commander Roland R. Riggs in 1916, the merchant sailor had become "a slender reed on which to lean in war." The complexity of modern warships, claimed Rear Admiral Charles S. Sperry, commander of the Great White Fleet during the latter portion of its 1908 circumnavigation of the globe, had changed "the character of the enlisted personnel of the navy. Even if the seafaring population of the coast[al] cities still existed[,] it would not be possible for them [*sic*] to do the work now demanded" of sailors. That shortage of trained man-of-war's men became more acute in 1910 even as Sperry wrote. In that year the navy was preparing to form reserve fleets of its overage battleships, and to achieve combat effectiveness in the event of war their skeletal crews would require a large infusion of trained sailors.[36]

Convinced by the Spanish-American War that the states' naval militia, regarded by regulars as useful only for coastal defense, provided no alternative to the merchant marine, naval officers quickly abandoned attempts to raise the militia to regular standards. Because militiamen generally opposed relegation to coastal defense, they viewed as a threat the navy's subsequent consideration of a federally controlled reserve of experienced man-of-war's men, and relations between naval militia and regulars gradually worsened.[37] In the Naval Militia Act of 1914, Congress compromised by applying the principles of the army's Dick Act to the naval service, but the subsequent outbreak of war in Europe prompted the legislators to apply another approach the army had already found wanting—creation of a reserve force of ex-servicemen.[38]

Rear Admiral Bradley A. Fiske, aid for operations to naval secretary Josephus Daniels, discounted the value of all such efforts. In Fiske's opinion, expecting to gain sufficient seamen from either a naval reserve or the naval militia was "a visionary notion, with no basis of fact to rest upon." Because full-time sailors were "the only men we can depend upon for naval work on board our ships," Fiske proposed a relatively modest 19,600-man increase in the regular navy. Even after 1914, however, such hopes remained illusory, and searching for a source of sailors to man its newly created reserve fleets, the navy tried an experiment derived from the army's use of summer training camps. In 1916 the Atlantic Reserve Fleet conducted a cruise during which a few interested civilians from coastal cities participated in maneuvers and received instruction in gunnery.[39]

As the relatively small size of Fiske's recommendation reveals, the navy's manpower needs remained rather modest. Once the ships of the active and reserve fleets had obtained the few men needed to bring them to full complement, the navy could quite easily train men to replace wartime losses, and the naval progressives' quest for efficiency consequently focused less on relatively minor manpower issues than on improvements to both warships and naval administration. Accepting the premise of Commander Yates Stirling that the "object for which a navy exists is, in the ultimate, war," naval reformers assessed their service's efficiency in terms of its capacity to succeed in combat with a great power.[40]

With that standard in mind, one group of reformers began work at the bottom, concentrating its criticism on deficiencies in the navy's equipment and training, while the other group continued its previous focus on the high command, seeking improvements in naval organization and planning. After traveling along converging paths, both groups ended by reemphasizing earlier calls for creation of a naval general staff to direct the work of the technical bureaus that reformers held responsible for the navy's inefficiency.

The career of Admiral William S. Sims, so ably recorded by Elting E. Morison, well illustrates the path to reform taken by the younger, equipment-and-training-oriented group of naval progressives.[41] Unimpressed by America's victory in the war with Spain, those officers carefully studied foreign warships—those the United States Navy must prepare to meet in battle—only to discover the inferiority of American gunnery techniques and equipment. The reformers at first responded to that discovery by forwarding their analyses and recommendations through official channels and publishing their views in professional journals. But when bureaucratic inaction frustrated their recommendations, Sims and several of his peers decided to steer a riskier course; they circumvented the entire chain of command by sending their criticisms directly to their commander in chief, President Theodore Roosevelt, who responded by ordering Sims's appointment as inspector of target practice. While holding that post, Sims introduced his reforms to the navy and successfully demonstrated their value.

Impressed by their victory in the struggle to improve gunnery, those same reformers cast a critical eye on the design of America's newest battleships, which seemed more vulnerable to enemy gunfire and shipboard accident than comparable foreign models. The gun turrets of American ships, claimed the reformers, lacked adequate protection, the armor plates protecting the hull had been improperly placed, and faulty interior arrangements increased the probability of fatal and disabling explosions in the ships' powder magazines.

When official appeals failed again to impress the navy's Washington bureaus, the reformers once more used extreme measures, now feeding their criticisms to writer Henry Reuterdahl, who published in *McClure's* his muckraking expose of "The Needs of Our Navy." The article led to both a Congressional investigation and a joint General Board–Naval War College inquiry. Though given a chance to state their case, the young reformers failed to repeat their earlier triumph, and the senior officers of the navy's technical bureaus successfully defended their decision to confine improvements to new ships rather than spend time and money remodeling inferior equipment already in service. That defeat led those reformers to conclude, in Sims's words, that the bureau chiefs had become mere "technical men [who] . . . resist[ed] all criticism that is disrespectful." The navy's "military men," who commanded the ships and "must ultimately be responsible for disaster in battle due to mechanical defects," must therefore seize control of the Washington bureaus and "determine the requirements of the weapons they are to fight with."[42]

The reformers' eventual decision to battle the bureau chiefs represented, however, no simple struggle between youthful reformers and aged bureaucrats, and in 1909 Sims specifically recognized that in moving from criticism of gunnery and equipment to attacks on departmental administration his group had finally merged its arguments with those of more senior reformers who had "begun this fight before we youngsters understood much about its object and importance." Statements about war as the determinant of naval policy and practice, like that of young Commander Yates quoted above, found, moreover, their antecedents in the assumptions that had guided older reformers like Captain Henry C. Taylor, who had described the navy as a "war machine" with only "incidental purposes of peace." Though that common premise had led older reformers, whose activities have been the subject of earlier chapters, to pursue naval efficiency through reorganization of the fleet, periodic maneuvers, and war planning, those senior progressives too had reached the conclusion that reform of the departmental bureaucracy had become the key to naval efficiency.[43]

The reformers' joint attack on the navy's bureau system also shows the extent to which naval officers shared the progressive outlook of many early-twentieth-century civil leaders. "It is a truism," wrote Lieutenant Commander Lyman A. Cotten, "that the chief function of a navy is to wage war upon the sea, and all other functions are but derivatives of this chief one." The navy's ultimate purpose being war, naval administration, the reformers maintained, must support preparation for war and be rationalized with that end in view. In addition to demanding rationalization of the naval service, the reformers likened the navy to a business and urged that naval affairs be conducted on sound, efficient business principles. That, they believed, required the navy to create a general staff of line officers—the only experts in that business— to ensure that the technical bureaus gave first priority to the combat side of the navy. Likening the navy to a large railroad, Captain Henry C. Taylor claimed that just as a railroad needed a board of directors "to *think* for the railroad, to observe rival lines, to consider the local laws of towns and states which their tracks traverse, and above all, to *watch the future* and prepare their [*sic*] system to draw all possible advantage from events," the navy needed a general staff to gather data concerning possible enemy fleets and likely theaters of war, to subordinate subsidiary naval tasks to the pursuit of the fleet's battle readiness, and to prepare and implement plans for naval operations.[44]

As with the fight for better gunnery and improved battleships, the naval progressives only gradually overcame the opposition of the naval staff. With a departmental order in 1909, however, Secretary of the Navy George von L. Meyer established a system of naval aids for fleet operations, personnel, materials, and inspections. Meyer then grouped the navy's existing bureaus, placing them under the supervision of the appropriate naval aid, in each case a senior line officer. Individually each aid coordinated the work of "his" bureaus and advised the secretary of their activities. Collectively the aids formed what Meyer described as a sort of "strategy board" representing the viewpoint of the military, or line, officers of the navy.[45]

Although Congress refused to establish the aid system on a legislative basis, the period from 1909 to the commencement of war in Europe was one of calm for the department. According to Daniel Costello, line officers had a "great amount of confidence" in both Secretary Meyer and the aid system as a means to coordinate the work of the bureaus and to ensure that the navy's peacetime activities fitted the service to support the war plans being drafted by the General Board.[46]

When a new administration assumed office in 1913, however, the aid system fell into disuse with a subsequent increase in line-staff controversy. In 1915, an ex-naval officer, hero of the Spanish-American War, and now member of Congress, Richmond P. Hobson, consequently sponsored a bill to create a naval general staff, a project assisted by Rear Admiral Bradley A. Fiske and other naval progressives. Although Congress finally established a chief of naval operations charged with "the operations of the fleet and with the preparation of plans for use in war," it refused to give that officer either specific authority to direct the bureaus or, initially, the assistants needed to accomplish his legislated duties. At last, however, the navy had taken the first legislative step toward creation of a naval general staff.[47]

In the years before World War I, the army too became the scene of a major line-staff controversy. Despite the 1903 creation of a general staff authorized to serve as the war secretary's principal military adviser and in his name to coordinate the work of the military departments, the service's bureau chiefs had used their handling of administrative routine and their extensive ties with powerful congressmen to retain effective control of the army and to limit the secretary's ability to run his department free of unofficial Congressional interference.

Ironically, two otherwise insignificant disputes over the appointment of recruiting officers and the retention of the army's unobtrusive muster roll became the occasion for a significant, if symbolic, decision on those wider issues.[48] Adding to the incongruity, both of the principal contestants—Major Generals Leonard Wood and Fred C. Ainsworth—having entered the army as contract surgeons were unlikely protagonists in a line-staff struggle for supremacy in the War Department. Yet, each had worked his way out of the medical service to become one of the War Department's two most powerful uniformed officials— Wood as chief of the General Staff and Ainsworth as adjutant general and unofficial leader of the bureau chiefs.

Though their dispute over the role of the General Staff had been brewing since Wood assumed his duties in 1910, it came to a boil in mid-1911 when Ainsworth made an insubordinate reply to Wood's legal but unprecedented intrusion into the selection of recruiting officers. Although Wood, who had previously urged President Taft to replace the adjutant general, undoubtedly hoped for sterner action, Henry L. Stimson, the moderately progressive war secretary who shared Wood's conception of the General Staff's proper role, gave Ainsworth only a vague reprimand. Still, Wood had less than a year to wait for final victory. When in February 1912 Ainsworth sent the chief of staff a much-delayed and thoroughly insulting response to General Staff queries into the necessity for the muster roll, Stimson ordered a court-martial, from which the adjutant general escaped by early retirement.

Though the nature of the immediate issues and the character of the chief participants brought to the incident an element of farce and some semblance of a personal vendetta, Ainsworth's defeat gave the chief of staff and the army's line a symbolic victory and marked a turning point in the General Staff's struggle to establish its and the secretary's legal control of the bureau chiefs, aptly described by Captain James G. Harbord as the "stumbling blocks of the progressive movement."[49]

Other, previously described, early-twentieth-century struggles for military reform also had a progressive character in that they sought to rationalize departmental affairs on behalf of military efficiency. Seeking economic efficiency through the closure of unneeded facilities, for instance, naval reformers struggled against both Congressional support for outdated local naval bases and resistance to the concentration of repair facilities at a few key points. Meanwhile army progressives with similar goals battled the legislators' opposition both to shutting down tiny "hitching post" forts with less than a few hundred men and to assembling the field army at several large garrisons. Previous chapters have also described the reformers' efforts to organize the army's regiments into combat divisions, to form the navy's vessels into battle fleets, and to hold periodic maneuvers to test the worthiness of the formations and their leaders.[50] While such reforms had an entirely military logic, they also illustrated the methods of civilian progressivism and were advocated in that language.

The military progressives did not, however, only look inward in their efforts to modernize America's military establishment. In their support for a Council of National Defense, the reformers suggested an agency for the coordination of foreign and military policies whose value the civilian community only fully recognized in the aftermath of a second world war. Although the council, as finally established by a rider to the August 1916 Army Appropriations Act, became little more than a cabinet-level committee comprising the secretaries of interior, agriculture, commerce, labor, navy, and war supported by a more important advisory commission to consider the economic aspects of a massive military mobilization, military officers had originally sought something quite different.[51]

As Louis Morton has explained, the armed services had wanted to lay the foundations and construct the administrative machinery for joint intragovernmental action and coordination of national policy. They had consequently proposed a council comprising the secretaries of war, navy, and state (with the latter as president pro tempore), the chairmen of the six Congressional committees on military, naval, and foreign affairs (relations), the presidents of the services' war colleges, and the senior officer of each service, with the president as an ex-officio member. Unfortunately, the civilian agencies of government then generally lacked any awareness of the need for such coordination, and the State Department specifically opposed what it perceived as an attempted military intrusion into its exclusive domain.[52]

The armed forces' concept of an agency for political-military coordination is at least as old as Rear Admiral Stephen B. Luce's 1892 condemnation of military policies dictated by either the willy-nilly action of Congress or the nature of the navy's peace duties. Believing that the nation's foreign policies must shape its naval establishment, Luce had urged Secretary of the Navy Benjamin Tracy to seek formation of an intragovernmental commission comprising representatives from each of the four Congressional military and naval committees, two army officers, two naval officers, and two eminent civilians—all under the chairmanship of the naval secretary. Service progressives meanwhile kept the idea of intragovernmental policy coordination alive, within the next fifteen years expanding it to include the State Department and Congressional foreign affairs committees. By 1907 the *Infantry Journal* listed a council "with large advisory powers" among a triumvirate of items jointly described as "Our Greatest Need." But the Council of National Defense first became a lively, if not immediately pressing, national issue only after 1910, when Congressman Richmond P. Hobson, a former naval officer, began periodically to introduce bills for establishing an agency along the lines desired by military officers.[53]

The services' reformers argued the case for the council from a variety of viewpoints. Speaking for the navy's General Board, Admiral George Dewey urged the council's creation because it would give other agencies of government some education in military needs, create public support for his service's programs, and "compel the adoption of a definite naval policy." With an element of service self-interest also in mind, Captain James G. Harbord, later General Pershing's chief of staff and subsequently supply and services chief for the American Expeditionary Force before becoming president of RCA, claimed that submission of military proposals to the scrutiny of a board of "distinguished men of both parties" would place the armed forces' programs "above criticism" and take them "out of politics." Like many civilian progressives who sought to remove decisions from the political arena and place them in the hands of disinterested experts, some military officers saw the council as a means to isolate military legislation from the deleterious influence of Congressional pork-barrel tactics.[54]

Others described the council as a rational preparation for war, which, like Commander Josiah S. McKean, they believed was "caused by conflict of national policies."[55] Recognizing that the United States had lately begun to pursue policies likely to lead to the sort of international clashes that produced war, those army and navy officers argued that the country could only avoid armed conflict by modifying the policies most likely to lead to war or by increasing its military power sufficiently to deter an attack and if necessary enforce the national will. Those officers maintained, moreover, that the services alone ought not make that choice. Nor must the State Department "do as it has done in the past," warned Commander Frank K. Hill, and "establish policies without regard to the military preparedness of the country" to support them.[56]

Making proper choices required intragovernmental coordination and accommodation: the president and his cabinet in the establishment of national policies; the army and navy in the design of military strategies for their support; and the Congress in the provision of the military means to implement those strategies. All, the officers argued, must cooperate, modifying initial positions on issues as necessary to win the support of other groups and giving the United States a rational and comprehensive military policy.[57]

In a sense, then, the Council of National Defense became the ultimate military reform, the editor of the *Infantry Journal* finding "no measure of greater national import . . . [confronting] the American people." A properly constituted council would authoritatively define America's national policies, give military strategists vitally needed political guidance, and eliminate the necessity for them to speculate about which national aims would be supported, if necessary, by force. Such a council would also lend weight to the military departments' requests for appropriate legislation, creating the public and Congressional support necessary to win approval for military programs. The council would bring, moreover, order and system to the creation of military policy and eliminate the inefficiencies stemming from a lack of coordination and the intrusion of local, personal, or partisan political considerations.[58] Ironically, when a modified council commenced operations during World War I, the chiefs of the services' bureaus still had sufficient power to resist council control of the wartime mobilization of the economy.[59]

In the decade before World War I, American military reformers continued their quarter-century study of technological change and international politics, still seeking to stay abreast of their joint effect upon America's military security. At the same time, those reformers became, in John Gates's happy phrase, "progressives in uniform," who increasingly employed the values, methods, and language of progressivism in their struggle for military modernization.[60] Efficiency, as measured by the services' capacity to achieve the ends of national policy without long and costly combat, the reformers made the goal of military policy. To that same end, they sought to rationalize military organizations and to provide expert advice to civil authority. Reliance upon experts and intelligent centralized direction, the reformers hoped, would serve the public interest and secure military policy against the chaos of political compromises designed to serve local or special interests.

Armed forces officers nevertheless realized that they only shared the responsibility for America's military security. The nation's civil leaders too must help the United States escape the "extravagance and inefficiency" that Major Palmer considered characteristic of American military history. In cooperation with the armed forces, elected officials must devise institutional arrangements for coordination of foreign and military policies, the accommodation of ends to means, and the reduction of "war preparations to a business-like system" with no requirement for the hasty improvisation that led to "political intrigue at the time of national crisis."[61] With those rhetorical goals for civil-military cooperation in mind, the next chapter will address the actual relations between America's civil and military elites.

CHAPTER 7

The Armed Services and American Society

ALTHOUGH MILITARY OFFICERS DESCRIBED their reforms as modest and essential responses to the ways that technology, societal change, and the evolution of international politics had transformed the character of war and exposed the United States to attack, some Americans considered any improvement in the regular forces as more likely to threaten than to protect the nation's fundamental interests. Alarmed by the services' expansion and drawing upon the hallowed antimilitary tradition that described America's civil and military institutions as antithetic, those citizens equated any modernization or increase of the army and navy with militarism. Powerful regular forces, the argument ran, imperiled American democracy. They would encourage citizens to glorify military values and institutions, involve the United States in needless foreign conflict, intervene in domestic affairs on behalf of a despotic chief executive, and, ultimately, dominate the national government.[1]

Though the antimilitarists' worst fears failed to materialize in the period before World War I, the stupendous expansion of America's armed forces during the last quarter century of cold war has caused more recent critics of the military establishment to reexamine the older arguments and to offer a more sophisticated analysis that similarly questions the benign and adaptive character of twentieth-century military reform. President Eisenhower's warning that a "military-industrial complex" sought to achieve "unwarranted influence" in "every city, every State house, every office of the Federal government" inspired some of those critics to assert a threat to democracy more subtle than the promulgation of military values or armed intervention in civil affairs. Those new antimilitarists traced that threat to possibly conspiratorial efforts by business leaders, military officers, and governmental officials to increase unnecessarily the size of military budgets with a view to enhancing their own economic or political power at the expense of both social amelioration and representative government. Though normally emphasizing the recent past, a few of those critics have joined Peter Karsten in characterizing the early-twentieth-century military reformers and their civilian allies as "Ancestors of the Military-Industrial Complex."[2]

While not entirely rejecting the existence of such a military-industrial complex, a second group of critics has described that concept as too narrow. Calling attention instead to the roles of class and ideology, those modern antimilitarists attributed the origins of America's military expansion to the nation's socioeconomic order. Early in the twentieth century, they claimed, America's business elite consciously created a powerful federal bureaucracy to guard monopolistic corporations against the consequences of unrestrained competition, to restore order to the nation's economic and political life, and to build an informal overseas empire that would provide an outlet for America's surplus of goods and capital. Sometimes regarding military officers as little more than tools of American businessmen, those critics traced military reform not to some external security threat but to the need for armed support for an imperialistic foreign policy aiming at the acquisition and control of the foreign markets that sustained America's economic growth and social stability.[3]

Because aspects of the armed forces' employment and their officers' relations with the nation's elites lend plausibility to the criticisms offered by both groups of modern antimilitarists, their argument deserves investigation. That investigation must, however, look beyond the superficial coincidences that might cause military reformers to appear as either coconspirators or guardians of a social class.

The least substantial part of the case for the military officers' role as defenders of a clique or class rests upon certain historical sequences. The early phases of America's military renaissance, for instance, did precede both the war with Spain and the acquisition of an island empire assumed to facilitate access to markets in Latin America and the Far East.

And, in the late nineteenth century, the United States government had begun to shift a few regular troops to the East, where they were subsequently used to suppress labor violence. As the country strengthened its armed forces after 1898, moreover, American presidents ordered army and navy participation in such imperial ventures as the China Relief Expedition, used a warship to facilitate Panamanian independence and acquisition of land for an interoceanic canal, initiated a series of interventions in the troubled affairs of Latin America, and, when the European powers had exhausted themselves in a seemingly endless conflict, intervened in a world war from which the United States gained global economic hegemony.

The common social origins and frequent contact between America's civil and military elites also lend credence to that case for civil-military cooperation. For contrary to the oft-repeated assertions that long periods of physical isolation—on the frontier or at sea—separated turn-of-the-century officers from "the main currents of American life" and that officers "were a cross-section of middle-class America . . . , [r]epresentative of everyone, . . . affiliated with no one,"[4] the nation drew its military leaders from its social elite, and they maintained close contact with leaders in politics, business, and intellectual life. Studies of the social origins of military officers have shown, in the words of Morris Janowitz, that service leaders came from "an old-family, Anglo-Saxon, Protestant, rural, upper middle-class professional background" only somewhat more rural and likely to be native born than the nation's businessmen. The services' generals and admirals, moreover, overwhelmingly represented the upper or upper-middle class and possessed social profiles very similar to those of business and political leaders.[5]

Drawn from the same social backgrounds, the members of civil and military elites maintained their unity by such diverse means as membership in the same clubs and intragroup marriages. The 1902 membership list of New York's University Club, for instance, contained the names of almost two hundred army and navy officers—a pattern repeated on the rolls of the Manhattan Club, Knickerbocker Club, and New York Club as well as in the Union and New Algonquin clubs of Boston, the Cosmos and Metropolitan clubs of Washington, D.C., and the Chicago Club, where that city's senior army officer lunched regularly with corporate and political leaders like George Pullman, Marshall Field, John Clark, Potter Palmer, and Robert Lincoln.[6] The ways that intermarriage united the nation's elites is well illustrated by the unions that made in-laws of: future United States senator Henry Cabot Lodge; Brooks Adams, intellectual, author, and scion of one of America's most prominent families; and Henley Luce, son of the reforming rear admiral. All had the same father-in-law, Rear Admiral Henry Davis. Nor were such unions rare. Future General of the Armies John J. Pershing married the daughter of Wyoming senator Francis E. Warren, and Admiral William S. Sims, Pershing's world war naval counterpart, wed the former Margaret Hitchcock. Her father was a wealthy manufacturer of plate glass who became America's first ambassador to Russia and secretary of interior for both McKinley and Roosevelt, whose own brother-in-law was William Cowles, a naval officer.

The unmarried members of the elite found more novel ways to keep in touch. In 1907 Captain Frank R. McCoy, a protege of Chief of Staff Leonard Wood and military aide to the president, joined two General Staff officers in the rental of a handsome townhouse at 1718 H. Street, NW, close by the White House and the new edifice shared by the Departments of War, Navy, and State. The three army bachelors, who entertained freely, quickly learned how much they had in common with the young progressives staffing the Washington bureaucracy, and their "Family" grew as the officers invited their civilian counterparts to take up residence at the townhouse on H. Street whenever military orders temporarily sent one or another of its army tenants away from the capital. Within a decade, 1718 had become the sometime home of a remarkable group of young men who then or later held positions of great influence and responsibility: Willard Straight, founder of the *New Republic* and a J. P. Morgan partner; Basil Miles, editor of *Nation's Business*; Arthur W. Page, editor of *The World's Work;* Benjamin Strong, governor of the New York Federal Reserve Bank; Andrew J. Peters, a Massachusetts congressman and Boston mayor; James F. Curtis, assistant secretary of the treasury; Henry P. Fletcher, a former Rough Rider who became ambassador to Mexico; Joseph Grew, ambassador to Japan; and so many other members of the State Department's inner circle that historian Robert D. Schulzinger described 1718 as "virtually a second foreign office." Whether in Washington or not, whether in government service or out, the Family kept in touch, helping to further one another's careers and its members' common hope that the United States might play a more active role in world affairs.[7]

The establishment of military ties to civilian elites was only rarely, however, left to the vagaries of love or friendship. Rather than rely upon chance and circumstance, army and navy officers focused their attention on specific groups within the national elite.

As early as the 1880s, for instance, military officers had begun to forge close links with the academic and intellectual communities by taking the platform at learned societies and contributing to their journals. Within a short time the *Army and Navy Journal* declared such contributions "so frequent and so valuable" that its pages lacked space "to give the attention due to their importance and interest."[8] The ninth annual meeting of the Academy of Political and Social Sciences illustrates the way armed forces officers, undeterred by that lack of service publicity, participated in the affairs of the academic community's emerging professional societies. At that 1905 gathering, academy members heard addresses on "The United States as a World Power" given by three future army generals—two of whom later became chiefs of the General Staff—and three present or future flag officers of the United States Navy. The American Historical Association similarly welcomed service participation in its meetings, published in its journal and reports the works of military writers, and in 1902 chose a naval officer, Alfred Thayer Mahan, as its president.[9]

Shared interests sometimes resulted in even closer cooperation. In 1916, for instance, Captain Arthur L. Conger and Major James W. McAndrew joined with Professors Robert M. Johnston, Albert Bushnell Hart, and Justin H. Smith to establish a short-lived journal, *The Military Historian and Economist.* Professor James R. Soley, formerly of the Naval Academy and an ex-assistant secretary of the navy, helped Captain Alfred Thayer Mahan find a publisher for *The Influence of Sea Power upon History, 1660–1783,* and Theodore Roosevelt promoted Mahan's work in the pages of the *Atlantic Monthly.* Mahan, in turn, assisted Josiah Strong in the preparation of *Expansion Under New World Conditions,* while Generals Adna R. Chaffee, John Story, and Leonard Wood contributed favorable introductions to the preparedness works of Homer Lea and Frederick Huidekoper.[10]

The 1886 Congressional legislation authorizing the appointment of twenty officers as university professors of military science and tactics provided yet another bridge to the academic community. With that authorization raised to one hundred by 1893, Lieutenant Alfred C. Sharpe wrote that his service had found the professorships a useful way to create a proper "military spirit" among both civilian faculty and students, who might in turn influence the country at large.[11]

As the preparedness movement took shape in 1913, former chief of staff Leonard Wood and several of his protégés sought to extend their service's influence on the students by, as previously described, establishing a series of summer camps of instruction. Although the encampments, Wood acknowledged, failed "to accomplish much in the way of detailed military instruction," they did allow the army to implant "a sound military policy" in the minds of thousands of young men and to maintain the service's association with academic leaders and university presidents like Benjamin Ide Wheeler (California), Arthur T. Hadley (Yale), Lawrence Lowell (Harvard), John Grier Hibben (Princeton), and Henry Sturgis Drinker (Lehigh), all of whom helped Wood recruit students for the camps.[12]

The summer camps also caught on as a way to reach business, professional, and political leaders. Working with Grenville Clark, Elihu Root, Jr., son of the former war secretary, and Captain Harry S. Howland, a former aide then serving on the West Coast, Wood in 1915 opened the summer camps to adults, some four thousand of whom sought military training that summer. The next year, the army quadrupled that figure and might have reached fifty thousand had not the National Guard's 1916 mobilization drawn preparedness advocates to the Mexican border. To those businessmen's camps came the likes of: former Secretary of State Robert Bacon; future Senator George Wharton Pepper of Pennsylvania; Harvard Professor Ralph Barton Perry; Delaware Congressman Thomas W. Miller; war correspondent Richard Harding Davis; Willard Straight, also Family member at 1718 H. Street; United States Steel's General Solicitor Raynal C. Bolling; New York City Mayor John Purroy Mitchel; and Dudley Field Malone, Collector of the Port of New York and close friend of President Wilson. The camps' participants found the experience so valuable that to keep their summer contacts alive and to further military preparedness they subsequently formed the Military Training Camps Association (MTCA), under the de facto leadership of Wood allies Drinker and Clark. Also in 1916, civilians who had participated in the navy's summer cruises created the Naval Training Association with similar ends in view.[13]

The summer camps did not, of course, produce the first close ties between the military elite and business leaders. In the 1880s, for example, the principal military societies began to invite businessmen to meetings that discussed such topics of mutual interest as the inability of American industry to fabricate heavy guns and the wartime management of the nation's railroads. To ensure cooperation with business professionals as well, the military departments had by 1915 established contact with such groups as the American Society of Civil Engineers, the American Institute of Mining Engineers, the American Institute of Mechanical Engineers, and the American Institute of Electrical Engineers.[14]

Taking such informal exchanges beyond limits presently considered proper, in the late-nineteenth-century active-duty naval officers entered the employ of shipping companies and the industries that supplied the services with ordnance, munitions, and armor plate. While still on active duty, Lieutenant Commander Francis M. Barber, for instance, served as agent for French armor manufacturer Schneider-Creusot, and Lieutenant William Jaques similarly represented Sir Joseph Whitworth, an English manufacturer of the hydraulic forges used in making armor plate. Secretary of the Navy Benjamin Tracy ordered Lieutenants Charles A. Stone and John F. Meigs and Commander Robley D. Evans to duty with the Bethlehem and Carnegie steel works. And it was apparently at Evans's suggestion that Carnegie "first seriously considered the question of starting a plate mill for the manufacture of ship plates."[15]

Other opportunities for cooperation between military and civilian elites grew out of the campaign for universal military training (UMT), which peaked shortly after the mid-1916 mobilization of the National Guard along the Mexican border seemingly demonstrated the weaknesses of that body as a reserve force. The Army League, the National Security League, the Association for National Service—led by retired chief of staff Samuel B. M. Young—General Wood's allies in the MTCA, and the new Universal Military Training League all made UMT an official part of their program. While Major Douglas MacArthur successfully lobbied the nation's newspapermen on behalf of universal training, the latter league secured the services of such leaders in business and politics as financier J. P. Morgan, manufacturer Charles G. Curtis, Roosevelt-ally George Perkins, former secretary of state Robert Bacon, and Senator George Chamberlain, who submitted a bill for six months' training based upon the proposals of Captain George Van Horn Moseley, a Wood protégé. Although advocacy of UMT undoubtedly facilitated public acceptance of selective service following America's April 1917 declaration of war, the Chamberlain-Moseley proposal made little headway in Congress, caught up as it was between the hostility of antimilitarists and the friendly opposition of officers like Chief of Staff Hugh L. Scott, who wanted a longer period of training, and his assistant, Tasker H. Bliss, who advocated submission of flexible alternatives more likely to win Congressional support.[16]

Linked to civilian elites by social origins, marriage, organizational memberships, and shared political and military goals, army and navy officers made use of their ties to hasten the progress of military reform. To establish a firm legislative foundation for the new Naval War College, for example, Rear Admiral Stephen B. Luce allied himself with Nelson A. Aldrich, a prominent Republican senator and future majority leader, in whose state the college was located. "The interests of the Navy and the people of Newport running in the same direction," Luce explained, "we can pull together for our mutual advantage." To that same end, Luce also enlisted the help of his daughter-in-law's in-law, then-Representative Henry Cabot Lodge, three other members of Congress—Representatives Washington C. Whitthorne and Charles R. Boutelle and Senator William E. Chandler—and a budding naval historian and occasional lecturer at the college named Theodore Roosevelt. Nor was Roosevelt's lecture an isolated phenomenon. Making no secret of his intentions and hoping to enlighten "the public generally as well as the Navy," Luce sought prominent speakers and invited to the college's lectures "leading citizens who make Newport their summer home" and might help advertise "the true character of the College." Luce's successors continued the practice, Captain Henry C. Taylor crediting the addresses and invitations to prominent civilians with "extending the influence of the War College, and indirectly familiarizing the public with its aims and methods, and so strengthening the claims of the Navy upon the intelligent support of the nation."[17]

Seeking to establish "a mutually beneficial relationship between the United States Army and the leading universities," army officers used similar techniques on behalf of their service's senior college. But army leaders not only invited sympathetic professors like Henry C. Emery (Yale), Robert M. Johnston (Harvard), and George C. Wilson (Brown) to speak at the war college, they offered to send army officers on lecture tours of civilian schools.[18]

Officers of both services also turned to their allies in Congress when seeking support for military reform. Naval officers William J. Barnette, William S. Sims, Bradley A. Fiske, Albert L. Key, Philip Andrews, William Swift, and Luce, for example, obtained the cooperation of Representative George E. Foss, chairman of the House Naval Affairs Committee, when they initiated their campaign for legislative changes amounting to de facto creation of a naval general staff. When that attempt failed, some of the same officers, plus John J. Knapp, John Hood, and Dudley Knox, turned to Fiske's close friend and ex-naval officer, Congressman Richmond P. Hobson, for submission of an even stronger naval staff bill, enacted on the eve of America's entry into the world conflict.[19]

Army officers, too, appreciated the legislative advantages of their close ties to civilian elites. In the struggle to modernize the coastal defenses, for instance, Brigadier General Nelson A. Miles, then commanding the Division of the Pacific, so successfully lobbied "the entire Pacific coast delegation" that he "received assurances from many . . . Senators and Congressmen that they will favor suitable appropriations for coast defenses" and "work in harmony and earnestly"to that end. On the East Coast, the Coast Defense Convention, which drew nineteen state governors to Tampa, Florida, selected Major General John M. Schofield to chair the committee charged with effecting a permanent organization to support the campaign for improved coastal defenses.[20]

To energize California's merchants as well as its politicians, Miles reminded the former that without adequate fortifications "[o]ur harbors could be blockaded . . . so quickly that commerce would be checked entirely." Schofield chose to approach eastern businessmen through Ambrose Snow, chairman of the New York Chamber of Commerce committee on defense of the seacoast, to whom the general sent Captain Eugene Griffith's paper on "Our Sea-Coast Defenses." Expressing gratification at finding "so powerful a body as the Chamber of Commerce of New York moving in this all-important manner," Schofield promptly offered to render "any further assistance."[21]

Sometimes, moreover, the services and business groups cooperated in pursuit of goals seemingly more beneficial to the latter. Beginning in the 1880s, for example, when naval officers still considered protection of commerce their service's principal mission, they boldly advocated federal subsidies for America's ailing merchant marine. "The navy and the merchant marine must go hand in hand," wrote Lieutenant Richard Wainwright. "Whatever capital is invested in shipping becomes interested in the navy, and without such an interest being created, adequate appropriations for a naval force cannot be obtained." Naval reformers consequently cooperated with the Atlantic Carriers Association, the Shipowners' Association of the Pacific Coast, the New York Board of Trade, the Society of Naval Architects and Marine Engineers, and the Merchant Marine Commission of the Congress to acquaint the public with the advantages of subsidizing the merchant fleet.[22]

When naval strategy early in the twentieth century shifted its focus from possible wartime attacks on commerce to the clash of battle fleets, however, the navy began to lose interest in the merchant marine just as the army was recognizing the merits of increasing America's available shipping—to move troops and supplies to overseas garrisons in the event of imperial conflict. Until the army, after 1905, once again emphasized coastal defense rather than expeditionary activity, that service frequently drew the attention of congressmen to its need for the wartime support of a powerful merchant marine.[23]

The classic example of military-business cooperation in the period before World War I remains, of course, the association so ably described by Dean G. Allard, Jr., in "The Influence of the United States Navy upon the American Steel Industry, 1880–1900."[24]

Allard traced the origins of that cooperation to the plight of the steel industry, 90 percent of whose output in the early 1880s went to the fabrication of low-quality steel rails. The erratic pace of railroad construction therefore repeatedly threw the industry into depression, suggesting the need for other major buyers to take up the slack. Compounding the problem, the surplus in the federal treasury encouraged opponents of the tariff that protected that inferior domestic steel from less-expensive, high-grade European imports, indicating the need for a vast outlay of capital to bring American equipment and techniques abreast of the industry's foreign competition. In both respects the armed services seemed willing to provide important help.[25]

The navy acted first and most significantly. Beginning with the first Naval Advisory Board, both that service and the Congress generally insisted that domestic steel be used in the construction of America's new navy, thus creating a demand for steel plates. At the same time, the high standards of the navy's ubiquitous steel inspectors prodded American producers to make greater use of the superior open-hearth process and to de-emphasize the Bessemer system, which yielded a low-grade steel of inconsistent quality. The navy knew, according to Rear Admiral Robley D. Evans, "that pot metal was cheaper than steel, and that our people would go on making pot metal until we forced them to do something better."[26]

Creating a new market for steel plates made with the open-hearth process, however, simply stimulated wider use of a technology already known to American producers. Of greater importance, the military services also induced American steel producers for the first time to acquire both the plant and the technical ability to manufacture both steel armor and the huge forgings for heavy guns. That new capability in turn enabled the industry later to fabricate high-quality steel for the mammoth

bridges and towering buildings soon to transform the American sky-
line and the high-speed machinery required by the nation's new industries.[27]

Congress and the navy joined with business to obtain the new technology in 1886 when the national legislature authorized construction of
an armored cruiser, the U.S.S. *Maine*, and an armored battleship, the
U.S.S. *Texas*, but provided that the armor contract go to an American
firm only if it could provide high-quality armor at a reasonable price.
Believing that the government had a duty to aid American industry,
Secretary of the Navy William C. Whitney set about ensuring that the
steel industry acquired the capacity to satisfy those terms. Because he
recognized that the French firm of Schneider-Cruesot then made the
world's best armor plate, Whitney used the bait of a large government
contract to entice Joseph Warton of the Bethlehem Iron Company to
purchase from the French producer the necessary patents, technical assistance, and machinery to duplicate its process. In addition to the implied promise of a contract, Whitney facilitated negotiations by em-
ploying the services of Lieutenant Francis M. Barber, USN, the exclusive
American agent of the French firm.[28]

Whitney played a similar role in regard to Bethlehem's acquisition
of heavy presses for forging the massive steel ingots needed for modern
naval guns and coastal artillery. The backdrop to that role had been
hung between 1883 and 1885, when the Congress and two governmental boards, the joint army-navy Gun Foundry Board and the Army Fortifications Board, determined that the services should purchase the forgings for their heavy guns from private industry but rely on two military
armories, one for each service, to fabricate coastal and naval artillery.
When the steel makers nevertheless held out for an order of sufficient
size to cover the costs of the investment in heavy presses, Whitney began to hoard the navy's annual appropriations for heavy guns. At the
same time he encouraged Wharton to purchase rights to the steam
presses patented by the English firm of Joseph Whitworth, again using
as an intermediary an American naval officer, Lieutenant William Jaques, who was also Whitworth's exclusive American agent. Although
four American firms subsequently bid on Whitney's accumulated contracts for armor plate and heavy forgings, Bethlehem's careful preparations made in virtual collusion with the Navy Department enabled that
firm to submit the low, four-and-one-half-million-dollar bid.[29]

Although the close ties between the services and the steel industry
survived the 1889 change of administrations, the delays Bethlehem en-

countered in converting its facilities to the new technology led new secretary of the navy Benjamin Tracy to induce a second American steel
maker to develop the capacity to produce armor plate and to fabricate
large steel ingots. Engaging in behind-the-scenes negotiations as Whitney had done, Tracy encouraged Andrew Carnegie of Carnegie, Phipps,
and Company to obtain the rights and equipment to manufacture the
new nickel-steel armor developed by Le Ferro Nickel of France. And like
Whitney, the new secretary had to use a large government contract with
the promise of more to come as an encouragement to Carnegie's large
capital outlay. Tracy even dispensed with the formality of asking for
competitive bids and instead signed an agreement with Carnegie at a
negotiated price.[30]

The navy's demand for armor, and to a lesser extent both services'
need of heavy guns, thus caused the military, wrote Allard, to enter
"into a close partnership with the steel makers." Though only fully developed in the case of the navy's tie with the steel industry, that military-industrial partnership exemplifies the host of other activities
involving cooperation between military and civilian elites, a degree of
collaboration that to some indicates that the military-industrial complex
emerged during the nineteenth century's last two decades.[31]

Dean Allard's description of the precipitous collapse of the "partnership" between the navy and the steel industry provides the first of
many indications that the relations between the nation's military and
civilian elites, however close, constituted no enduring, quasi-conspira-
torial network promoting class or group interests to the conscious detriment of national needs. Even while asserting the temporary existence of
close government-industry collaboration, Allard acknowledged that the
navy never became "completely enamored with its partner in the armor
venture," and he traced the affair's breakup to Bethlehem's 1894 an-
nouncement of a contract to sell armor plate to Russia at roughly half
the price charged the Navy Department. However perfidious in the eyes
of naval leaders, Bethlehem's action was not entirely without justification. As the *Army and Navy Journal* pointed out, the Russian contract
required neither the fabrication of the complicated shapes nor the application of the expensive hardening process demanded by the American navy. After using the cost-price contract to gain access to the European armor market, moreover, Bethlehem made subsequent foreign
sales at prices comparable to domestic levels. Neither the navy nor the

Congress, however, became reconciled to the steel industry's business practices, and, wrote Allard, the American government "proceeded to dissolve . . . [its] partnership with the steel makers."[32]

The navy's experience with the steel industry also served to rekindle within that service the military officers' typical late-nineteenth-century attitude toward businessmen. In the early eighties, before the naval secretaries forged the links temporarily uniting the navy with the steel makers, the army and navy officers sitting on the Gun Foundry Board expressed the typical view by calling attention to the "whims, caprices, and conveniences" of private enterprise and warning that American manufacturers might conspire either to set the prices or lower the quality of government work. By appearing to do just that, Bethlehem and Carnegie reconfirmed the military officers' earlier low opinion of businessmen and initiated a new phase in the navy's relations with steel makers. When naval secretary Hilary Herbert's efforts to obtain a large price reduction bore no early fruit, his department put pressure on the two companies by opening negotiations with French and English firms, and the chief of naval intelligence indorsed the 1899 proposal of his service's attache in Rome that the United States buy Italian armor plate in order to "weaken the grasp of the [American] armor combination." Congress helped too, increasing the pressure on armor makers by authorizing the navy to build a government steel works and to establish a maximum price for armor plate. In the end, both Secretary Herbert and his successor, John D. Long, convinced the two American companies to supply the government at reasonable prices. In a typically progressive approach to government-business relations, wrote Allard, the government adopted the policy of "neither abolishing [the private armor] business nor allowing it unchecked freedom."[33]

The reasons for even that cautious cooperation with American business provide a second indication of the fragility of military-industry relations. Whenever army and navy officers studied possible American involvement in great-power war, they assumed that such a conflict would commence with the bombardment and subsequent blockade of the nation's coastal cities, a situation the country must endure until the armed services mobilized and armed a force sufficient to clear the coasts and commence offensive operations. The conclusion was obvious; so long as the United States relied upon foreign sources for the heavy guns and armor plate needed to create a modern military force, warned the members of the 1885 Endicott board, "war would at once put a stop to such importations and leave us helpless in the emergency." The government ought consequently to dispense its defense appropriations within the United States, where they "would encourage home industries, promote the national wealth, and render our defenses independent of other countries." Other military boards made the same point; without the capacity to fabricate steel armor or heavy forgings, the United States lacked a vitally important defense industry. Military officers therefore gave cautious support to the "partnership" described by Allard.[34]

Convinced that the United States must develop domestic sources for its military hardware, army and navy officers had but three choices— rely upon private manufacture, government arsenals, or some combination. That officers in the end recommended primary reliance upon private industry is less evidence of a conspiracy to aid business than of their assessment of contemporary industrial and political realities.

On the one hand, the experience of European states had convinced American officers that private armaments companies generally achieved higher levels of both quality and technological innovation than government armories. Reflecting the fears of many officers, the *Army and Navy Journal* also speculated that a government-owned plant would require supervision by enough naval officers to man a warship, prompt a Congressional investigation (with consequent loss of the plant's secrets) every time an armor plate failed to pass inspection, and end as the victim of political patronage when the party in power put its supporters in lucrative positions. Armed forces officers doubted, moreover, that Congress would ever vote the money to establish a government facility adequate for the manufacture of armor plate and heavy steel forgings.[35]

On the other hand, service leaders correctly surmised that a steady annual appropriation for guns and armor would induce businessmen to invest in the needed technology and equipment. If so, the nation would benefit, claimed the members of the Gun Foundry Board, from "the ingenuity and inventive talent of the [private industries of the] country" while the economy generally prospered from the stimulation of the domestic distribution of federal monies and the private acquisition of new technology. To ensure that the government avoided becoming "the slave of the corporation . . . dependent entirely upon the private industries of the country, which might combine to the detriment of the public service," the board also recommended establishment of two new federal arms factories. Those arsenals, which in peacetime could preclude such combinations by threatening to switch to foreign suppliers, would serve to check the greed of private steel makers—presumed to be the source of new ideas and superior workmanship.[36]

If the national interest unavoidably required a degree of government-industry cooperation, military supervision of the resulting contracts revealed how the services' determination to serve their own interests strained the association. When, for instance, the navy let its first
steel contracts, it set strength and ductility standards higher than those
demanded by foreign navies. After successfully resisting industry pressure to lower those standards, the navy sent its own officers to verify the
quality of the contractor's work. The high early rejection rate suggests
that the inspectors performed their task with diligence, ultimately forcing the steel makers to meet and then exceed government standards.
Andrew Carnegie's description of the inspectors as "martinets" who insisted on "technical points to an absurd degree" suggests their determination to place government interests well ahead of a steel maker's
profits.[37]

If the modern complex allegedly uniting military officers, governmental officials, and America's industrialists has a nineteenth-century
ancestor, one must look elsewhere than at the services' relation with the
steel industry. A more likely candidate is the long-standing cooperation
of the Congress, a host of small businessmen, and certain military bureaucrats.

In the navy, that partnership united the owners, managers, and em-
ployees of many outdated naval yards and small private shipbuilders behind the local member of Congress—who shared the interest of the
former in maintaining the nation's obsolete, wooden-hulled fleet. The
$1,123,000 total spent on repairs for the U.S.S. *Kearsarge*, built in
1861 for only $286,000, well illustrates Samuel Bryant's contention that
contracts to maintain the navy's "ancient hulks," "if awarded to the
right people, would bring in campaign contributions and ready cash."
He might also have added votes and patronage. Nor was the *Kearsarge*
an isolated case. Between 1865 and 1882 the navy disbursed some $385
million but built virtually no new ships, except for a few repaired so extensively as to constitute a new vessel with an old name. Senator "Pitch-
fork Ben" Tillman, no friend of business or the armed services, suc-
cinctly stated the views of many members of Congress: "I am trying to
get a little for Port Royal because, if you are going to steal, I want my
share." The Navy Department, anxious to protect its annual budget,
acquiesced, allowing its individual bureau chiefs to lend their support
to "pork barrel" tactics. The influence of those naval bureaucrats in
Congress—and their success in slowing the course of naval reform—re-

flected their willingness to award repair contracts that produced desired political results.[38]

A similar situation affected the army. ''The presence of a[n army] post in a locality,'' explained Captain Merch B. Stewart, ''means a steady source of income, a business asset, to an influential element in the vicinity.'' Local congressmen, Stewart claimed, guarded such assets ''with great care,'' for any detrimental military action was ''sure to raise a storm strong enough to blow a protest—and probably a delegation— to Washington.'' The army's bureau chiefs too yielded to Congressional desires on army facilities and contracts. Although, for example, virtual- ly all the army's cavalry served in the Far West, Quartermaster General James B. Aleshire maintained a cavalry remount station at Fort Royal, Virginia, in the district of James Hay, senior Democrat of the House Military Affairs Committee.[39]

Far from seeking to continue this profitable ''complex'' of bureau chiefs, members of Congress, and local businessmen, reform-minded officers advanced technological and strategic concepts that would dis- rupt that long-standing relationship. To succeed, the reformers had in fact to destroy, rather than create, a partnership that better served pri- vate greed and political success than public interests. Naval reformers thus threatened the very cornerstone of an old relationship when their concern for economy and security led them to advocate concentration of the navy's repair work at a few large, modern facilities—one on the Pa- cific coast and two on the Atlantic. The General Board consequently met heavy opposition from both the bureau chiefs and Maine's senator Eugene Hale when it proposed closure of the uneconomical Portsmouth Navy Yard, a ''strategic aberration'' that sufficed to complicate defense of the New England coast while contributing little to maintenance of the fleet because of the yard's inability to accommodate modern battle- ships.[40]

Army reformers hoping to improve training and enhance their serv- ice's ability to respond quickly in emergencies met similar resistance when they proposed to concentrate infantry and cavalry regiments at a few large posts nearer the coasts, population centers, or major rail junc- tions. When Chief of Staff Leonard Wood, for example, resubmitted proposals for concentration not unlike those made decades earlier by General William T. Sherman, the chief of staff brought ''a swarm of hornets about the ears of the Secretary [of War.]'' According to the cal- culations of the general's biographer, ''Two-thirds of the senators and half of the representatives cherished garrisons which helped to feed the faithful." The *Army and Navy Journal* thus echoed the voices of the reformers when it editorially condemned such selfishly motivated opposition to reform and asserted that "local interests must yield to the general welfare of the nation."[41]

As the dispute over the closing of unneeded and obsolete military facilities suggests, the new element in the relations among military officers, politicians, and businessmen during the three decades before World War I seems less the creation of a sinister network for the cooperative pursuit of group interests than the disruption of an older partnership that benefited local or parochial interests at the expense of the nation as a whole. To the extent that something new appeared in the relations among military, political, and business leaders the change involved the way that technology focused the reformers' attention on the largest and most modern industries and drew it away from politically powerful local interests incapable of equipping or supporting a modern armed force—a shift from localism to reliance upon nationally focused organizations that was typical of American society in the four decades preceding World War I.

Local opposition to military reform, which only added to the low esteem in which army and navy officers held the typical businessman and politician, reflected an attitude that would have frustrated any efforts to bring into existence the ancestor of an alleged military-industrial complex. "Distrust of, and disdain for, the world of stock exchanges and marketplaces," Peter Karsten has found, became "standard features of military men . . . [who] left a trail of abuse for business civilization as long as their ink would permit." Uneasy about certain of the economic and social trends observable in late-nineteenth-century America, military thinkers like Captain Alfred Thayer Mahan grew impatient when the government did little to halt "the concentration of wealth and power in the hands of a protected few," and Major General Oliver O. Howard described business leaders as "narrow souled men . . . accompanied with inordinate pretension and ostentatious display" and "exponents of tendencies which our wise men must study to repress." Upon "the ghoul-like despotism of capital," a younger army officer, Captain Otho E. Michaelis, placed responsibility for the social tensions inflicting "insidious and grievous wounds on the body-politic," and naval lieutenant William S. Sims, who blamed the period's violent strikes on "the greed of the capitalists," expected that only "some fearful lesson—let us hope . . . in some other country—[will] set people thinking and . . . convince them that these labor troubles are not due to any change in the nature of the laborers."[42]

With few exceptions, army and navy officers held the businessman's political allies in even greater disrepute. Naval captain Charles S. Sperry, for example, described Senator Eugene Hale of Maine as "a despicable character . . . [who] has for years been the political boss of the navy and has expended, or forced the expenditure, of the shipbuilding money to suit himself and his henchmen." Army officers, claimed one major, acquired at West Point their "contempt for mere politicians and their dishonest principles of action." The professional politician, wrote Captain Edward Field, was the "most formidable obstacle to any thorough or genuine scheme of national defense." The typical politician favored military reforms "just so far as he could make capital or influence out of them or handle the appropriations—which stuck tightly to the hands they passed through." Speaking for many in the armed services the *Army and Navy Journal* characterized the typical member of Congress as a backwoods statesman or sentimentalist. The former was narrow, illiterate, and boisterous with a horizon limited to those projects that helped his district; the latter was thinskinned, scholarly, visionary, and wrong-headed. Both types, though for different reasons, opposed military reform.[43]

Those sentimentalists, whether politicians, businessmen, or intellectuals, were a particular thorn in the side of America's military leaders. For contrary to the implications of those analyses of the American past that identify class interest as the basis of America's foreign and military policies, the similar social origins of the country's civilian and military elites failed to unite them in support of military reform. Quite the opposite, being a member of America's social elite more often than not led one to adopt a strongly antimilitary stance.

Samuel P. Huntington has aptly described as "business pacifism" the prevailing philosophy of the age that paradoxically witnessed America's military renaissance. The nation's intellectuals—and most of their countrymen—generally regarded war and armed forces as twin evils, the one squandering valuable resources in senseless wartime slaughter and the other diverting men and money, even in peace, from constructive employment. According to Huntington, most thoughtful Americans expected the continued growth of international trade to make war unthinkable by binding nations with ties of mutual economic interest. As interpreted by most American businessmen and many political and intellectual leaders, the earlier Darwinian struggle for existence had by the late nineteenth century become an economic competition in which success would go to the pacific, that is industrial, societies that sociologist Herbert Spencer claimed would replace those increasingly anachronistic societies of a militant character. "The dichotomy between militarism and industrialism," wrote Huntington, "was unchallenged dogma in the intellectual world at the close of the nineteenth century, accepted by all business pacifist thinkers . . . [who] assumed a natural progress from the militant to the industrial society coupled with the gradual elimination of war."[44]

Nothing better illustrates the split within the nation's elite than the American peace movement, which attracted many prominent politicians, business leaders, newspapermen, and university professors. Although the peace movement's leaders sprang from the same social roots as the advocates of an active foreign policy and more powerful armed forces, the former, far from being supporters of military reform, personified the nation's traditional antimilitarism. Among intellectuals, for example, university presidents David Starr Jordan (Stanford) and Nicholas Murray Butler (Columbia) became leaders in an antiwar movement that gained strength steadily between the 1890s and America's entry into World War I, and industrialist Andrew Carnegie used some of the millions he acquired from sales of armor plate to endow the largest of the peace societies. Many members of the political elite too became peace advocates; between 1905 and 1916 two presidents, five secretaries of state, and a host of judges and congressmen were active members of at least one peace organization.[45] In regard to war's inevitability and the use of force in international affairs, military officers and many members of the civilian elite thus remained poles apart intellectually—hardly the close relationship needed to sustain conspiratorial class action on behalf of military reform.

Such divisions within the nation's elite and the services' hostility to politicians and businessmen did not of course preclude occasional cooperation, a result that has been characterized as an "intriguing paradox."[46] That paradox dissolves, however, upon examination of the different motives that led to common action. Regarding international trade as beneficial to the nation as a whole, for example, military officers readily gave their support to its growth, even though they expected that the expansion of exports would as likely lead to increased conflict as to world peace. Believing similarly in the need for order and stability, military officers willingly intervened at home and abroad to quell violence and to restore order, even while they believed that the government must eventually preclude future outbreaks by restraining the greedy, exploitative behavior that produced such attacks on the social order. Indeed, military officers saw themselves as the world's policemen charged with restraining lawbreakers, maintaining order, promoting stability, and encouraging the spread of civilization. Neither conscious nor intentional allies of America's Robber Barons, military officers sought to preserve the nation and to guard its interests. Governments, not military forces, had an obligation to eliminate the social injustices that led to outbreaks of violence; military officers saw theirs as the responsibility to maintain that degree of stability essential to orderly social progress. If that latter duty sometimes required cooperation with business and political leaders, or furthered their interests, military officers approached their temporary associates with caution, skepticism, and occasionally disdain.

Though writing of the recent past, sociologist Morris Janowitz has cast a clearer light on the military officers' relation to American society than the one shed by emphasis on a conspiracy of either class or group.

> To believe that the military profession in the United States anticipates no future alternative but an inevitable major atomic war is to commit a crude error. To believe that the military have become integrated with other leadership groups into a monolithic national political establishment is to commit a sophisticated error. But to believe that the military are not an effective pressure group on the organs of government is to commit a political error.

The contacts, described earlier in this chapter, between military and civilian elites are better perceived in the light of that insight, as are the military reformers' efforts to overcome the traditional view that officers were "not in the service to instruct the people . . . [but] simply to die when the occasion requires."[47]

Indeed, as the twentieth century progressed, army and navy officers began to circumvent such restraints. At first they privately took their case for reform to select individuals and groups, which the officers hoped would carry the military point of view to the public—a technique somewhat akin to the earlier practice of leaking self-serving information to journalistic or political allies. The army should, Captain George F. Price told the readers of the *Journal of the Military Service Institution of the United States*, convey its message primarily through writings in military journals, a practice in fact initiated in the last quarter of the nineteenth century, and by "official and personal relations with the militia," which Price saw as occupying "the middle ground separating the army from the people."[48]

Efforts of armed forces officers to acquaint America's intellectual, business, and political leadership with the needs of the services had a similar indirect and behind-the-scenes character, as did military approaches to journalists and patriotic societies. The navy's General Board, for instance, hoped in that circumspect manner to arouse, "throughout the country," "a general interest in the creation of a General Staff for the Navy." In the same frame of mind, the army's General Staff furnished certain of its reports to newspapers, syndicated writers, magazines, universities, business and civic clubs, boards of trade, and prominent individuals, thereby hoping to overcome the "ignorance of national military problems amongst the most intelligent men and leading newspaper writers."[49] To that same end, the services used the Army League, the Navy League, and the host of prewar preparedness organizations.[50]

Although such methods remained in use, military officers eventually adopted the assumption that guided the progressive era's muckraking journalists. "When the public, however intelligent," explained Major General Nelson A. Miles in his 1890 annual report, "are kept in profound ignorance of the real condition of affairs, or are living under an illusion concerning it, apathy, inaction, and national danger must necessarily be the result." Commodore Edward Simpson, who in 1898 directed the American fleet blockading Santiago Harbor, made the same point when he asserted that the public had "a right to complain of the deceit . . . practiced upon them [sic]" by not being "kept properly informed . . . of the decay of their [sic] naval power."[51] It being "the literal truth," wrote Lieutenant Arthur L. Wagner, "that in the United States the people govern," the services had only to remedy the public's lack of accurate information to lay the "foundation of wise military legislation." In the face of an informed and aroused public, claimed retired Major General Alexander S. Webb, "the representatives of the people will be forced to move as men of straw." As a corollary to that proposition, the editor of the *Infantry Journal* placed the responsibility for the slow pace of military reform on "the soldier and the military student . . . [who] have largely failed in the duty of eliminating military ignorance by spreading real military knowledge."[52]

Keeping in mind such assumptions about the ability of an informed public to achieve military reform, military officers had begun, by the eve of World War I, to appeal directly to their fellow citizens. Using, for example, the contact between soldiers and civilians provided by the post-1913 students' camps of instruction, Major General Leonard Wood hoped "to develop a sense of responsibility in the young men of this country." "This is the biggest opportunity we have," Wood wrote to Major James G. Harbord, who was to command one of the camps on the West Coast, "to educate the coming generation." The later businessmen's camps gave Wood and other army reformers a similar opportunity to carry their message directly to participating civilians. The 1916 mobilization of the National Guard gave army progressives like Captain Frank R. McCoy yet a third chance; "if we are able to hold them [the guardsmen] only a few months longer," he advised Wood, we "will have accomplished much the same sort of training and propaganda as you have so successfully done at Plattsburg."[53]

Nor were the military officers' efforts limited to those civilians who participated in military programs. Following the outbreak of war in Europe, military officers used books, articles, and public addresses to carry their message of preparedness directly to an even wider audience. Between December 1915 and May 1916, for example, General Wood— despite President Wilson's efforts to muzzle him—addressed audiences totaling more than 130,000 in over one hundred separate speeches. On the West Coast, another former chief of the General Staff, Major General J. Franklin Bell, similarly but less obtrusively appealed to civilian audiences to support the army's efforts to correct America's military weaknesses.[54]

The preparedness literature also indicates that younger officers, often aided by more senior sponsors, and retired officers also sought to reach the public, for instance: *Fundamentals of Military Service*, prepared by Captain Lincoln C. Andrews under the supervision of General Wood; *An Army of the People*, written by Major John McAuley Palmer at the urging of Major General Tasker Bliss; *Why Preparedness*, ex-Captain Henry J. Reilly's report on a tour of Europe's battlefields; and *The Present Military Situation in the United States*, by ex-General Francis V. Greene. Senior officers were similarly involved, as indicated by Major General William H. Carter's *The American Army* and Wood's two works, *Our Military History: Its Facts and Fallacies* and *The Military Obligation of Citizenship*.[55]

Such direct public challenges to the nation's political leadership, which many regular officers condemned, were nevertheless quite rare and usually limited to the most political officers, of whom Leonard Wood was the archetypical example. The exceptional behavior occurring during the fight over preparedness thus did little to alter the traditional military reluctance openly to enter the political sphere in the face of official disapproval.

During the early phases of America's military renaissance, armed forces officers began to exploit, on behalf of army and navy reform, their contacts with the nation's political, business, and intellectual elite, with whom the services' leaders shared a common social background. The resulting useful but wary cooperation between military and civilian elites did not mean, however, that army and navy reformers formed part of a political-military-business complex or monolithic social elite. Rather, military cooperation with other groups generally extended no further than achievement of service and national interests as perceived by military leaders, and the members of America's upper class as often opposed as supported military reform. When even that cautious cooperation with civilian elites failed to achieve the full program of military reform, army and navy officers turned to the general public, hopeful that the latter, once properly informed, would supply the services' needs. In both instances, in fact, the military services acted much as pressure groups, exploiting their contacts with those in positions of influence and using public-relations techniques to create general support for military reform.

CHAPTER 8

The Response to War

I N INTERNATIONAL AFFAIRS, the Realist* would join naval reformer Stephen B. Luce in describing war as "the heritage of man" against which every prudent nation prepares by an appropriate development of its military potential.[1] In the early twentieth century, most Americans did not share that view. Both a unique historical experience and the development of the national culture had convinced them that the means existed for men not only to guarantee their own security but to put an end to war. The inevitable spread of democratic institutions, for example, would dispose governments around the world to love peace. If a Spencerian proliferation of industrialization and free trade, with its corollary specialization and interdependence, failed sufficiently to reinforce democratic institutions and make war impossible, the creation of institutions to define and judicially enforce international law would make it unnecessary. Should even those remedies not suffice, appeals to prin-

---

*In accord with the usage determined by Robert E. Osgood in *Ideals and Self-Interest in America's Foreign Relations: The Great Transformation of the Twentieth Century* (Chicago: University of Chicago Press, 1953), the capital "R" indicates that Realist refers to a pessimistic view of human nature and international affairs rather than, necessarily, an accurate assessment of reality.

151

ciple or similar nonviolent approaches resting on faith in humanity's fundamental goodness would certainly preclude a resort to force—at least among civilized states. To American eyes, the international struggle for power was an aberration, and some combination of education, enlightened diplomacy, institutional reform, or, especially, increased popular control of government would surely lead to war's eradication. Americans consequently exhibited great hostility, Robert Osgood has discovered, to mitigating international conflict "by balancing power against power and by cultivating a circumspect diplomacy that knows the uses of force and the threat of force as indispensable instruments of national policy."[2]

America's military reformers, unlike many of their fellow citizens, generally accepted the Realist's philosophy, described international relations in Osgood's terms, and used such views to justify a modest development of the national military potential. "Moral suasion, neutrality treaties and the principles of international law," claimed Lieutenant Colonel Henry T. Allen, provided the United States "insufficient protection against the aggression of unscrupulous nations. Righteousness may exalt," he told the Tennessee Sons of the Revolution, "but it will not protect a defenseless nation against the brutal attack of a greedy neighbor." Even in the absence of aggressive neighbors, mere devotion to peace and justice could not guarantee protection of the nation's fundamental interests, warned army lieutenant Henry J. Reilly; "abstract right or wrong has little to do with international affairs." Although nations have frequently waged war "under the pretext of altruism, philanthropy and utopian sympathy for the downtrodden," wrote army captain Howard R. Hickok, "a close examination will frequently reveal self-interest in some form concealed in the mailed fist." By the early twentieth century, most military reformers shared with Commander Josiah S. McKean the view that "All modern wars are caused by conflict of national policies." Far from seeing war as an aberration, the General Staff in 1912, described armed struggle as a recurring "phase of international politics." A decade earlier, Brigadier General Theo Schwan had anticipated that conclusion when he explained that the primary purpose "for which the complex body known as an army is kept on foot is to compel by force action of some kind . . . which the government is unable to bring about by pacific means." That did not mean, however, that the United States must raise forces comparable to those of Europe's militarized powers. "The conditions under which, and the purposes for which, armies are maintained," wrote army captain Carl Reichmann, "depend on the conditions surrounding the nations maintaining them; in other words, they depend on the national policy, and they are, therefore, bound to change with that policy." It did mean—and according to Colonel Allen the 1914 outbreak of war in Europe confirmed—that "the basic character of man remains what it was at the dawn of history." Wars should consequently "be treated as all other existing evils and must be prepared against."[3]

Attention to that preparation had for several decades prior to 1916 guided the endeavors of America's military professionals—and with important results. By the eve of United States entry into the World War, both services had created at least the rudiments of a modern general staff capable of developing war plans appropriate to the nation's foreign policies and determining the necessary organization, training, and equipment of both regular and reserve forces. Because the services recognized that successful accomplishment of those tasks would engage civil as well as military authority, army and navy reformers had urged the establishment of agencies for the executive coordination of national and military policies and the legislative support of their implementation. Aware, like Captain Carl Reichmann, that "[a]ny change in a military system cuts deep into the life of a nation and should not be undertaken without necessity and without mature consideration," army reformers had sought to adapt America's military traditions to modern warfare's requirement for the rapid mobilization of large numbers of trained men.[4] To enhance, meanwhile, the war readiness of the existing forces—however inadequate—military progressives had advocated improved training, the concentration of troops and ships in large tactical formations, an improved system of officer education, and frequent maneuvers, which would both sharpen the soldiers' and seamen's skills and prepare officers for high command and staff positions. In such ways, Realistic army and navy officers had endeavored to prepare their forces for support of national policies.

No less urgent than the prewar creation of an adequate regular force and manpower reserve, preparation for modern war required plans for the mobilization of the nation's economy. According to Grosvenor B. Clarkson, director of the Council of National Defense during World War I, however, the American army had unrealistically made no such plans, indeed "had made no study, and, as a body, had no comprehension, of the fact that in modern war the whole industrial activity of the

Nation becomes the commissariat of the army." Modern critics have repeated that dismal judgment, extending their censure to the navy as
well. Russell F. Weigley, for instance, wrote of the "limitations of [mil-
itary] vision" when he described prewar "planning by the armed forces
for the economic demands of war . . . [as] conspicuously and completely
absent."[5] Such claims, it would seem, challenge the perception if not
the Realism (and realism) of American officers. *

Although such assertions contain more than a germ of truth, they
fail both to reveal the military officer's views on the home front's role in
modern war and the reasons for the inadequacy of the armed services'
economic planning. Those assertions, moreover, simply ignore statements by officers such as former chief of staff Leonard Wood, who in
1916 wrote that

> Modern war involves the organization of the financial and material resources of
> a nation as well as the training, discipline, and equipment of its soldiers. This or-
> ganization must be such that the nation can apply its maximum strength in the
> minimum time, and maintain it at top pressure for the maximum period.

Assistant Chief of Staff Tasker H. Bliss seemed similarly alert to economic realities when he accurately forecast two significant wartime
problems. Whenever "material of a certain kind," he predicted, is "required in different classes of articles supplied by the different purchasing departments," it "will sometimes happen . . . that one bureau . . .
will find the manufacturers supplying it have tied themselves up for a
long time in contracts with another bureau." Without centralized contracting, Bliss thought the War Department likely to find that scarce
raw materials and manufacturing resources had become committed to
the production of less essential goods. Similarly, army demands on the
rail system for "the movement of great numbers of troops and great
quantities of every kind of material of war," Bliss wrote in anticipation

---

*This section on industrial preparedness highlights the nature of army thought, an em-
phasis made appropriate by the navy's lesser interest in economic mobilization. As the
smaller of the services, the navy's requirements had less effect on the national economy,
and the long lead time of naval construction and that service's first claim on the nation's
resources during America's first year of war shifted most of the burden of adjustment to
the army. See Paul Y. Hammond, *Organization for Defense: The American Military Establishment in the Twentieth Century* (Princeton: Princeton University Press, 1961),
pp. 36–37. All naval officers were not, however, unaware of the economic dimension of
the European conflict, which Naval Constructor Richard D. Gatewood described as its
"great military lesson." Modern warfare, he added, required "organization to the last
detail of *all* the resources of the nation in men and material." See "The Industrial in
Modern War," *PUSNI*, XLII (May-June 1916), 757.

of another major wartime bottleneck, must take into account the "economic life of the natio.." and create "the very minimum of interruption" in the normal peacetime traffic. That, Bliss correctly observed, was "a problem of vast complexity."[6]

Nor did military officers first perceive the need for governmental mobilization of the economy only on the eve of America's 1917 declaration of war. As early as 1888 the *Army and Navy Journal* had urged creation of an Engineer and Railway Transportation Staff Corps, a reserve of railroad executives with previous military experience who would advise the War Department how their lines might cooperate in the nation's defense. When the Russo-Japanese War demonstrated "the immense bearing that public lines of communication and transportation have on military operations," Captain Charles D. Rhodes of the army staff's Military Intelligence Division recommended that "in future wars . . . one of the earliest enactments of Congress . . . place the railroads, steamship lines, telegraph and telephone lines of the country . . . under the direct control and supervision of the President." Two years before the outbreak of war in Europe, Brigadier General Tasker H. Bliss made much the same point. "[T]he railway systems of the United States are an essential part of our military resources," he told the thirty-third annual meeting of the Military Service Institution. Informing army officers that they faced "no greater problem" than devising a "scheme for the orderly handling by railways of both military and civil business," Bliss warned prophetically that "no such attempt will be made or permitted until the undue [wartime] strain upon the railroads has resulted in the paralysis of both commercial and military business, with consequent disaster to both."[7]

Despite early recognition of the need for wartime coordination of transportation and communication, the army staff made few such plans—a failure that Captain Glenn H. Davis in 1911 attributed to the military's belief that planning might not (for lack of staff, perhaps could not) commence prior to the passage of enabling legislation defining the nature of the government's wartime powers and authorizing the appointment of an army superintendent of rail transportation. The next year Quartermaster General Henry G. Sharpe nevertheless took a first hesitant step by establishing with the help of the American Railway Association a system for placarding railroad cars that would give wartime priority to marked military shipments.[8]

Significant planning, even within parameters defined by the lack of Congressional authorization, nevertheless began only after August

1914. The outbreak of war in Europe prompted further meetings with the American Railway Association and individual railroad presidents to investigate the possibility of forming both a railway construction corps and a transportation corps comprising civilian reservists who, donning uniforms in wartime, would continue to perform railroad work under governmental direction. Responding to Quartermaster Sharpe's prompting, in 1915 the association formed a special War Department–Railway Association liaison committee, whose early success during the 1916 mobilization of the National Guard along the Mexican border caused Sharpe, too extravagantly, to predict that in future conflicts "rail congestion, which was the bugaboo of the mobilization of troops in 1898, . . . [would be] entirely eliminated." Looking seaward, the Quartermaster Corps also began to survey the military usefulness of all American merchant ships in excess of two thousand tons, and Rear Admiral William S. Benson helped form a joint army-navy board to prevent "complication and confusion" by ensuring that each service had not planned for the wartime use of the same ships.[9]

In the same 1905 article that drew army attention to the need for wartime control of transportation, Captain Rhodes, who would command a division in the World War, addressed another aspect of mobilization planning when he proposed a Congressional appropriation for the purchase and storage of enough uniforms and equipment for a 350,000-man increase in the army. Though still being advocated by the army staff and resisted by Congress as late as 1916, that proposal in the latter year had grown sufficiently to foresee the outfitting of a force of one-and-a-half million new soldiers.[10]

Chief of Ordnance William Crozier demonstrated his concern for yet another facet of economic mobilization in 1914 when he asked Congressional authority to supplement the production of ammunition at government arsenals with small purchases from private industry. Crozier sought thereby to have the country's manufacturers acquire the equipment and expertise for the rapid emergency conversion of their facilities to governmental ordnance work. Prior to America's intervention in the World War, other officers developed Crozier's concept. Lieutenant Colonel W. Irving Taylor, for example, publicized an appeal for authority to conduct "an immediate survey of the manufacturing plants of the country and their classification according to the character and quality of work they can turn out. All articles required for war," he urged, "should be standardized, so far as possible, and detailed plans, specifications and samples prepared and distributed in time of peace

. . . ; jigs, dies and special tools . . . should be issued." Distribution of samples and dies and the purchase of small quantities of military supplies from a variety of private sources would, claimed Captain Jairus A. Moore, make "as many private manufacturers as possible familiar with the peculiar nature of army supplies and [en]able [American businessmen] to produce enough of them for the use of the army in any emergency."[11]

By 1915 army and navy officers had also become interested in proposals to extend the responsibilities of any future Council of National Defense beyond intragovernmental policy coordination in peace to include authority for federal direction of private industry in war. To that end, the army helped publicize the suggestion of Martin J. Gillen of the Mitchell Wagon Company, who wished to create an advisory commission of businessmen and governmental officials charged with writing standby contracts for the items the services would need in an emergency and coordinating execution of those contracts following the outbreak of war. To further speed mobilization in the event of war, the army's War College Division in 1915 asked Congress to authorize the War Department, in an emergency, to place contracts with private industry without first advertising and requesting bids, to oblige industry to give those contracts first priority, and to permit the government to set, if necessary, a fair price for the purchased goods. Only the pressure of war, however, eventually convinced Congress to grant the president such powers.[12]

Though American military officers had not fully grasped the significance of modern warfare's economic dimension before 1917, they cannot fairly be charged with a total lack of comprehension. Well before America's entry into the World War, military officers had generally come to accept the War College Division's 1915 view that "[s]teps should be taken looking toward a national organization of our economic and industrial resources" because of "all the features disclosed by the war in Europe none stands more clearly revealed than the power to be derived from national economic organization behind the armed forces of a nation." Such an "organization of the industrial resources of the country," wrote Major General Leonard Wood, "would place the government in possession of full knowledge concerning the capacity of each industrial plant . . . and . . . place in the possession of the various industrial organizations an exact knowledge of what was expected of them and . . . see to it that they are properly equipped."[13] Prior to 1917, moreover, the services had—though with little success—requested of

Congress the funds, the authority, and the staff needed to achieve the necessary wartime mobilization of industry—a fact that must modify criticisms like those of Clarkson and Weigley.

However vigorously individual army and navy officers may have advocated preparedness and however clearly some may have perceived the economic dimension of modern warfare, the War and Navy Departments nevertheless remained shockingly unprepared for American military intervention in the World War.

The army's five, semi-independent supply bureaus suffered not only the inevitable inefficiencies accompanying their vast wartime expansion—the Quartermaster Corps rose from 8,100 officers and men to nearly 140,000—but the avoidable consequences of competing with one another for raw materials, industrial facilities, storage space, and transportation. With little thought for the overall needs of the army, the commander of the Rock Island Arsenal, for instance, quickly gained control of the nation's entire supply of leather—an admittedly mistaken action that he nevertheless took in order to "look after . . . [his] particular job." Even when faced with critical shortages stemming from such misplaced initiative, the bureaus resisted general staff proposals to create a steering committee to coordinate purchases. Competitors for transportation as well as raw materials, the uncoordinated efforts of the Ordnance Department and Quartermaster Corps also produced crippling congestion in all the important railway freight centers and created an artificial shortage of rolling stock as unloading facilities became jammed. Though the quartermaster general avoided camp construction and subsistence scandals like those of the Spanish-American War, an inability to supply uniforms forced him to ask for a delay in the induction of new recruits, and the chief of ordnance reluctantly armed American soldiers with British rifles and helmets, French artillery and machine guns, Allied aircraft and tanks, and foreign munitions. Nor did the bureaus successfully cope with such difficulties until extensively reorganized by the secretary of war in cooperation with the chief of staff, who replaced prewar bureau chiefs with officers from outside their departments and gave civilian planners extensive authority over army purchasing and contracting.[14]

"The declaration of war," recalled Peyton C. March, who returned from France in February 1918 to head the army staff, "found the United States, from a military, industrial, and economic standpoint, thoroughly unprepared for the great task which confronted it.'' Passing through Washington in 1917 while enroute to France, the commander of the American Expeditionary Forces (AEF) reached a similar conclusion. ''It had been apparent to everybody for months that we were likely to be forced into war, and a state of war had actually existed for several weeks, yet scarcely a start had been made to prepare for our participation.'' Consequently ''chagrined'' to learn ''that so little had been done in the way of preparation,'' John J. Pershing described the War Department as ''suffering from a kind of inertia,'' and he later complained of the General Staff's apparently uninspiring ''lack of foresight.'' A young member of that staff, Hugh S. Johnson, who achieved fame as chief of the New Deal's National Recovery Administration after he left the army, validated that view when characterizing the winter 1917–18 supply situation ''as nearly a perfect mess as can be imagined.'' Almost as Tasker Bliss had earlier predicted, Johnson found that army purchasing practices had ''clogged . . . efficient factories . . . and practically paralyzed them by shortages of labor, fuel, raw material, power, and transportation.'' Despite more than two years to master the lessons of the world conflict, the army lacked both war plans and an adequate scheme for economic mobilization.[15]

American intervention found the navy little better prepared. Admiral William S. Sims, Pershing's naval counterpart, claimed his service entered the conflict ''with no well[-]considered policy or plans and with . . . [its] forces on the sea not in the highest state of readiness.'' Despite the navy's subsequent reputation for farsightedness and efficiency, at least as compared to that of the army, Sims charged that it had failed ''for at least six months to throw . . . [its] full weight against the enemy'' and instead ''pursued a policy of vacillation, . . . a hand-to-mouth policy, attempting to formulate . . . plans from day to day.'' Without ''a definite plan to work on,'' confirmed Captain Harris Laning, a wartime staffer in the Office of Naval Operations, ''the various parts of the Navy Department could make no co-ordinated effort to carry on the war, but, on the contrary, each part was obliged to do what that part thought best, with the result that . . . the effectiveness of the naval effort [was] greatly reduced in the early stages of the war.''[16]

In light of three decades of agitation for military reform and the preceding period of preparedness propaganda, evidence of such mismanagement and lack of foresight seems paradoxical. Though staffed at least in part by officers who had given extensive thought to the problems of modern war, who recognized the need for prewar planning, and

who perceived war's new economic dimension, America's military headquarters nevertheless found themselves in 1917 almost totally unprepared for armed intervention in Europe—a contradiction that deserves
resolution.

The continued failure of the two armed services to modernize their
bureau systems—long a target of military reformers—accounts in part
for that paradox. As many military progressives had predicted, the uncoordinated and competitive purchasing practices of the departmental
bureaus, which the general staffs had little power to correct, quickly
fouled the military supply system and by early 1918 contributed to the
growing paralysis of the national economy.[17]

Throughout 1917, Secretary of War Newton D. Baker ignored both
the mounting evidence of that system's inefficiency and the advice of
outgoing chief of staff Hugh L. Scott to use the opportunity provided
by the wartime crisis to give the General Staff "ample authority for securing the coordination of all the activities of the military establishment." Although the recipient of a stream of war college proposals for
reorganizing "the supply service under General Staff control," Baker
refused to face that issue. Then, with Scott's mid-1917 retirement for
age and the dispatch of his successor to Europe for Allied conferences,
the secretary left the General Staff virtually leaderless, thereby exacerbating an already confused situation.[18]

Navy secretary Josephus Daniels showed a comparable hostility to
reform, probably because of distrust for his admirals and a reluctance to
delegate authority. Baker, however, seems to have hesitated for fear of a
fight with his bureau chiefs—and their powerful Congressional allies—
and felt constrained by the statutes that defined the bureaus' extensive
independent authority. A voluntarist and traditionalist who preferred
to work within existing institutions by means of informal arrangements
made in private conferences, Baker also opposed giving any new intragovernmental agency, like the War Industries Board, power both to coordinate purchases by the army, the navy, and the Allies and to control
the civil economy.[19]

Only after the supply breakdown of the winter of 1917–18 and subsequent senatorial investigation did Baker finally yield to the progressives' demands. He replaced several of the older staff chiefs with
younger men, often from outside the bureau, and appointed the aggressive Peyton C. March to succeed Bliss, who had reached retirement

age in December 1917. Then in cooperation with March, Baker used the extensive power of the May 1918 Overman Act to reorganize the War Department, at last giving the General Staff a significant measure of control over the department's military bureaucracy and modernizing the unwieldy system for making military purchases that had hindered mobilization of the economy.[20]

Such bureaucratic inertia did not alone cause the two services' lack of readiness for intervention in Europe. The military reformers themselves must shoulder a portion of the blame. Rather than respond to the 1914 outbreak of war with the preparation of new contingency plans keyed specifically to the possibility of American involvement, the services' progressives instead used the World War as an argument adding urgency to their long-standing advocacy of general military reform. Army and navy officers consequently saw the European conflict as a "most opportune time," an "opportunity," a "golden opportunity," and even "the opportunity of a lifetime" rather than an immediate military problem requiring solution by the services' planners. "Fortunate will be our country," explained the editor of the *Cavalry Journal*, "if advantage is taken at the high tide of this [preparedness] hysteria that is rampant throughout the land . . . to get on our statute books a well[-]digested and wise military policy which will provide for a suitable and reasonable army and navy."[21] Most army reformers also hoped that the preparedness "hysteria," and the later imminent participation in the European war, would persuade Americans, in the words of Chief of Staff Scott, to "see the benefits" of compulsory military training. Similarly, members of the navy's General Board hoped that the World War would convince their countrymen to build "a fleet powerful enough to prevent or answer any challenge to . . . [national] policies."[22]

Officers who might have used the interval between the outbreak of war and America's intervention to prepare extensive plans for the nation's possible armed involvement instead expended their energies agitating for Congressional passage of their prewar program of military reforms. As a letter to the editor of the *Cavalry Journal* suggests, army and navy officers quickly perceived that "[t]he present war in Europe is causing many of our thinking citizens to sit up and take notice on [of?] military affairs." And Captain William S. Sims, USN, expected the international conflict to convince Americans "that arbitration treaties will not stand in the way of aggression unless they are backed by adequate force . . . ; the peace at any price policy of Bryan and the President will fail to satisfy." Eager to exploit the public's interest in military affairs,

army and navy officers took their decades-old case for military reform to
the American people, convinced, according to Major James A. Ryan,
that "Congress will have to concede what the people demand." The
"present difficulties," predicted Lieutenant Colonel George T. Langhorne, will "give us a real military policy."[23]

Nor did reformers place all their hopes on the European war. The
Infantry Journal anticipated equally beneficial results from the country's trouble with Mexico; "[n]ever before have so many opportunities
for enlargement and advancement presented themselves to the
army."[24]

The outbreak of war in Europe in that sense brought little change in
American military thought. Not perceiving the World War as an immediate threat to American interests, one that required some adjustment
in the nation's war plans, army and navy officers regarded the European
struggle as an opportunity to gain Congressional and popular support
for the military policies they had long advocated.

Contrary to the old cliché suggesting that in peacetime generals
invariably spend their energies in vain preparation to refight the last
war, during the three-year period before America's intervention in the
world conflict, its military leaders prepared neither for the last war, nor
indeed for the present war, but instead for the next. Convinced, explained the *Army and Navy Journal*, that "new dangers" would confront the United States at the conclusion of the World War,[25] American
officers turned their attention to the future, exacerbating the previously
discussed tendency to see the European conflict as an opportunity and
to emphasize general reform at the expense of planning that might have
prevented the services' poor performance in the year following America's declaration of war.

That sense of future danger derived from at least two sources. At the
onset of war in Europe, military officers doubted the conflict would end
in either a clear victory or—presciently—in a lasting peace. "[N]one of
the principal nations involved can be destroyed," Lieutenant Colonel
Henry T. Allen advised the secretary of war in 1914, and the "great
questions" that divided Europe would survive the termination of hostilities. That being the case, the war cannot "reconcile the vanquished to
the victors" and postwar Europe will quickly return to its former troubled state. Affairs in the Far East, too, Allen predicted, would become
more threatening as a result of the "terrible catastrophe" that had di-

vided the Western powers. If the "white races" weaken one another, Allen confided to his wife, "the yellow races will have their innings." The Europeans' use of colored troops in the West's internecine struggle only made matters worse, erasing as it would belief in "the superiority of the white man" and leading to "a struggle between the West and the East in due course of time." Speaking strategically as well as racially, Allen added that Japan's "very distressing" seizure of Germany's holdings in China and the Pacific placed that already threatening Asian neighbor astride America's lines of communication with the Philippines. Nor did the situation in Latin America give cause for hope. On behalf of the General Board, Rear Admiral Austin M. Knight expressed the military's typical fear that the World War would result in "changes of sovereignty in possessions on or adjacent to the American continent," which would both challenge the Monroe Doctrine and provide bases from which to assault the United States.[26]

When the fighting in Europe failed to reach a speedy climax, American military officers sensed dangers also in the possibility of a long war and an eventual clear victory. At the conclusion of a prolonged struggle —with the United States having engrossed most of the world's overseas trade and American industries enjoying a price advantage over their heavily taxed European competitors—the victors' "large armies . . . , now trained in modern warfare," predicted Colonel Charles A. Bennett, would become a "standing menace" as the Old World sought to reclaim its former commercial and financial dominance. Nor would the victors' "exhaustion," warned Lieutenant Commander John P. Jackson, render the United States "immune from attack after the present war is over." The disruption of the European balance of power, predicted Major General Hugh L. Scott, would compensate for wartime losses suffered by the victors and free them to employ a larger portion of their armed forces abroad.[27]

Although few officers were indifferent to the war's outcome, that analysis revealed a threat from whichever side emerged victorious. Officers with such varied backgrounds as army staff chief Scott, former naval attaché Edward Blakeslee, and army major George Van Horn Moseley, a leading reformer, contended that an English triumph would make possible a two-ocean, Anglo-Japanese attack on the United States. Describing the English as a "cool and calculating people," Blakeslee considered their alliance with Japan a "club held over" the United States. Already threatened by troubles along the Mexican border, warned Moseley, the United States might in the future find its newly powerful "neighbor on the north in a position to speak with authority as never before."[28]

Should Germany be the winner, other dangers would arise. In a 1915 book, former Major General Francis V. Greene warned of a hypothetical German invasion of the East Coast, a possibility given official sanction when the General Staff used such an assault as the measure of American preparedness, the primary contingency against which the United States must prepare. Germany, Captain William S. Sims told his wife, would surely attempt to "establish a naval station in the West Indies." Should American weakness force acquiescence in that expansion, Germany could use the new base to "create crown colonies in any South American country." The Germans could thereafter "take the Panama canal and charge us for using it." If the United States still "would not fight," Germany might eventually demand a naval station on Long Island, "regulate the tariff we charge on her goods (as foreigners did in the case of China and Japan), and . . . make our foreign and domestic policy subject to her approval." With less exaggeration, army officers Charles S. Farnsworth and James Parker expressed similar fears. Should the war's end leave Germany with "sufficient strength to act aggressively in South America," Parker expected Europe's other powers to stand aside and "see us fight it out with Germany, with the idea of stopping it later."[29]

With concern for such dangers drawing attention away from possible intervention in the present conflict (in any case a contingency incompatible with President Wilson's stated national policy), army and navy officers instead advanced long-range proposals designed to enhance, over the course of the next decade, the armed forces' ability to guard the continental United States, its overseas possessions, and their lines of communication.

In a 1915 proposal for incremental "development year by year," the navy hoped by 1925 to make the United States Navy "equal to the most powerful maintained by any other nation of the world." Also in 1915, the General Staff gave its programs a similar long-range character when proposing legislation calling for 379,000 fully trained reservists backed up by a 500,000-man partially trained citizen army. The army would accumulate its reserve gradually by having the 121,000-man regular force train soldiers for two years before releasing them for six years of standby duty, which meant that the entire ready force would reach full strength only at the end of eight years. Even the partially trained citizen army was to be built in three annual increments and would require an additional three months of training before commitment to active service. Similarly looking to the future, the army staff proposed plans for procurement of arms and equipment for the reserve and citizen forces that took eight years to complete. Noting that tendency to ignore the possibility of intervention in the present conflict, John P. Finnegan has accurately described the 1916 National Defense Act that derived from the army's proposals as "a decision that the United States would *not* arm immediately to meet the menace of a world at war."[30]

With military officers contemplating a defensive war well in the future rather than the immediate prospect of overseas intervention, war planning continued along traditional lines. Plan ORANGE, the strategy for war with Japan, assumed an initial Japanese assault on the Philippines, in response to which the United States would move its fleet to the Pacific, win naval supremacy, and reestablish communications with the beleaguered Philippine garrison. With consideration of such an attack drawing attention away from the possibility of offensive operations against the Japanese homeland, army and navy planners instead debated the location of America's principal Pacific naval base, the disposition of the American fleet, and the length of time the ground forces might hold out without reinforcement.[31]

The plans for war with BLACK (Germany), which assumed Germany would initiate hostilities by invading either the continental United States or, as a preliminary, some Caribbean island suitable as a base for subsequent operations against the continent, had a more pronounced defensive orientation. Even the wartime revision of BLACK envisioned no intervention in the European war and consequently focused on detailed estimates of the German capacity to move troops to the Western Hemisphere and the size of the American ground force needed to crush the initial German landings. "[S]uch strategic war plans [as] existed for war with Germany," concluded a later Department of the Army study, "were designed for a defensive war, were general in nature, and were totally inapplicable to the situation on 6 April 1917."[32]

Like strategic planning, economic arrangements for future war failed in part because officers assumed a termination of hostilities in Europe prior to any American involvement in great-power conflict, thus precluding the possibility of any crippling economic competition as both Allied and American governments sought to exploit the nation's industrial strength.

Having made that assumption, Major General Leonard Wood confidently advised Congress that the "present European war . . . developed [in the United States] . . . an enormous amount of machinery in many plants suitable for the manufacture of war material.'' With the proper preservation of such machinery, Quartermaster General James B. Aleshire estimated that American industry could equip 600,000 to 900,000 soldiers, and Chief of Ordnance William Crozier took a comparable position on the needs of his bureau. To Wood, Aleshire, and Crozier, then, adequate industrial preparedness for a future conflict required little more than maintaining ''nuclei plants at . . . various establishments,'' and Aleshire consequently advanced plans to recreate within ninety days the productive capacity achieved while supplying the European belligerents. Anticipating combat only within the United States, Aleshire also foresaw no transportation difficulties because of the lack of civil traffic in the war zone.[33]

The military's tendency to plan for what in the end became the wrong war—an inclination closely related to the services' description of the European conflict as an opportunity to achieve general reform rather than a threat to be countered—helped account for the chaos and inefficiency following American intervention in the world conflict. If in hindsight such behavior seems incomprehensible, condemnation of the services' assumptions and their consequences must be moderated by the fact that civilian preparedness literature similarly emphasized that America must prepare for a defensive struggle in the wake of World War I.

In a host of books, Frederick L. Huidekoper, Hudson Maxim, J. Bernard Walker, Julius W. Muller, Robert M. Johnston, and many others pointed not to the need to intervene but to the dangers likely to face America at the close of the war in Europe. ''After the present belligerents have settled their scores with the sword,'' wrote Maxim in anticipation of a postwar attack on the United States, ''there will be other scores to be settled between the victors and the neutral nations.'' According to Maxim, ''the acts of the neutrals that at present seem quite insignificant may be magnified to advantage as *casus belli* . . . ; whichever side wins, the United States will likely have to fight the winner within a short time after the war is over.''[34]

Like most military officers, the civilian advocates of preparedness generally gave first thought to the German menace, whether or not that nation triumphed in Europe. ''The grave danger,'' wrote historian George Louis Beer, ''is that after the war, an unchastened and unbeaten, though not victorious, Germany may seek to retrieve its fortunes by annexing Southern Brazil." In the resulting German-American conflict, Beer expected that "England, weary of the incessant wrangling and not averse from having German ambitions deflected from Africa and Asia, will no longer interpose her fleet as a barrier."[35]

Relatively few civilians, however, accepted the logical extension of Beer's analysis: wartime aid to Great Britain to prevent a German victory and an Anglo-American alliance to deter postwar aggression. Civilian thinkers instead followed the path taken by army and navy leaders and urged military preparations to counter the anticipated postwar attack on the continental United States. Writing of that civilian preparedness movement, John P. Finnegan has observed that the "striking thing . . . was its lack of relation to foreign policy." Virtually ignoring the issue of intervention in Europe, "preparedness was put forward largely as a long-range peacetime proposition, directed at various bugaboos that might threaten the United States after the end of the World War." The movement had in fact "aimed at the wrong war."[36]

Generally avoiding discussion of intervention and the use of force to shape the outcome of the European conflict, military and civilian advocates of preparedness chose the politically less divisive and the rhetorically more dramatic course: preparing the American army and navy to repulse a future invasion of the continental United States. That choice permitted military leaders to speak publicly about defense policy, and it enabled civilian leaders more easily to enact military legislation seemingly unrelated to divisive foreign policy issues. That choice also, Finnegan has written, "threw a subtle distortion into all military planning."[37]

Had such distortions not existed, other influences might still have impeded effective planning for war in Europe. With the General Staff limited by statute to fewer than sixty officers, for instance, the United States Army could not hope to match the extensive studies accomplished by the immense prewar staffs of the principal European belligerents, which ranged in size from 171 (Great Britain) to 929 (Austria-Hungary) and found France and Germany near the mean with 645 and 537 respectively.[38]

In 1912 and again in 1916, Congress had further weakened the American staff by limiting not only its total size but the number of its officers that might serve in Washington. Consequently, only nineteen general staff officers were assigned there in April 1917, and of those only eleven worked in the War College Division—the army's principal war-planning agency. Between 1903 and 1917, moreover, that small General Staff had commonly devoted a larger portion of its energies to administrative matters related to establishing its right to coordinate the War Department's bureaus than to the study of war plans.[39]

The navy suffered comparable handicaps. Until 1915, the naval secretary's aid for operations, assisted by the Naval War College—inconveniently located in Rhode Island—had attempted to plan for the navy. Having only two assistants, a host of other duties, and a civilian superior who refused even to discuss the possibility of war, Rear Admiral Bradley A. Fiske, who held that post during the first years of the war in Europe, accomplished almost nothing. The 1915 bill for the establishment of a naval general staff sought to correct that situation by creating a planning agency with a chief and fifteen assistants. As finally enacted, however, the legislation initially authorized only a chief of naval operations. "We were so short of officers," claimed Admiral William S. Benson, the first to hold the new job, "it was almost impossible to organize a planning section."[40]

America's troubled relations with Mexico between 1911 and 1916 created a second impediment to the preparation of extensive plans for a European war. Perceiving that America's uneasy relations with Mexico carried a grave risk of hostilities, military officers devoted attention principally to study of that problem, supervising the concentration of the National Guard along the Mexican border, planning two armed incursions into Mexican territory—at Vera Cruz and in pursuit of Pancho Villa, and estimating the requirements of a general war with Mexico. Such activities left America's tiny general staff little time for planning against the possibility of intervention in Europe.[41]

The attitude of the Wilson administration placed yet another check on effective military planning. The president and his two service secretaries regarded military contingency planning as faintly immoral and certainly unneutral, and they resolutely thwarted the services' efforts to prepare for the possible consequences of American foreign policy.

During the 1913 crisis with Japan over California's alien land law, for example, Wilson furiously resented recommendations from members of the interservice Joint Board to redeploy several American cruisers and to improve the services' military posture in the Pacific—recommendations that led to a presidential order that the board not meet again without Wilson's specific approval.[42]

The next year, following the incident at Tampico and the navy's seizure of the Vera Cruz customs house, Chief of Staff Leonard Wood called on the president, intending to brief him on army planning against the possibility of war with Mexico. As Wood's biographer recounted that conference, the president dismissed Wood in minutes "horrified at the thought of making any plans. Planning would not be neutral."[43]

The administration followed a similar policy in regard to the European war. When Wilson learned of Army War College studies on war with Germany, Assistant Secretary of War Henry Breckinridge was called to the White House to find the president " 'trembling and white with passion.' " He ordered Breckinridge to investigate and, if such studies had been made, "to relieve at once every officer of the General Staff and order him out of Washington." The assistant secretary ignored the order but directed Acting Chief of Staff Tasker H. Bliss to " 'camouflage' " future war planning, which resulted, Bliss recalled, "in practically no further *official* studies."[44]

As late as March 1917, Wilson demonstrated a similar attitude toward naval planning, that month warning Assistant Secretary of the Navy Franklin Roosevelt: "I do not want the United States to do anything in a military way, by way of war preparations, that would allow the definitive historian in later days . . . to say that the United States had committed an unfriendly act against the central powers."[45] That historian has instead condemned the nation's lack of foresight, and war planning.

Through the service secretaries, President Wilson conveyed the same message to his military planners. "From the time I went to Washington [1916] until we were nearly in the War," Secretary of War Newton Baker told his biographer, "the President gave me the idea—although I could not quote anything he said—that to him the function of the United States was to be the peacemaker, and that the idea of intervening in the War was the last thought he had in the world." Intervention, Baker explained, "was just not in the range of . . . [the president's] mind," and any War Department suggestion "that we increase appropriations with a view to putting the American Army on a better footing in case of hostilities would have been regarded as provocative." Naval lieutenant Tracy B. Kittredge, a member of Admiral Sims's wartime staff, described that service's experience in similar terms, asserting that Secretary Josephus Daniels "refused to listen to talk of war or of preparedness," imposing "on the Navy a pacifist interpretation of neutrality which made any real preparedness measures for our war with Germany impossible before March 1917." As Colonel T. Bentley Mott recalled the period, "the President had said that nothing must be done; nothing was done."[46]

Though exceptionally hostile to military contingency planning, the Wilson administration was merely continuing a long-standing practice when it also failed to advise the armed services of those circumstances in which the United States might resort to war, leaving the strategists, noted John Grenville and George Young, "to establish the basic premises for themselves." An incident of November 1913 well illustrates the frustrations military planners met even when they specifically sought policy guidance. After calling upon Secretary of War Garrison and Secretary of the Navy Daniels in an unsuccessful effort to learn if the administration contemplated the use of force in Mexico, Chief of Staff Leonard Wood went to the secretary of state.

> He [Wood] asked Bryan what the situation was [in Mexico] and what might be expected.
> Bryan looked vague. "I don't understand."
> "In order to know what to prepare for, Mr. Secretary, I merely would like to know what your policy is in regard to Mexico."
> "Search me," answered the Secretary.[47]

Such lack of political guidance had a particularly harmful effect in the spring of 1917, leaving military planners in the dark as to the role the administration wished the services to play as a consequence of American intervention. Chief of Staff Hugh L. Scott wrote in despair to his son, also an army officer: "You know as much as we do about war with Germany. . . . Of course, we are doing everything here to get ready . . . that we can, but having no money or authority to do anything outside the War Department we can not do very much." Claiming to be "perfectly alive" to the need to let contracts for supplies, Scott protested that Congress still believed that it could "meet suddenly and vote $500,000,000 for defense [and] we would at once have it." Following the American declaration of war, Scott complained to his daughters that he was still waiting to be told "what kind of a force they propose for us to raise. It is remarkable that in every crisis . . . we have . . . to go to Congress for a policy, which ought to have been laid down some time before." To Major General John J. Pershing, Scott confided the same thought: "It seems remarkable that we should have been at war for nine days and still be without a policy."[48]

The Navy Department struggled with a similar lack of guidance.

Admiral William S. Sims, sent to London in March 1917 to coordinate American naval assistance to the Allies, complained that for over three months he had no policy guidance to direct his efforts. The navy had little knowledge of how it was to prosecute the war, Sims later told a Senate subcommittee, despite the fact that "war had been a possibility for at least two years and was, in fact, imminent for many months before its declaration."[49]

Lacking personnel, without clear policy guidance from civilian superiors often hostile to planning, and distracted by events in Mexico, America's military staffs had little opportunity to prepare elaborate plans for a possible intervention in Europe.

A sense of urgency, an imperative belief in the pressing importance of planning for American intervention in Europe, might have inspired military officers to overcome even such impediments as inadequate staff, an unsympathetic administration, and an eagerness to exploit the World War in the interests of preparation for a future, and quite different, conflict. The armed services' misperception of the true military situation in Europe, however, precluded the development of an accurate view of immediate necessities. To the contrary, army and navy officers at first thought the World War had little direct relevance for long-run American interests, and service leaders therefore found no justification for their nation's involvement. Later, when they began to perceive advantages for the United States in certain possible outcomes of the European war, their erroneous belief in the inevitability of an Allied victory made intervention seem unnecessary. No sense of urgency therefore compelled either the army or the navy to commence careful planning for America's armed intervention in Europe.

Like most Americans in 1914, military officers participated in what former Major General Francis V. Greene described as the "universal sigh of relief" that three thousand miles separated them from Europe. Seeing "no great danger in the present situation . . . , no need of excitement . . . , no cause for hysteria," Greene denied that "the European war . . . affect[ed] the United States in any vital way." Hunter Liggett, who as a lieutenant general would command an American army in France, agreed, later recalling that he had found the outbreak of worldwide war only slightly less "incredible" than the idea that the United States "ever could be drawn into it." Another wartime army commander, Robert L. Bullard, initially considered the conflict none of "our business," and like Henry T. Allen, who later commanded an army corps, counted the United States "fortunate" to be "out of this world wide war."[50]

Almost a year later, in May 1915, future chief of staff Tasker H. Bliss still hoped the United States would "have no necessity to raise armies and go to war in connection with the unhappy situation in Europe." Characterizing the conflict as "a frightful spectacle," William S. Sims, soon to be America's senior naval commander, told his wife of America's good fortune in being "free from all the wretched European entanglements." An older naval officer, Rear Admiral Raymond Rodgers, also hoped the United States might remain aloof, waiting to see "how this great, awful war will terminate."[51]

Consequently expecting the "President's proclamation . . . of strict neutrality [to] . . . fall on receptive ears," the editor of the *Infantry Journal* nicely summarized the military's early assessment of developments in Europe; "owing to our geographical situation, we are not immediately concerned in these serious events."[52]

That initial reaction resulted in no small part from the American political tradition, in which army and navy officers shared no less than their countrymen. Major General James G. Harbord, the AEF's chief of staff, spoke for many officers when he recalled that they "had never conceived participation in war of any importance outside our continental limits." Although America's "military leaders," Harbord claimed, were not "unaware that an offensive is sometimes the best defense," they remained, like their fellow citizens, imbued with the nation's traditional aloofness from European affairs, even when the latter directly involved American interests. Thinking of the offensive as a "tactical principle, and not in connection with . . . foreign policy," American military officers gave little consideration to intervention as a means of achieving a favorable outcome to the World War. Had any officer predicted that an American army of two million men would one day conduct operations in Europe, wrote Brigadier General John McA. Palmer, one of the army's most progressive and cerebral officers, the War Department would have "committed [him] to St. Elizabeth's [a Washington mental hospital] for observation and treatment."[53]

Even had army and navy officers immediately perceived that the European war affected major American interests and shown a willingness to abandon a national tradition, no burst of planning would necessarily have resulted. For American officers told one another that should the unlikely necessity for intervention ever develop, the "well-trained armies" of its prospective European allies would "stand between us and disaster while we are preparing," thus permitting the United States to plan and execute a relatively unhurried mobilization.[54]

Until at least the eve of America's military involvement, moreover, intervention seemed an unlikely prospect, and military officers persisted in their misplaced confidence in the unaided Allied victory they generally thought best suited American interests. Captain Albert Gleaves, USN, for instance, thought the "Kaiser must be insane. He has now declared against Russia, Belgium, France and England, and as Italy has proclaimed neutrality, he has for his only ally, poor Austria." More realistically expecting "the 'Alleys' . . . [to be] worsted for a while," William S. Sims nevertheless thought "they must win out in the end." While those two naval officers may have been influenced by the power of the British fleet and their belief in Admiral Mahan's seapower theories, Rear Admiral Raymond Rodgers based his similar conclusions on faith in yet a higher power, refusing to "believe that it is in the scheme of the Almighty that such a Gov[ernmen]t [as Germany's] shall be victorious." By mid-1915, Rodgers had become more firmly convinced "that Germany is going to lose," and Sims confidently asserted that Germany had "reached her maximum effort. . . . [E]ven if Russia, France and Italy made peace with her, Great Britain could bring her to terms in time." Army staffers held similar views, and even in early 1917 Brigadier General Joseph E. Kuhn, chief of the War College Division of the General Staff, could confidently advise naval secretary Daniels that Germany would surely fall by April first.[55] In such circumstances, preparing for intervention held a low priority.

Even the few officers who anticipated the need for greater American aid to the Allies had little reason to conclude that such assistance would require mobilization of a large expeditionary force. Like most Americans—and most members of the Wilson administration—army and navy officers generally assumed that their nation's contribution would be one of money, food, raw materials, and manufactured goods—not large bodies of troops or fleets of ships. Learning unofficially of claims like Senate Appropriations Committee chairman Thomas S. Martin's assertion that "Congress will not permit American soldiers to be sent to Europe," members of the War Department in July 1917 nevertheless advanced proposals for raising a large land force only to draw the presidential warning "that the country would be shocked by, and would never stand for, a draft of a million men." With little reason, therefore, to anticipate an immediate and substantial commitment of American

troops in Europe, army officers had little incentive to hasten preparation of such plans.[56]

Most American naval officers, too, in the spring of 1917, expected
their nation's contribution to be largely moral and financial. The
United States Navy, they thought, would aid the Allies by patrolling
the waters of the Western Hemisphere, a limited task the British mission to Washington in April 1917 did little to expand when it requested
only a small destroyer force to show the flag in European waters. Due to
Allied propaganda and feeble American intelligence efforts, naval officers, reported Admiral William S. Sims, had originally "felt little fear
about the outcome [of the European conflict]. All the fundamental
facts in the case made it appear impossible that the Germans could win
the war." Consequently, in early 1917, it seemed "altogether probable
that the war would end before the United States could exert any material influence upon the outcome." Until Sims reached London in March
1917, in fact, nothing about America's prospective role in the World
War suggested that the service's planners had been seriously remiss.
When Lord Jellicoe revealed the actual situation, Sims became the first
American naval officer to learn that "the Navy Department did not understand the seriousness of the submarine situation . . . ; unless the ap-
palling destruction of merchant tonnage . . . could be materially
checked, the unconditional surrender of the British Empire would inevitably take place within a few months." Awakened to the truth, Sims
began a Herculean struggle to convince the Navy Department and his
fellow officers of the grave misperception that had convinced prewar
planners that any American naval role would be a peripheral one.[57]

Unlike Sims's experience in London, talks with an Allied mission to
Washington in April 1917 did little to alter the army's views on its
probable role in the World War. Secretary of War Baker's biographer
has written that the Allied military representatives led the department
to believe that "the United States should merely contribute war materials, financial aid, and volunteers for Allied armies." Brigadier General
Hugh S. Johnson remembered that the "Allied military missions . . .
felt that we could neither arm, train, equip, nor transport an army
[to Europe]." Moreover, "our attempt to do so would interfere with
the availability of our raw material and manufacturing resources to
them."[58]

In view of the small size of the American army and the Allies'
250,000-man margin of superiority in France, the Allied argument
seemed sound, and as late as May 1917 the army's planning agency, the

war college, recalled Major General James G. Harbord, had "no thought . . . that the sending of troops abroad was imminent." Even after the American declaration of war, therefore, the United States Army lacked an incentive to plan for an immediate and massive commitment of American ground forces in Europe.[59]

Accepting Allied assurances at face value, American officers also vigorously resisted Allied proposals to boost British and French morale by the prompt dispatch of a single division to Europe. The General Staff did not believe, Acting Chief of Staff Tasker Bliss told the war secretary, "that the Entente Allies were in such a condition as to make . . . [that] desirable or necessary." If victory eventually demanded that America send a large army to Europe, the Allies should in the meantime, Bliss wrote, "stand fast and wait until our reinforcements can reach them in such a way as to give the final, shattering blow." Bliss, like the War College Division, found no need to rush American troops to France and argued that the trained personnel of the requested division were needed in the United States "for the expansion and training of the national forces," to maintain the overseas garrisons, and to guard against "disturbances on the Mexican border and in Cuba."[60]

Only late in 1917 did American army officers acquire that sense of imminent disaster that lent urgency to planning for an immediate and massive armed intervention in Europe. Russia's departure from the war, Britain's costly offensives in Flanders, and Italy's defeat at Caporetto—unforeseen disasters that enabled the Germans to achieve numerical superiority and the chance for a decisive victory in France—brought the shift in American plans. The likelihood of Allied defeat—unperceived until late in 1917—finally forced army planners to increase significantly the rate at which American troops would be mobilized and committed to Europe and fully revealed the folly of having failed to prepare more extensive plans for American intervention in the World War. During the winter of 1917–18, the army consequently altered the previous summer's plans to have a thirty-division force (1.3 million men) in France by December 1918 and developed a program to provide fifty-two divisions (2.3 million men) by December and a total of eighty divisions the following July.[61]

Although possessing a Realistic view of international politics, one that should have recognized the possibility of American intervention in Europe, army and navy officers gave little thought to that contingency.

Partially absorbed by the more proximate danger of war with Mexico, military officers instead used the outbreak of war in Europe to validate their world view and argue for the prompt enactment of their long-standing program of military reforms. Should the European war—or more likely its aftermath—ultimately touch the United States, the speedy completion of the reform program would ensure the good order of the nation's defenses and prepare the services for any eventuality. In the meantime, not only did the European conflict pose no threat to the United States but its continuation in fact enhanced American security.

With no obvious need to break free of the traditional preoccupation with continental defense, military planners made little effort to overcome other obstacles to consideration of intervention in Europe. The Wilson administration, for example, not only failed to confide its political objectives to military leaders, it specifically forbade them to consider war with a European power. Confident of an Allied victory and lacking sufficient personnel in their planning agencies, the armed services had little reason to defy the president. Even American participation in the war, moreover, did not necessarily imply any requirement to plan for the immediate, massive commitment of men and ships. In 1917 even the Allies anticipated only a financial and material contribution on the part of the United States.

The United States thus found itself unprepared, in late 1917, for the war it must fight. The consequences of that lack of preparation must not, however, obscure the overall success of a mobilization effort that surprised friend and foe alike. Any assessment of the responsibility for the services' shortcomings, moreover, must consider that the military's somewhat misdirected prewar reforms, if adopted by Congress and the administration, would have placed the army and the navy in a far better position to wage the World War's unanticipated struggles—both those on the battlefield and those on the home front.

CHAPTER 9

The Afterclap of the First World War

Surveying the international havoc left by the First World War, American military officers, recalled Major General James G. Harbord, seemed "haunted by forebodings of insecurity." The former chief of staff of the American Expeditionary Forces (AEF) also described his colleagues as "dazed by . . . changes" which seemed to foretell "the passing of an era." Fearful of the "red tidal wave of Bolshevism . . . rolling in from Russia" and uncertain of "the future relations between [*sic*] white, yellow and dark races," military officers believed they could feel the "[a]ncient structures . . . trembling" and worried lest "Christian civilization [fail to] steady itself on new courses mapped for it during four years of war." Wondering if the West could "weather another such storm," military men speculated about an end to America's isolation, the nation's role in postwar reconstruction, "the prospects of permanent peace," and "the future of democratic institutions." A contemporary study by Lieutenant Tracy B. Kittredge, a wartime member of Admiral Sims's London staff, indicated that naval officers felt similar anxiety. In his postwar summary of naval opinion, which Kittredge prepared under Sims's direction, the lieutenant stated that the war to end wars had instead "thrown the world into confusion." The resulting "new world . . . with new tendencies, new forces, new problems" con-

177

vinced naval officers, who continued to believe that war would remain "the ultimate test of a nation," that the United States had entered "upon a period of history in which the soundness of its institutions and the strength of its people will be subjected to crucial tests."[1]

Despite such forebodings, many of the military proposals advanced for the postwar reorganization of the armed services followed customary lines. Believing, as did the editor of the *Infantry Journal*, that no world war "would have occurred"—or "would have ended at our threat of going in"—if only we had "been as well prepared when this war started as we were at its close," army and navy officers suggested many proposals for reform that simply extended into the postwar period the programs of the preceding four decades.[2]

Describing the "lack of officers who had experience in handling . . . large units" as the "greatest handicap we had at the start of this war," Chief of Staff Peyton C. March in 1919 urged Congress to authorize improvements along several long-established lines: restoration and expansion of the prewar military educational system, the concentration and reorganization of units along tactical lines, and the conduct of frequent large-scale maneuvers, all of which would give officers vicarious experience in the control of large units in combat. "[A] reasonable efficiency in peace time training for war," added March, "can never be secured until the present system of small, isolated battalion and company posts . . . is replaced by a system which enables entire divisions to be trained together and to be consolidated frequently for the maneuvers of larger units." During that same period, the navy's General Board made a similar argument when it called for sufficient funds and authority to assemble "the active fleet at least once a year" for naval war games lasting "not less than three months." To bring its educational system abreast of the army's, the navy in 1919 finally gave its senior college a permanent staff and commenced the annual assignment of sixty student officers for an established twelve months' course. That same year the Army War College broadened its curriculum to give greater emphasis to the civil dimension of war and war preparation. The problem of modern war, explained Commandant Edward F. McGlachlin in 1921, "is one of the nation: of the Army, of the Navy, of the Departments of Government and the leaders of industry and politics." Captain Ridley McLean, a naval exchange student, consequently found that the college's curriculum "covers war in its broadest aspect, the studies are national in character, all problems involve combined [army-navy] operations, the world[,] rather than a limited area on land, is the theatre; naval strategy enters quite as much as land strategy."[3]

Not surprisingly, either, military officers argued that the World War had demonstrated the need of each service for the guiding hand of a strong general staff, the lack of which the *Infantry Journal* described as the country's "outstanding weakness at the outbreak of the late war." In 1919 service reformers consequently resumed their campaign to strengthen the army's Chief of Staff and the navy's Chief of Naval Operations. Supplementing older arguments with references to wartime shortcomings, reformers urged Congress and the Wilson administration to give those staff chiefs enough officers to prepare effective war plans and sufficient authority to retain their wartime control over the departmental bureaus that must implement the plans' administrative and logistical aspects. A modern war being "a war of nations rather than armies," General March wanted to plan for "mobilization of the entire resources" of the country and coordination of the "needs of the War Department" with those "of other governmental agencies and of the general public." To that end the services also gained legislative approval for a joint Army and Navy Munitions Board that would prepare plans for the mobilization of American industry, and the War Department received authority to appoint an assistant secretary, who would coordinate the procurement activities of the supply bureaus, and to establish an Army Industrial College, which Russell Weigley has written would prepare its students for "more systematic study of industrial mobilization planning."[4]

In at least two respects, however, military reform abandoned its usual focus as officers advocated programs that had become widely popular among service leaders only after the outbreak of the war in Europe: international naval supremacy and a large standing army backed by universal military training (UMT). In so doing, military reformers behaved somewhat like their predecessors during that brief period following the war with Spain, when army and navy officers had sought to prepare the armed forces for a perceived shift in national policy, one that would require the services to give less attention to continental defense and to plan instead for the imperial projection, on a global scale, of America's new military might.

The armed services' grandiose schemes of 1919 seem based on the belief that Americans generally had learned from the World War what officers thought they had. The war indicated, explained Peyton C.

March, that America had lost its geographic protection against "the military operations of any possible powerful enemy." The United States, moreover, had emerged from the war with "tremendously increased [international] responsibilities," most of which required maintenance of a much larger army. Speaking for an equally outward-looking General Board, Secretary of the Navy Edwin Denby claimed that the navy must become sufficiently powerful to "make every effort, both ashore and afloat, to assist the development of American interests."[5]

By resting programs for a vast postwar expansion of the American military establishment on an assumed active involvement in world affairs and a perceived increase in the likelihood of major conflict, however, army and navy officers demonstrated a grave misunderstanding of both international affairs and the national mood, and they advocated programs that ill served the needs of both the nation and the armed services.

Not all army officers, of course, advocated UMT and a large standing army. A few, for example Tasker H. Bliss, ex-chief of staff, former U.S. military representative to the Supreme Allied War Council, and in 1919 minister plenipotentiary to the Peace Conference, hoped that full American participation in the League of Nations and the world court and strong national support for disarmament and an end to conscription would reduce the risk of war sufficiently to enable the United States Army to return to prewar levels.[6]

Overwhelmingly, however, the army's leaders placed little faith in the league. Even its "staunchest supporter," Major Richard Stockton reminded the readers of *North American Review*, "does not claim that it will do away with war." The president himself, Stockton added, "makes no such claim," and his opponents charge that the league would more likely "serve as a cause of war." Americans must therefore realize that they "may again be involved therein" and adequately prepare "to meet the issue when it is forced upon [them]." Nor should they again expect others to guard America's interests, as had the armies of England and France, while the United States readied its forces.[7]

Such thinking led army officers to assume that they must prepare their service to fight a war not unlike the just-completed struggle in Europe—the next time without allies. To preclude another, at least initially, inefficient and ineffective response, army officers maintained that such preparation must include a means to raise, with a minimum of delay, a well-trained force in excess of a million men.

Excluding the followers of Bliss, who rejected such extensive prepa-ration, a tiny minority of officers supported plans like those of Brigadier General George Van Horn Moseley, who wished to achieve that level of preparedness by submerging the regular forces in a vast citizen army on the Swiss model—a small cadre of full-time soldiers, that is, backed by all the furloughed veterans, each assigned to a unit near his home but, except for emergencies, pursuing a civilian career.[8]

Most officers, however, supported one of two other approaches. Chief of Staff March and Secretary of War Newton D. Baker lent their names to the first, official proposal: a large standing army slightly in ex-cess of a half million men backed by UMT. That number would suffice to bring units in the overseas garrisons, like the Philippines, to full strength but would provide less than half the troops needed for a con-tinental field army of five corps. The remainder, enough men to bring that force to a war strength of 1.25 million, would come from a reserve of soldiers prepared by several months of training in a program of uni-versal service. Baker and March thus implicitly slighted the National Guard, which opposed a plan demoting it from the regulars' principal backup to an ill-defined third line of defense. The War Department perhaps saw in its inclusion of UMT a means to counter the guards-men's anticipated criticism with support from the many civilian advo-cates of universal training, who were often more interested in the sup-posed socializing effects of military service than in increased readiness for war.[9]

The real blow to the March-Baker proposal, however, came not from the guardsmen but from a well-known army progressive, Colonel John McA. Palmer, and the former commander of the AEF, General John J. Pershing, who together provided the rallying point for those officers who either rightly perceived that their fellow citizens would never sup-port so large a standing army or rejected the concept of an expansible regular force requiring an infusion of partially trained reservists to make it a usable military body.

In contrast, Palmer and Pershing recommended a standing army of fewer than three hundred thousand, organized as a force-in-being whose full-strength units would be immediately ready for field service. Their proposal would create an army capable of serving in the overseas garrisons as well as responding to such emergencies as had occurred along America's border with Mexico or had required the mounting of small expeditionary campaigns like those in the Caribbean. Palmer's plan also required the standing army, in support of UMT, to train a mass citizen army that, in the event of a major conflict, would organize for active service behind the shield of the small regular force.

Palmer, too, thus clung to UMT, about which Congress and the public were becoming increasingly skeptical, and to a federalized reserve force, which threatened the position of the states' guardsmen. And like March, he assumed the feasibility of recruiting enough volunteers to fill a standing army of at least a quarter million men.

From the many competing plans and a commitment to national traditions too easily ignored by most regular officers, Congress fashioned the National Defense Act of 1920. Taking the estimates provided by Palmer and Pershing, Congress created a 280,000-man standing army, which it tasked to garrison the overseas possessions, supply small expeditionary forces, and train the citizen forces. To defend the country in a major war, the act provided for the country's organization into nine corps areas, each of which would contain one skeletal division of regulars, two of National Guardsmen, and three from a new organized reserve. Those nine corps formed, in turn, three understrength field armies. For the first time in peace, the American army had a modern tactical organization. Yet, Congress had also preserved the traditional role and independence of the National Guard and, by rejecting UMT, continued the nation's reliance upon volunteers, the source of recruits for the standing army as well as the partially trained citizen soldiers who were to bring the regular, National Guard, and reserve divisions to full strength in an emergency.[10]

Too quickly regular officers gave that act their enthusiastic endorsement. Major General William G. Haan called the new army law "the best and most rational ever placed on our statute books," and a young student of military policy, Lieutenant Colonel Paul S. Bond, described the act as "a great advance on all previous military legislation . . . and . . . on the whole the best . . . we have ever had."[11]

Such enthusiasm strangely ignored the fact that Congress had rejected UMT—surely the only means, short of a revolution in American attitudes toward peacetime military service, to maintain the guard and reserve units at full strength and to provide enough trained men to bring the nine regular divisions to a war footing. While expressing satisfaction that Congress had placed the American "military establishment . . . on a big war basis," officers like Major William Bryden also overlooked the new shadow army's consequent inability to act in any significant emergency short of the "big war" crisis that alone would bring out the volunteers or justify the conscription of the men needed to fill its ranks. Perhaps the large pool of war-trained veterans caused army officers also to ignore the fact that neither an emergency return to conscription nor a crisis-induced outburst of voluntarism would yield trained soldiers once the heroes of the World War had become overage or grown unfamiliar with military drills. More likely the army's leaders falsely assumed that the World War had taught Americans the lesson of preparedness, causing them henceforth voluntarily to maintain an adequate peacetime force. If so, the prewar army's inability to recruit even 100,000 volunteers should have given them pause and raised doubts about the possibility of keeping the 280,000-man army at full strength. America's increasingly antimilitary mood should also have caused officers to wonder if Congress would continue its support of the new policy.[12]

Only as both regular and citizen forces failed to meet their recruiting goals, however, and the appropriations of an economy-minded Congress in effect cut regular strength to less than half the original 280,000-man authorization, did army officers seem to sense their error. While writing of the reduced appropriations early in 1923, former secretary of war Elihu Root's old adviser, Major General William H. Carter, put his finger on the problem. "The net result of the reorganization now being carried out," he told readers of *North American Review*, "is to leave the nation with a policy in theory, but with a military force, in practice, unable to fulfill its peace mission, and more expensive in proportion to its efficiency than any military establishment we have ever had." Despite that warning, the War Department compounded the problem by preserving all nine of the expansible regular divisions. With the National Guard at less than half its 435,000 authorization and an organized reserve containing 100,000 officers but virtually no enlisted men, that decision left the United States with a standing army whose skeletal organization rendered it ineffective in small emergencies and with too few trained men to fill the units of either the regular or reserve forces in a major crisis.[13]

The drive for a superior navy, as measured by the strength and number of its battleships, led the majority of naval officers similarly to limit the effectiveness of their service. With the support of the Wilson administration—which may have wished to use the threat of a naval arms race either to wring concessions from Great Britain at Versailles or to win support for the League of Nations from senators at home—navalists like Chief of Naval Operations Robert E. Coontz and General Board member Charles J. Badger urged upon Congress construction of the world's largest navy. In reaching for that goal the battleship admirals were also aided by America's wartime building program and Britain's relative inattention, after 1914, to the construction of capital ships. With supremacy within reach, the admirals justified its pursuit by arguing that Germany's defeat released the Royal Navy for offensive action anywhere on the globe. Defense of the Philippines and support of American commercial interests in China, they added, might also produce a clash with Japan, England's ally in the Far East, and force the United States to engage the combined fleets of the other two principal naval powers. Strangely, however, the battleship admirals failed to press hard for funds needed to construct an impregnable naval base at Guam or the Philippines, without which no American battle fleet, however powerful, could hope to control the western Pacific.[14]

That pursuit of naval supremacy went forward despite the criticism of a small but vocal minority of officers led by such prewar reformers as William S. Sims, Caspar F. Goodrich, William F. Fullam, and Bradley A. Fiske. In their opinion, explained Goodrich, "stern necessity, not the sentimental cry for the biggest, should rule." Describing war with Great Britain as "unthinkable," Goodrich characterized efforts even to match its fleet as "sheer folly;" the United States Navy needed ships enough only to counter "any fairly probable (not remotely possible) attack." Those officers also wished to exploit technology by supplementing a small American battle fleet with improved coastal fortifications and large numbers of submarines and bombing aircraft, which they thought could increase the usefulness of naval efforts to interdict the commerce of a maritime enemy like England or Japan and render a seaborne invasion of the United States or its possessions all but impossible. To guard the Philippines, for instance, Fiske proposed a fortified naval base, a fleet of submarines, and "a force of say one hundred first-class airplanes" that would "concentrate at any threatened point on the coast before the invading troops could start from the transports to the shore." While such weapons might be less effective in exercising control of the western Pacific, they would provide defense at far less cost than building the world's preponderant battle fleet.[15]

Such prestigious criticism failed, however, to scuttle the plans of the battleship admirals. That task fell to the Harding administration's drive for economy in government and a popular revolt against navalism, which led to the 1921-22 Washington Conference. Over the protests of naval officers, the administration there negotiated an arms-limitation treaty in which the United States accepted simple parity in capital ships with Great Britain and a five-to-three advantage over Japan. The concurrent termination of the Anglo-Japanese alliance somewhat sweetened that bitter pill by eliminating the possibility of a two-ocean war with those powers, but a total capital-ship tonnage below what naval experts thought safe and a prohibition on fortification of a naval base in the western Pacific negated the alliance's abrogation as well as the military value of American superiority vis-à-vis Japan. For the defense of the Philippines, warned Rear Admiral William V. Pratt, the United States "must now rely upon the spirit of good understanding entered into through the offices of this Conference."[16]

Still fascinated with the battleship, naval officers generally ignored the possibilities suggested by the advocates of aircraft and submarines. The former thus left the Philippines, now well beyond the operating range of a fleet based at Hawaii, virtually undefended. As with the army's overambitious plans, Congress then further weakened the navy by failing to appropriate sufficient funds to maintain the battleship fleet at authorized levels.

From the perspective of a second world war, the military officers' proposals for the world's premier navy and a large, expansible army backed by UMT may seem unusually prescient. That perspective assumes, however, that statesmen had no subsequent opportunity to crush the obvious seeds of discord in the Versailles settlement and that prudence demanded extensive preparation for the next global conflict even while the world lay prostrate from the last.

Neither assumption seems valid; in the context of the 1920s, the military officers' advocacy of UMT and global naval supremacy suggests that service thought had for the moment lost touch with reality. In the first instance, military officers based their proposals upon a largely inaccurate analysis of the strategic situation. British interests in fact closely paralleled those of the United States, and such differences as existed hardly served as grounds for war. Although Japan had clearly imperial ambitions, its immediate interests focused on the Asian mainland to the north, away from the Philippines, a fact from which few officers drew any satisfaction. In any event, both England and Japan remained too vulnerable to commercial warfare, which could cut their links with overseas markets and sources of raw materials, to consider war with the United States except in extremis.[17]

In addition to those strategic errors, American officers failed to take account of the public's increasing disillusionment with both the peace settlement and American intervention in Europe. In the postwar world, traditional antimilitarism and isolationism as well as a drive for economy in government shaped national policy, eroding support for any extensive military establishment and rendering the services' proposals singularly inopportune. Faced with such attitudes, army and navy officers might better have opted for smaller forces-in-being and urged Congress to use the savings in part to satisfy the voters and in part to invest in the latest military technology.

Mechanization of war and the introduction of new weapons—especially the submarine, the airplane, and the tank—counseled a period of reflection and testing prior to the adoption of a firm military policy. Though America's successful overseas intervention in Europe had demonstrated to some the feasibility of a future assault on the United States from abroad, the submarine and bombing aircraft vastly increased the power of coastal defenses, raised doubts about the practicality of such an attack, and thus the need for so large an army. Should the course of events require that the United States again intervene massively in Europe, certainly no immediate prospect, surely the nation would have allies that might once more provide time for mobilization.

Tanks and aircraft should also have caused thoughtful officers to question the usefulness of a skeletal army brought to strength with a flood of reservists having only three months' training and little knowledge of mechanized warfare. A small regular force with the latest equipment and organized for immediate employment might better have served America's postwar needs than plans to recreate the wartime army.

Although new naval weapons challenged the role of the battleship in future naval contests and hinted at the possibility of new strategies for winning effective control of the seas and defending the Philippines—despite the restrictions imposed by the Washington Conference—naval officers generally reinforced the army's technical errors by giving inadequate thought to inexpensive alternatives more likely to satisfy Congress and ensure its continued support.

Postwar military programs, designed, wrote Walter Millis, "to repeat, more efficiently and with less time-lag, the great feat of 1918 . . . [and] to resume construction of the big battleship and battle-cruiser programs," simply ignored the international situation, the national mood, and the evolution of weaponry.[18] America's military leaders unfortunately failed to consider modest programs that both incorporated the latest technology and conformed to the public mood as well as postwar foreign policy. Perhaps such programs might similarly have met defeat at the hands of Congress; we shall never know. But surely the plans for a large military establishment were doomed from inception. Whereas Congress and the executive had often blocked needed military reform in the decades preceding 1917, in the immediate aftermath of World War I they joined, perhaps unconsciously, to rescue military men from their extravagant hopes and the folly of applying old solutions to new problems. In so doing, the nation's civil leadership presented the armed services with an unpleasant surprise.

In contrast to that postwar tendency to ask for more force than required, the military reformers of the four prewar decades had usually advanced modest programs seeking to adapt the armed forces to both a changing domestic and international environment and anticipated shifts in American national policy. That adaptation had begun in the nineteenth century's last quarter as army and navy officers debated the appropriate military responses to a changing environment. Two domestic developments—the end of the Indian wars and the decline in the American merchant marine—encouraged such a debate, suggesting to many officers that both services were about to lose their traditional reasons for existence: keeping peace on the frontier and guarding overseas trade. Technological changes, which had reduced to obsolescence the army's forts, the navy's ships, and the guns of both services, also spurred reform by indicating that America's armed forces lacked the strength to perform their secondary, wartime duties.

That situation produced a fleeting interest in such nonmilitary programs as subsidies and privileges designed to stimulate the American merchant marine—thereby justifying the navy's existence—and closer links with the civil community—which might demonstrate to a skeptical public the army's usefulness as either a constabulary to control urban violence or a school to train civilian militiamen.

By the 1890s, several considerations nevertheless prompted both army and navy officers to conclude that the only proper peacetime mission for each force had become preparation against the possibility of war with a major power. In the navy's case, the studies of Alfred Thayer Mahan and a number of like-minded officers demonstrated how a nation at war might employ a modest fleet-in-being to defend its coasts and, by thus keeping its ports open, use neutral shipping to maintain the flow of international trade. That navy might accomplish its old peacetime duties, those officers wrote, with but a few cruisers that would co-

operate with the navies of the other major trading powers in keeping order in the nonindustrialized world—the only place in peacetime where
violence threatened international trade and investment. Otherwise, the
navy had little need to perform its traditional duties, and it might safely
turn its attention to preparation against great-power war.

A distaste for riot duty and an obligation to assist in the defense of
America's coastal ports and cities—thus freeing the navy for limited offensive action against an attacking force—similarly turned army officers
away from civil functions and reinforced their preference for readying
their service for modern warfare. Near the close of the century, after the
Sino-Japanese War of 1894 had demonstrated the need for a mobile
land force to supplement coastal fortifications in repelling an overseas
invasion, cavalry and infantry officers increasingly joined members of
the artillery and engineers in studying the defense of America's coasts.

A third factor, the changing nature of warfare, influenced officers of
both services to give greater priority to the military or wartime functions
of the armed forces. Several recent wars, most notably Japan's successful
invasion of China and Prussia's clashes with Austria and France, had
demonstrated that powers with highly trained, readily mobilized forces
could quickly overcome even demographically and industrially superior
adversaries. That ability of smaller states to win decisive victories in the
early stages of a conflict placed at a considerable disadvantage those nations, like the United States, which planned to postpone the mobilization of its military potential to the months following a declaration of
war. The complexity of modern weapons, which had begun to require
both special facilities and many months for their construction as well as
lengthy training in their use, only compounded the dangers of defer-
ring preparation until the outbreak of war. Military officers viewed technological change, then, as yet another reason for modernizing America's armed forces and improving their peacetime training for war.

Though institutional self-interest undoubtedly contributed to the
military officers' advocacy of modernization, only their world view and
their perception of the changing strategic environment account for the
timing and direction of the military reform movement. Abandoning
programs that might have preserved the services by increasing their nonmilitary functions, army and navy officers pursued reform in the belief
that war was inevitable and that security required advanced preparation.
To get the public to share those beliefs, officers pointed out that a number of great powers possessed real or anticipated grievances that might
lead to conflict with the United States. Believing that late-nineteenth-
century imperialism, especially, magnified the likelihood of American

involvement in great-power war—in defense, for example, of the Monroe Doctrine—army and navy officers worked closely with like-minded civilians to warn of the dangers and to procure the ships and guns required for a successful defense of the national domain. The services' leaders also called attention to the threat posed by those smaller states whose modern weaponry gave them at least a temporary military advantage over the United States.

The commitment to peacetime preparation for war also went hand in hand with efforts to create a more professional officer corps and to improve the services' training, organization, and administration. Both the army and the navy consequently established a system of schools for the education of their officers, and with only partial success the services sought Congressional approval for the elimination of those individuals unfit for advancement and wartime command. The military reformers also proposed reorganization of the combat forces through creation of units that facilitated both realistic training and rapid commitment to battle. At the same time, reformers intensified their assault upon the system of powerful departmental bureaus, which they regarded as suited only for a subservient role as providers of administrative and logistical support. Those bureaus lacked, according to the reformers, a sympathetic understanding of the needs of the combat forces, the capacity to plan for anticipated conflict, and any agent, short of the service secretaries, capable of ensuring a coordinated response to the demands of modern warfare.

Despite America's easy victory in the war with Spain, that conflict facilitated military modernization by validating the reformers' warnings about the possibility of war and demonstrating the services' administrative and organizational shortcomings. In its aftermath, sympathetic civilians helped the army win Congressional approval for creation of a General Staff Corps with authority to prepare war plans and to advise the civilian secretary on the coordination of bureau activities. In addition, the army improved its educational system with the establishment of its own war college. In contrast, naval reformers achieved secretarial support for only an ad hoc General Board that might work closely with the Naval War College in the performance of certain general staff functions. Congress did, however, authorize increases in the strength of both services, and it appropriated funds for the modernization of their equipment.

For some half dozen years after that conflict, many army and navy officers also lost their earlier preoccupation with defense of the continental United States. Convinced that the administration had adopted a more aggressive foreign policy and would now join with the imperial powers in bearing the white man's burden, a significant number of officers began to study preparation of their services for frequent small-scale intervention abroad. Sharing the progressive views of many civilian expansionists, those same officers also worked to bring the blessings of liberal democracy and modern technology to the nonindustrialized societies with which they came into contact—even if that mission required that those societies provisionally lose their right to self-government.

By 1905, however, the armed services' older, defensive orientation began to reassert its dominance over American military thought. That reorientation had, on the one hand, an internal source. Artillery officers had never lost their interest in coastal defense, and a large minority of officers within the army had always held doubts about the wisdom of territorial expansion. Many naval officers, moreover, had opposed the big-navy plans of the most expansionist-minded men in their service. Additionally, firsthand experience with imperialism produced disenchantment among the majority of officers, who slowly began to oppose the frequent interventions in Latin America and personally felt the frustration of service in the Philippines and elsewhere overseas.

International developments, on the other hand, also prompted a renewed interest in territorial defense. While never quite abandoning the view that human depravity or the working of natural laws caused international conflict, military officers began to give their beliefs focus by tracing war's origins to the clash of national policies and, in so doing, gained a better understanding of America's most likely enemies. That shift in perception occurred during the same period that military officers came to see Germany and Japan as expansionist and thus likely to challenge the Monroe Doctrine in Latin America and the Open Door in the Far East. Increasing international tension also cast doubts on the earlier assumption about the possibilities of great-power cooperation in control of the nonindustrialized world. To all those concerns, the Russo-Japanese War of 1905 gave a convenient focus, illustrating once again the feasibility of an overseas invasion of the United States, the need for mobile land forces to support coastal fortifications and naval defenses, and the possibly decisive advantages of highly trained and ready forces, which enabled even a small power to defeat an unprepared giant.

Military officers consequently returned to the defensive themes they had stressed in the years before the war with Spain. After 1905, moreover, service writers increasingly clothed their appeals for reform in the language of progressivism. The reformers now spoke of the efficiency that would result from improved tactical organizations and extensive field exercises. Military administration must also be placed under the control of line officers, those experts in war and preparation for war, the reformers claimed, who would reduce the influence of politically motivated congressmen systematically working through the chief of a military bureau to secure the interests of their district rather than serve what reformers regarded as the needs of the entire nation. As yet another means to achieve efficiency, army officers recommended centralization—especially a federal militia or increased regular control of the National Guard. Like many civilian progressives, army and navy officers also turned to the press, confidently exposing military deficiencies in the belief that an informed public would demand suitable corrective legislation. As perhaps the ultimate reform, officers advocated an interdepartmental Council of National Defense capable of coordinating foreign and military policies and ensuring Congressional support for essential programs.

That army and navy officers turned to the concepts of the progressive movement to reinforce their arguments for reform contains few surprises. Officers as well as civilian advocates of military modernization had employed similar language since the late nineteenth century. More important, military leaders had always maintained close social and intellectual ties with America's business, professional, and political elites and shared their outlook. That outlook also encouraged officers to join with civilian progressives in describing the armed services as schools for citizenship. When, for example, advocating larger regular forces or universal military training, armed forces officers declared that a period of military service would inculcate America's youth with patriotism and respect for law while simultaneously combating the materialism and selfishness characteristic of civil society. Progressive officers also believed that military service would improve the health and physiques of city-bred youngsters and prepare them for industrial employment by encouraging obedience to authority and attention to detail. Equally important, the intimate contact among young men of all social strata during a period of military service would promote mutual respect among classes, reducing the likelihood of domestic conflict and exposing the foreign born to American values.

The August 1914 outbreak of war in Europe lent further support to the movement for military reform. The conflict seemingly validated the military officers' claims about the persistence of war—to include the possibility of great-power conflict—and a host of preparedness advocates joined progressives in urging an expanded and improved military establishment. With such support, naval officers hoped to achieve a navy of the first rank, and army officers expected that Congress would eventually enact a program of universal military training. The World War also encouraged officers and civilians to give increased attention to the economic and industrial dimensions of modern warfare. While never losing interest in better-trained and better-equipped regular forces and a more effective reserve, military officers also came to recognize that modern wars might be of long duration and demand a high level of industrial mobilization to ensure ultimate victory.

A few soldiers and civilians had, as early as 1915, advocated American military intervention in the European war, and the preparedness agitation of the next two years undoubtedly contributed to American success after April 1917. Nevertheless, most civilian and military backers of preparedness had not supported service reform with intervention in mind. Instead, they had sought to prepare the army and the navy for defense of the United States and the Western Hemisphere against an anticipated postwar challenge to the Monroe Doctrine. Consequently, the reformers' programs generally required from three to eight years to achieve the desired level of readiness.

In that sense, American intervention caught the services by surprise. Despite difficulties in the supply bureaus, however, the army and navy quickly adjusted to the new turn in national policy, and using the declaration of war as a unique opportunity, progressive officers pressed the administration and Congress to accelerate the pace of military reform. Conscription, for example, appeared to many army officers as but the first step toward universal peacetime service. When the army's General Staff stepped in to unsnarl the tangle in that service's supply system, reformers used the opportunity to strengthen the line officers' control of the departmental bureaus. Regular control of the reserve forces also occurred as the president called the National Guard into federal service and Congress authorized the creation of a federally controlled, professionally officered National Army. And the World War, by demanding a larger and better-equipped army and navy, led many officers mistakenly to conclude that the United States would in the future maintain comparable forces.

By advocating postwar programs that included the pursuit of global naval supremacy and the creation of a large, expansible army backed by universal military training, however, military officers revealed that they had temporarily lost touch with reality. For the foreseeable future,

American foreign policy seemed unlikely to demand creation of a swollen military establishment appropriate primarily for participation in a second global war.

Great Britain and Japan, the only powers with enough naval strength to pose a significant threat to the United States, seemed eager to compose any potential clash of interests, and both nations lacked the financial strength and secure national base from which to wage a successful campaign against the United States. Naval leaders, generally obsessed with battleships, also failed to give due attention to aircraft and submarines, possibly more effective and certainly less costly supplements to the existing fleet than more battleships.

While rightly continuing to work on plans for industrial mobilization, increasing the efficiency of the reorganized combat forces, improving educational systems, and strengthening general staff coordination—the only reforms to survive the Congressional cuts of the 1920s—army officers contemplating the unlikely event of a major emergency failed to rely upon the World War's pool of trained men while creating and equipping a small, mechanized, full-strength regular force with which to test the strategic and tactical implications of new weapons and the impending mechanization of war. Indeed, too many officers of both services entertained the fantasy of an imminent conflict with Japan or Great Britain and recommended creation of a military establishment bearing little relation either to America's international needs or to the mood of its citizens.

In a sense, Congress and the Republican administration rescued America's military leaders from their folly by making drastic cuts in both services. So long as officers clung, however, to the skeleton of a much larger land force and a naval organization based upon the supposed superiority of the battleship, even the cuts stimulated little real progress toward the adoption of new weapons and the application of new tactical concepts. Both adjustments had to await the eve of a second world war.

Misjudging the national mood, military officers ignored the gradual creation of modest forces incorporating the actual lessons of the recent conflict in favor of maintenance of a large army and navy built along traditional European lines. By asking for more strength than the situation demanded and of a type suited more to the past war than foreseeable future needs, America's postwar military leaders may well have denied Congress the opportunity to approve a more modest force organized to exploit both the forthcoming mechanization of warfare and the airplane's introduction of a third dimension to battle.

Nevertheless, as budget cuts and developments abroad eventually forced the American armed forces to face the dawn of a new era in warfare, their leaders could fall back upon a tradition of modest and realistic adaptation of the nation's military policy to national traditions, the international situation, and technological change.

That earlier practice had avoided any effort to reproduce the vast military establishments of the European states, despite the very real dangers posed by the militarism and imperialism characteristic of the four decades preceding World War I. To compensate for the relatively small army and navy recommended by prewar reformers, military officers had recognized and relied upon the advantages inherent in America's geographic and political position and its great industrial and financial power, and they simply adapted America's modest military establishment to anticipated changes in the international order.

After exposure to the costs of a too active globalism during the decade following the war with Spain, officers had once again focused their attention on the defense of the Western Hemisphere and depended upon less violent instruments of policy to secure interests lying outside the nation's sphere. Though emphasizing the deterrent value of adequate armed strength, those officers also acknowledged the futility of seeking absolute security. Regarding preparedness as a form of national insurance, reformers had prudently balanced the social and economic costs of the military establishment against a carefully calculated assessment of both the possible harm of remaining less than fully prepared and the probability of an attack upon the United States.

The officers who guided the reform of American military policy from the Grant era through the close of the Wilson administration often erred in the fine points of their analyses and the details of their programs, but they set American military policy upon the proper path during the decisive period when the nation and its armed forces came of age. Their modest, adaptive approach, which gave full attention to both the international and domestic dimensions of military policy, established a pattern suitable for emulation by subsequent generations of military leaders.

APPENDIX

List of Equivalent Ranks

United States Army and United States Marine Corps	United States Navy*
General	Admiral
Lieutenant General	Vice Admiral
Major General	Rear Admiral
Brigadier General	Commodore†
Colonel	Captain
Lieutenant Colonel	Commander
Major	Lieutenant Commander
Captain	Lieutenant
First Lieutenant	Lieutenant (Junior Grade)‡
Second Lieutenant	Ensign

*A naval staff officer had both a title descriptive of his duty and a relative rank comparable to one of the line officer ranks listed above. The Pay and Medical Corps titles were: PAY and MEDICAL DIRECTOR (Captain); PAY and MEDICAL INSPECTOR (Commander); PAYMASTER and SURGEON (Lieutenant Commander); PASSED ASSISTANT PAYMASTER and SURGEON (Lieutenant); and ASSISTANT PAYMASTER and SURGEON (Ensign). The Engineer (until its 1899 amalgamation with the navy's line officers) and Construction Corps titles were: CHIEF ENGINEER and CONSTRUCTOR (Lieutenant Commander, Commander, or Captain); PASSED ASSISTANT ENGINEER (Lieutenant); ASSISTANT ENGINEER (Ensign); and ASSISTANT CONSTRUCTOR (Ensign or Lieutenant). The chief of each staff bureau normally ranked as a Commodore or Rear Admiral.

†Commodore was discontinued in 1899.

‡Lieutenants, junior grade (j.g.), were known as Masters until 1884.

195

Abbreviations

AGO	Adjutant General's Office
A&N Journal	*Army and Navy Journal*
Annals	*The Annals of the American Academy of Political and Social Science*
AR (year)	*Annual Report* for (year), Association of Graduates, U.S. Military Academy
Army Register (year)	*Official Army Register* (issued annually)
Army Regulations (year)	*Regulations for the Army of the United States* (issued periodically)
ARND (year)	*Annual Reports of the Navy Department* (issued annually; title varies)
Arty, J. or *Artillery Journal*	*Journal of the United States Artillery*
ARWD (year)	*Annual Report of the War Department* (issued annually; title varies)
Atlantic	*Atlantic Monthly*
Cav. J. or *Cavalry Journal*	*Journal of the United States Cavalry Association*
Century	*Century Magazine*
Cong. Rec.	*Congressional Record*
DAB	*Dictionary of American Biography*
Forum	*The Forum*

Harper's	*Harper's New Monthly Magazine*
Inf. J. or *Infantry Journal*	*Journal of the United States Infantry Association*
JMSIUS	*Journal of the Military Service Institution of the United States*
LOC	Library of Congress (Manuscript Division), Washington, D.C.
Military Affairs	*Military Affairs: The Journal of the American Military Institution*
N. Amer. Rev.	*North American Review*
Navy Register (year)	*Register of the Commissioned, Warrant, and Volunteer Officers of the Navy of the United States, Including Officers of the Marine Corps, and Others* (issued annually)
Navy Regulations (year)	*Regulations for the Government of the Navy of the United States* (issued periodically)
NG	National Guard
NHF	Naval Historical Foundation collections deposited with the Library of Congress (Manuscript Division), Washington, D.C.
N.S.	New Series
PUSNI	*Proceedings of the United States Naval Institute*
RG 38	National Archives, Record Group 38, Records of the Office of the Chief of Naval Operations
RG 45	National Archives, Record Group 45, Naval Records Collection of the Office of Naval Records and Library
RG 80	National Archives, Record Group 80, General Records of the Department of the Navy
RG 94	National Archives, Record Group 94, Records of the Adjutant General's Office, 1780s–1917
RG 107	National Archives, Record Group 107, Records of the Office of the Secretary of War
RG 108	National Archives, Record Group 108, Records of the Headquarters of the Army
RG 165	National Archives, Record Group 165, Records of the War Department General and Special Staffs
Scribner's	*Scribner's Magazine*
United Service	*The United Service: A Quarterly Review of Military and Naval Affairs* (subtitle varies)
USA	United States Army
USMA Register (year)	*Register of Graduates and Former Cadets of the United States Military Academy* (issued annually)

USMC	United States Marine Corps
USN	United States Navy
USNR	United States Naval Reserve
USV	United States [Army] Volunteers
WCD	War College Division, War Department General Staff

Notes

Preface, pp. xi–xv

1. Richard D. Brown, *Modernization: The Transformation of American Life, 1600–1865* (New York: Hill and Wang, 1976), has applied that characterization to nearly three centuries of national life.
2. Brown, *Modernization*, pp. 12–16.
3. This and the next three paragraphs are based upon: Walter T. K. Nugent, *From Centennial to World War: American Society, 1876–1917* (Indianapolis: Bobbs-Merrill, 1977); Robert H. Wiebe, *The Search for Order, 1877–1920* (New York: Hill and Wang, 1967); Samuel P. Hays, *The Response to Industrialism: 1885–1914* (Chicago: University of Chicago Press, 1957).

Chapter 1: The Turning Point, pp. 3–18

1. "Gen. Liggett Dies; World War Hero," *New York Times,* December 31, 1935, p. 15; "Obituaries," *A&N Journal,* January 4, 1936, p. 356.
2. *AR* (1936), p. 125; *USMA Register* (1970), pp. 276–77; *ARWD* (1879), I, 18–31; Frederic V. Abbot, *History of the Class of 'Seventy-nine* (New York: G. P. Putnam's Sons, 1884); Robert M. Utley, *Frontier Regulars:*

The United States Army and the Indian, 1866–1891 (New York: Macmillan, 1973).

3. Ibid., pp. 80–87; Major General James Parker, USA, *The Old Army: Memories, 1872–1918* (Philadelphia: Dorrance, 1929), p. 24.

4. Utley, *Frontier Regulars,* pp. 88–90; Lieutenant Colonel Otto Hein, USA, *Memories of Long Ago* (New York: G. P. Putnam's Sons, 1925), p. 140.

5. Sherman, *ARWD* (1883), I, 45; Lincoln, *ARWD* (1884), I, 5; Schofield, *ARWD* (1890), I, 43–44.

6. *United Service,* XI (November 1884), 567; Holabird, "Some Thoughts about the Future of Our Army," *United Service,* VIII (January 1883), 17; Captain Carl Reichmann, "In Pace Para Bellum," *Inf. J.,* II (January 1906), 4.

7. Russell F. Weigley, *The American Way of War: A History of United States Military Strategy and Policy* (New York: Macmillan, 1973), p. 167; Sherman, *ARWD* (1880), I, 5.

8. Schofield, *ARWD* (1887), I, 115; Colonel Henry L. Abbot, *Course of Lectures upon the Defence of the Sea-Coast of the United States* (New York: D. Van Nostrand, 1888), p. 141; Chief of Engineers Thomas L. Casey, *ARWD* (1891), II, part 1, 4; U.S., War Department, "Report of the Board on Fortifications or Other Defenses," *ARWD* (1886), II, part 1, appendix 3, 499; Emanuel R. Lewis, *Seacoast Fortifications of the United States: An Introductory History* (Washington, D.C.: Smithsonian Institution Press, 1970), pp. 37–72.

9. Utley, *Frontier Regulars,* pp. 69–77.

10. *ARWD* (1879), I, 18–22.

11. *ARWD* (1879), I, 18–31; Russell F. Weigley, *Towards an American Army: Military Thought from Washington to Marshall* (New York: Columbia University Press, 1962), pp. 137–38, 340–41; General Staff to Lieutenant General John M. Schofield, November 3, 1903, Schofield Papers, LOC, Subject File, container 66.

12. Lieutenant General John M. Schofield, *Forty-six Years in the Army* (New York: Century, 1897), pp. 520–21.

13. James E. Hewes, Jr., *From Root to McNamara: Army Organization and Administration, 1900–1963* (Washington: Center of Military History, 1975), pp. 3–6.

14. Walter Millis, ed., *American Military Thought* (Indianapolis: Bobbs-Merrill, 1966), p. xxxiii.

15. Kautz, "What the United States Army Should Be," *Century,* XXXVI (October 1888), 935.

16. Material on Sims in this and subsequent paragraphs has been drawn from Elting E. Morison, *Admiral Sims and the Modern American Navy* (Boston: Houghton Mifflin, 1942).

17. Harold Sprout and Margaret Sprout, *The Rise of American Naval Power,*

1776-1918 (Princeton: Princeton University Press, 1939), pp. 166–68.

18. Ibid.; Kenneth J. Hagan, *American Gunboat Diplomacy and the Old Navy, 1877-1889* (Westport: Greenwood Press, 1973).

19. Fiske, *From Midshipman to Rear Admiral* (New York: Century, 1919), p. 71.

20. Ibid., pp. 22, 26.

21. Weigley, *American Way of War,* p. 186; George T. Davis, *A Navy Second to None; The Development of Modern American Naval Policy* (New York: Harcourt, Brace, 1940), pp. 176–77.

22. Weigley, *American Way of War,* p. 167; Charles O. Paullin, "A Half Century of Naval Administration in America, 1861-1911," *PUSNI,* XXXIX (September 1913), 1217–33; Edward W. Very, *Navies of the World* (New York: John Wiley, 1880), pp. 131, 134.

23. Porter, *ARND* (1881), pp. 95–96, 99; Chandler, *ARND* (1882), I, 7; *DAB,* VIII, pp. 85–89.

24. *ARND* (1882), I, 33, tabulated the decline of the American merchant marine's share of the nation's carrying trade as follows:

Year	Portion (%) of U.S. Trade Carried in American Ships	Year	Portion (%) of U.S. Trade Carried in American Ships
1840	82.0	1865	27.7
1845	81.7	1870	35.6
1850	72.5	1875	25.8
1855	75.6	1880	17.4
1860	66.5	1881	16.0
	CIVIL WAR	1882	15.5

25. Kelley, *The Question of Ships: The Navy and the Merchant Marine* (New York: Charles Scribner's Sons, 1884), p. 140; Calkins, "Our Merchant Marine; the Causes of Its Decline and the Means to Be Taken for Its Revival," 1882 Honorable Mention Essay, *PUSNI,* VIII (1882), 73.

26. Wagner, "The Military Necessities of the United States, and the Best Provisions for Meeting Them," Prize Essay, *JMSIUS,* V (September 1884), 238.

27. Boies, "Our National Guard," *Harper's,* LX (May 1880), 918 [Boies's italics].

28. Sampson, "Outline Scheme for the Naval Defense of the Coast," *PUSNI,* XV (1889), 178; Griffin, "Our Sea-Coast Defences," *JMSIUS,* VII (December 1886), 416.

29. Schofield, *ARWD* (1894), I, 62. See also Jim Dan Hill, *The Minute Man in Peace and War: A History of the National Guard* (Harrisburg: Stackpole, 1964), pp. 132–36, 141–44, 173, 180ff, and Harold T. Wieand,

"The History of the Development of the United States Naval Reserve, 1889–1941" (Ph.D. dissertation, University of Pittsburgh, 1953), pp. 14–17, 20–23, 42–77.

30. Foster Rhea Dulles, *Prelude to World Power: American Diplomatic History, 1860–1900* (New York: Macmillan, 1965), pp. 163–64.

31. Evans, *A Sailor's Log: Reflections of Forty Years of Naval Life* (New York: D. Appleton, 1901), pp. 171–72; Schroeder, *A Half Century of Naval Service* (New York: D. Appleton, 1922), p. 74.

32. "The Chilians at Callao," *A&N Journal*, XVII (June 12, 1880), 922–23; "Bombardment at Callao, Peru," *A&N Journal*, XVII (July 3, 1880), 989–90; "Engagements off Callao, Peru," *A&N Journal*, XVII (July 10, 1880), 1002–3; "Let Alone Policy," *A&N Journal*, XVII (July 17, 1880), 1026; "Coast Defence," *A&N Journal*, XVIII (October 9, 1880), 186; "Our National Danger," *A&N Journal*, XX (February 24, 1883), 671–72; Captain Francis V. Greene, USA, "Our Defenceless Coasts," *Scribner's*, I (January 1887), 63.

33. Russell F. Weigley, *History of the United States Army* (New York: Macmillan, 1967), pp. 560–61, 567–68; *ARND* (1880), pp. 6, 10; *ARND* (1922), pp. 12, 17, 765; Passed Assistant Engineer N. B. Clark, "Discussion," *PUSNI*, VII (1881), 454, was one of the naval officers ranking the U. S. Navy below that of Chile.

34. Note 1, above; *DAB*, XI, part 1, 494–95; *AR* (1936), 125–27.

35. *DAB*, XI, part 2, 616.

36. *AR* (1936), 126; Morison, *Admiral Sims*, p. 4.

Chapter 2: The Debate Over Missions, pp. 19–40

1. Ensign Washington I. Chambers, USN, "The Reconstruction and Increase of the Navy," 1884 Prize Essay, *PUSNI*, XI (1885), 7 [Chambers's italics deleted].

2. Kenneth J. Hagan, *American Gunboat Diplomacy and the Old Navy, 1877–1889* (Westport: Greenwood Press, 1973), pp. 3–9.

3. Ibid., pp. 9–10.

4. *ARND* (1881), p. 29.

5. Ibid., pp. 35–36, 38.

6. Walter LaFeber, *The New Empire: An Interpretation of American Expansion, 1860–1898* (Ithaca: Cornell University Press, 1963), pp. 1–53; Foster Rhea Dulles, *Prelude to World Power: American Diplomatic History, 1860–1900* (New York: Collier Books, 1965), pp. 37–42, 76–96, 119–33.

7. Hunt, *ARND* (1881), p. 3; Thompson, *ARND* (1880), p. 25; Captain Edward Field, USA, "Our Coast Defenses," *United Service*, N.S., III (January 1890), 2–3; Harold Sprout and Margaret Sprout, *The Rise of*

American Naval Power, 1776–1918 (Princeton: Princeton University Press, 1939), pp. 183–86; George T. Davis, *A Navy Second to None: The Development of Modern American Naval Policy* (New York: Harcourt, Brace, 1940), p. 37.

8. *ARND* (1881), pp. 29, 37; Walter R. Herrick, Jr., *The American Naval Revolution* (Baton Rouge: Louisiana State University Press, 1966), pp. 27–28.

9. U.S., Congress, Senate, *Letter from the Secretary of the Navy Transmitting . . . the Report of the Naval Advisory Board, Organized Under the Act of August 5, 1882,* S. Ex. Doc. 74, 47th Cong., 2d sess., 1883.

10. Sprout and Sprout, *Rise of Naval Power,* pp. 188–89.

11. Miller, "Discussion of the Prize Essay of 1881," *PUSNI,* VII (1881), 457.

12. *ARND* (1881), pp. 44, 102; Dewey, *Autobiography of George Dewey, Admiral of the Navy* (New York: Charles Scribner's Sons, 1913), pp. 159, 161–62; Lieutenant Richard Wainwright, USN, "Our Naval Policy," *United Service,* N.S., II (September 1889), 234–39; Rear Admiral Albert Gleaves, USN, *Life and Letters of Rear Admiral Stephen B. Luce* (New York: G. P. Putnam's Sons, 1925), pp. 254–64.

13. *ARND* (1881), p. 39; Porter, *ARND* (1883), I, 393; Barber, "A Practical Method . . . ," *PUSNI,* XII (1886), 421 [Barber's italics]; Chambers, "Reconstruction," *PUSNI,* XI, 27–30.

14. Ibid., pp. 14–21, 35, 45–46; Rear Admiral Stephen B. Luce, USN, "Our Future Navy," *PUSNI,* XV (1889), 541–59; Professor James R. Soley, USN, "Our Naval Policy—A Lesson from 1861," *Scribner's,* I (February 1887), 223–35.

15. Clark, "Discussion," *PUSNI,* VII (1881), 454.

16. Simpson, "The Navy and Its Prospects for Rehabilitation," *PUSNI,* XII (1886), 7; Mason, "Discussion," *PUSNI,* XI (1885), 70–71; Smith, "Disposition and Employment of the Fleet . . . ," 1891 Honorable Mention Essay, *PUSNI,* XVII (1891), 122; Porter, *ARND* (1887), p. 42, and *ARND* (1885), I, 274.

17. Lieutenant Frank M. Bennett, USN, *The Monitor and the Navy under Steam* (Boston: Houghton Mifflin, 1900), pp. 256–62; Tracy, *ARND* (1889), pp. 3–13.

18. Ibid., pp. 3–5, 11.

19. Ibid., pp. 11–13.

20. Ibid., p. 4.

21. U.S., Congress, Senate, *Report of the Policy Board,* S. Ex. Doc. 43, 51st Cong., 1st sess., 1890, pp. 3–11, 56–58.

22. Ibid., pp. 3–4.

23. (American Century Series ed.; New York: Hill and Wang, 1957), chap. 1.

24. Ibid., pp. 22–25.

25. Ibid., p. 23.

26. Ibid., pp. 37, 73.

27. Ibid., pp. 23, 29–30, 37, 40–43.

28. Ibid., p. 75.

29. Chester, "Standing Armies a Necessity of Civilization," *United Service*, IX (December 1883), 666.

30. Schofield, *ARWD* (1894), I, 59; Howard, *ARWD* (1894), I, 102.

31. "What the Army Asks," *A&N Journal*, XXXII (November 24, 1894), 198; Sherman quoted in Samuel P. Huntington, *The Soldier and the State: The Theory and Politics of Civil-Military Relations* (Cambridge: Belknap Press of the Harvard University Press, 1957), p. 231; Lieutenant Arthur L. Wagner, USA, "The Military and Naval Policy of the United States," *JMSIUS*, VII (December 1880), 396.

32. *ARWD* (1887), I, 118ff; *ARWD* (1888), I, 65; *ARWD* (1894), I, 58–59.

33. E. g., Captain Henry R. Brinkerhoff, USA, "A Plea for the Increase of the Army," *United Service*, N.S., XIV (December 1895), 493–94; Lieutenant Colonel Harry C. Egbert, USA, "Is an Increase of the Regular Army Necessary?," *United Service*, N.S., XVI (November 1896), 380–84; Major George S. Wilson, USA, "The Army . . .," 1896 Infantry Society Prize Essay, *JMSIUS*, XVIII (May 1896), 477–506.

34. *Address by General W. T. Sherman, General-of-the-Army, to the Class of 1880, United States Artillery School, Fort Monroe, VA, April 28th, 1880* (n.p.; n.d.), p. 6, in Sherman Papers, LOC, Letterbooks, vol. 94.

35. Sherman to Secretary of War William C. Endicott, March 31, 1885, Sherman Papers, LOC, Letterbooks, vol. 97; Schofield to Secretary of War Stephen B. Elkins, January 26, 1893, Schofield Papers, LOC, Letters Sent, cont. 57.

36. "Artillery Practice," *A&N Journal*, XXI (August 25, 1883), 71; Sherman to Endicott, March 31, 1885, Sherman Papers, LOC, Letterbooks, vol. 97; Schofield to Elkins, May 7, 1892, Schofield Papers, LOC, Letters Sent, cont. 56.

37. "The Regulars and the Militia," *A&N Journal*, XVIII (January 29, 1881), 526–27; "Eighteen Hundred and Eighty-four, *A&N Journal*, XXII (January 3, 1885), 439; "The Militia Bill," *A&N Journal*, XXVII (January 18, 1890), 423; Commanding General Philip H. Sheridan's speech to the Philadelphia Centennial Celebration reprinted in *A&N Journal*, XXV (October 1, 1887), 188.

38. *ARWD* (1895), I, 70.

39. Lieutenant Colonel Joseph P. Sanger to War College Board, September 12, 1900, RG 94, AGO File No. 311224; Lieutenant Alfred C. Sharpe, USA, "Military Training In Colleges," *JMSIUS*, VIII (December 1887), 405–13; Gene M. Lyons and John W. Masland, "The Origins of ROTC," *Military Affairs*, XXIII (Spring 1959), 1–12.

40. "What the United States Army Should Be," *Century*, XXXVI (October

1888), 934–39, and "Military Education for the Masses," *JMSIUS*, XVII (November 1895), 492–93.

41. Major General Nelson A. Miles, *ARWD* (1895), I, 70; "What We Need," *A&N Journal,* XXVI (November 24, 1888), 251.

42. Luce to his son-in-law, Lieutenant Boutell Noyes, USN, July 19, 1883, Luce Papers, LOC, General Correspondence, cont. 8; Huntington, *Soldier and the State,* pp. 230–54; Timothy K. Nenninger, *The Leavenworth Schools and The Old Army: Education, Professionalism, and the Officer Corps of the United States Army, 1881–1918* (Westport: Greenwood Press, 1978), pp. 21–52; Gleaves, *Life and Letters of Luce,* pp. 98–103, 168–71.

43. Russell F. Weigley, "The Elihu Root Reforms and the Progressive Era," in William Geffen, ed., *Command and Commanders in Modern Warfare* (Washington: U.S. Government Printing Office, 1971), pp. 15–17; Magali S. Larson, *The Rise of Professionalism: A Sociological Analysis* (Berkeley: University of California Press, 1977), pp. 1–12, 17, 25–31; Corinne L. Gilb, *Hidden Hierarchies: The Professions and Government* (New York: Harper and Row, 1966), pp. 16–17.

44. Robert H. Wiebe, *The Search for Order, 1877–1920* (New York: Hill and Wang, 1967), pp. 111–32; Samuel P. Hays, "The New Organizational Society," in Jerry Israel, ed., *Building the Organizational Society: Essays on Associational Activities in Modern America* (New York: The Free Press, 1972), pp. 1–15.

45. Larson, *Rise of Professionalism,* pp. 17, 136–77.

46. Richard A. Andrews, "Years of Frustration: William T. Sherman, the Army and Reform, 1869–1883 (Ph.D. dissertation, Northwestern University, 1968), chap. viii; Huntington, *Soldier and the State,* chaps. i, ix.

47. *Address of General W. T. Sherman, to the Officers and Soldiers Composing the School of Application at Fort Leavenworth, Kansas, 25 October 1882* (n.p.; n.d.), p. 5, Sherman Papers, LOC, Letterbooks, vol. 96.

48. Schofield to the Military Service Institution, 1880, Schofield Papers, LOC, Speech, Articles, and Book File, vol. 93.

49. Sherman, *Address . . . to Class of 1880 . . . ,* p. 5 [Sherman's italics]; "The Needs of the Army," *A&N Journal,* XXVI (August 17, 1889), 1046.

50. Chief of Engineers Horatio G. Wright, USA, *ARWD* (1882), II, part 1, 5.

51. U.S., Congress, House, *Report of the Board on Fortifications or Other Defenses,* H. Ex. Doc. 49, 49th Cong., 1st sess., 1886, I, 3, 28–29.

52. *ARWD* (1891), I, 57.

53. "Some Hints for the Army," *A&N Journal,* XXI (October 20, 1883), 231; "Divisions and Departments," *A&N Journal,* XXVII (July 19, 1890), 879; Major General John M. Schofield to Secretary of War William C. Endicott, March 18, 1886, Schofield Papers, LOC, Letters Sent, cont. 60.

54. Dulles, *Prelude,* pp. 81–93.

55. Schofield, *ARWD* (1894), I, 61–63; Miles, *ARWD* (1895), I, 67.

56. Lieutenant George P. Scriven, USA, "The Army and Its Relation to the Organized and Unorganized Militia," *United Service*, N.S., I (May 1889), 521–25; Lieutenant Joseph B. Batchelor, Jr., USA, "A United States Army," Graduating Thesis of the United States Infantry and Cavalry School, *JMSIUS*, XIII (January 1892), 54; "Japan's Ambition," *A&N Journal*, XXXIV (August 21, 1897), 954.

57. *ARWD* (1890), I, 44, 47–48; *ARWD* (1894), I, 63; *Forty-six Years in the Army* (New York: Century, 1897), p. 528.

Chapter 3: The Reform Impulse, pp. 41–62

1. Lieutenant George B. Duncan, USA, "Reasons for Increasing the Regular Army," *N. Amer. Rev.*, CLXVI (April 1898), 545; Major George S. Wilson, USA, "The Army: Its Employment During Time of Peace, and the Necessity of Its Increase," 1896 Infantry Society Prize Essay, *JMSIUS*, XVIII (May 1896), 494 (18); Brigadier General John C. Kelton, USA, "Requirements for National Defense," *Forum*, VIII (November 1889), 317; Lieutenant General John M. Schofield, USA, undated, c. 1896, memorandum entitled "The Monroe Doctrine," Schofield Papers, LOC, Speech, Article, and Book File, cont. 94; Captain Alfred T. Mahan, USN, "The Future in Relation to American Naval Power," *Harper's*, XCI (October 1895), 775, and "The United States Looking Outward," *Atlantic*, LXVI (December 1890), pp. 817–18, 820–22; Captain William T. Sampson, USN, "Outline of a Scheme for the Naval Defense of the Coast," *PUSNI*, XV (1889), 179; Lieutenant Chapman C. Todd, USN, "Some Needs of the Navy," *United Service*, VII (July 1882), 87; Admiral David D. Porter, USN, *ARND* (1887), p. 33.

2. Price, "The Necessity for Closer Relations between the Army and People, and the Best Method to Accomplish the Result," 1884 Prize Essay, *JMSIUS*, VI (December 1885), 321.

3. Gorringe, "The Navy," *N. Amer. Rev.*, CXXXIV (May 1882), 487.

4. Lieutenant Henry W. Lyon, USN, "Our Rifled Ordnance," *PUSNI*, VI (1880), 13; Sampson, "Outline Scheme," *PUSNI*, XV, 178–79; Mahan, "Looking Outward," *Atlantic*, LXVI, pp. 819–22; Brig. Gen. Samuel B. Holabird, USA, "Some Thoughts about the Future of Our Army," *United Service*, VIII (January 1883), 26; Lieutenant John A. Harman, USA, "Our Frontier Canals," *United Service*, N.S., XIV (October 1895), 362; "Our Control of an Inter-Oceanic Canal," *A&N Journal*, XXII (December 20, 1884), 399.

5. Wilson, "The Army," *JMSIUS*, XVIII, 494 (18)–496 (19). On diplomacy see Foster Rhea Dulles, *Prelude to World Power: American Diplomatic History, 1860–1900* (New York: Macmillan, 1965), pp. 61–181.

6. "The Duty of Congress," *A&N Journal*, XXXIII (December 21, 1895), 271.

7. On antimilitarism, see Arthur A. Ekirch, Jr., *The Civilian and the Military* (New York: Oxford University Press, 1956).

8. *A&N Journal*, XXVII (May 31, 1890), 760.

9. ARND (1882), I, 8–9, 27–31; *ARND* (1883), I, 32–41, 406–9; *ARND* (1884), I, 46–48; *ARND* (1889), I, 46–48; "The Navy and the Revenue Marine," *A&N Journal*, XX (September 16, 1882), 150; "The Revenue Marine and the Navy," *A&N Journal*, XXIV (July 9, 1887), 998–99; Lieutenant Carlos G. Calkins, USN, "How May the Sphere of Usefulness of Naval Officers Be Extended in Time of Peace with Advantage to the Country and the Naval Service?," 1883 Prize Essay, *PUSNI*, IX (1883), 155–94.

10. "The Navy and the Diplomatic Service," *A&N Journal*, XXXII (October 27, 1894), 140–41.

11. *A&N Journal*, XXIX (May 14, 1892), 662, and XXIX (May 21, 1892), 683.

12. General William T. Sherman, USA, to Major General John M. Schofield, USA, November 21, 1888, Sherman Papers, LOC, Letterbooks, vol. 98; Assistant Quartermaster General Samuel B. Holabird, USA, "The Future of Our Army," *A&N Journal*, XX (March 24, 1883), 767; Lieutenant General Philip H. Sheridan, USA, to Senator John A. Logan, March 25, 1886, Sheridan Papers, LOC, Letterbooks, cont. 44, and *ARWD* (1887), I, 79; Schofield to Secretary of War Redfield Proctor, January 30, 1891, Schofield Papers, LOC, Letters Sent, cont. 55, *ARWD* (1887), I, 120–21, and *ARWD* (1889), I, 65; Adjutant General George D. Ruggles, USA, "The Proposed Increase of the Army," *N. Amer. Rev.*, CLIX (December 1894), 728–34.

13. Brigadier General William H. Carter, USA, "The War Department: Military Administration," *Scribner's*, XXXIII (June, 1903), 669; *ARWD* (1883), I, 46–47; *ARWD* (1884), I, 48; *ARWD* (1889), I, 23; *ARWD* (1891), I, 16; *ARWD* (1895), I, 10, 14–15, 123.

14. *ARND* (1889), I, 35, 87–88; *ARND* (1894), pp. 22–24; "The Squadron of Evolution," *A&N Journal*, XXVII (October 19, 1889), 146–47; "Naval Programme for the Summer," *A&N Journal*, XXXIII (May 16, 1896), 668; "Naval Maneuvers Proposed," *A&N Journal*, XXXIII (August 1, 1896), 872.

15. Captain Joseph P. Sanger, USA, "Resumé of Artillery Target Practice in the Division of the Atlantic, 1887," Schofield Papers, LOC, Letters Sent, cont. 52; Major General John M. Schofield, USA, *ARWD* (1887), I, 114–15; Lieutenant William S. Sims, USN, to his mother, January 24, 1898, Sims Papers, NHF, Personal Correspondence, cont. 4; Rear Admiral Yates Stirling, USN, *Sea Duty: The Memoirs of a Fighting Admiral* (New York: G. P. Putnam's Sons, 1939), pp. 94, 104–5; Commodore John G.

Walker, USN, to Rear Admiral Stephen B. Luce, USN, September 30, 1887, Luce Papers, LOC, General Correspondence, cont. 8.

16. Captain Alfred T. Mahan, USN, *From Sail to Steam: Recollections of Naval Life* (New York: Harper & Brothers, 1907), p. 271; Rear Admiral Stephen B. Luce, USN, typescript of address at Naval War College, June 2, 1906, Luce Papers, LOC, Subject File, cont. 19; "Autumnal Manoeuvres," *A&N Journal*, XXV (August 6, 1887), 29; "Training for Field Service," *A&N Journal*, XXVI (March 16, 1889), 581; "Military Instruction," *A&N Journal*, XXXIV (January 9, 1897), 318.

17. Wagner, "The Fort Riley Maneuvers," *JMSIUS*, XXXII (January–February 1903), 70; Hermann Hagedorn, *Leonard Wood: A Biography* (2 vols.; New York: Harper, 1931), I, 116–17; "Practical Instruction for the Army," *A&N Journal*, XXV (September 3, 1887), 107.

18. Scott, *Some Memories of a Soldier* (New York: Century, 1928), p. 137; Captain J. B. Babcock, USA, "Field Exercises and the Necessity for an Authorized Manual of Field Duties," *JMSIUS*, XII (September 1891), 942–46; Pope, "Comment and Criticism," *JMSIUS*, XII (September 1891), 1033; Don E. Alberts, "General Wesley Merritt: Nineteenth Century Cavalryman" (Ph.D. dissertation, University of New Mexico, 1975), pp. 389–92.

19. Livermore, "Military and Naval Maneuvers," *JMSIUS*, IX (December 1888), 421, 426–27; Schofield to Luce, November 29, 1887, and Luce to the secretary of the navy, July 28, 1888, Luce Papers, LOC, General Correspondence, cont. 8 and 9; "Autumnal Manoeuvres Provided For," *A&N Journal*, XXV (January 21, 1888), 510; Lieutenant J. F. Meigs, USN, to the secretary of the navy, January 4, 1890, RG 45, Entry 464, OJ, Box 3; "Union of Army, Navy and Militia," *A&N Journal*, XXV (August 6, 1887), 27.

20. Lieutenant William L. Sachse, USNR, "Our Naval Attaché System: Its Origins and Development to 1917," *PUSNI*, LXXII (May 1946), 661–72; Elizabeth Bethel, "The Military Information Division: Origin of the Intelligence Division," *Military Affairs*, XI (Spring 1947), 17–24.

21. Belknap, "Some Aspects of Naval Administration in War, with Its Attendant Belongings of Peace," *PUSNI*, XXIV (June 1898), 269–70.

22. Luce to his son-in-law, Lieutenant Boutelle Noyes, USN, July 19, 1883, Luce Papers, LOC, General Correspondence, cont. 8.

23. *Address of General W. T. Sherman, General-of-the-Army, to the Class of 1880, United States Artillery School, Fort Monroe, VA, April 28th 1880* (n.p.; n.d.), Sherman Papers, LOC, Letterbooks, vol. 96; Lieutenant General Philip H. Sheridan, USA, to Secretary of War William C. Endicott, November 10, 1885, Sheridan Papers, LOC, Letterbooks, cont. 44; Colonel John C. Tidball, USA, *ARWD* (1887), I, 190.

24. Wagner, "The Military Necessities of the United States, and the Best

Provisions for Meeting Them,'' 1883 Prize Essay, *JMSIUS*, V (September 1884), 241; Dewey, *Autobiography of George Dewey, Admiral of the Navy* (New York: Charles Scribner's Sons, 1913), p. 154.

25. *Army Register* (1890), pp. 85, 105, 145; *Navy Register* (1890), p. 24.

26. Dewey, *Autobiography*, p. 158; Major General James Parker, USA, *The Old Army: Memories, 1872-1918* (Philadelphia: Dorrance, 1929), pp. 23–31; Carter, "Infantry in War," *United Service*, 3d Ser., IV (July 1903), 7; Marsh to Lieutenant (j.g.) Washington I. Chambers, USN, August 18, 1883, and June 10, 1886, Chambers Papers, NHF, General Correspondence, cont. 5.

27. Colonel William A. Ganoe, USA, *The History of the United States Army* (New York: D. Appleton, 1924), pp. 355, 461; Peter Karsten, "Armed Progressives: The Military Reorganizes for the American Century," in *Building the Organizational Society: Essays in Associational Activities in Modern America*, ed. by Jerry Israel (New York: The Free Press, 1972), pp. 197–232, and *The Naval Aristocracy: The Golden Age of Annapolis and the Emergence of Modern American Navalism* (New York: The Free Press, 1972), chap. vi.

28. Karsten, "Armed Progressives," *Organizational Society*, pp. 203, 217–19, and *Naval Aristocracy*, pp. 289n and 326n. Calculations are based upon: articles used in preparation of this study; *Army Register* (1890), pp. 245–55; and *Navy Register* (1890), pp. 4–33.

29. Karsten, "Armed Progressives," *Organizational Society*, pp. 208–9, 221. Positions of various officers on reform are drawn from sources used in preparation of this study.

30. Walter Millis, *Arms and Men: A Study in American Military History* (New York: G. P. Putnam's Sons, 1956), pp. 134, 141, 147–48, 158; Russell F. Weigley, *The Amerian Way of War: A History of United States Military Strategy and Policy* (New York: Macmillan, 1973), p. 169.

31. Sherman, *ARWD* (1880), I, 5; Gibbon, "The Danger to the Country from the Lack of Preparation for War," *JMSIUS*, XI (January 1890), 21 [Gibbon's italics]; Greene, "Our Defenceless Coasts," *Scribner's*, I (January 1887), 52–53; Sampson, "Outline Scheme," *PUSNI*, XV, 172.

32. Mahan, "Looking Outward," *Atlantic*, LXVI, p. 82; Carter, "Interdependence of Political and Military Policies," *N. Amer. Rev.*, CXCIV (July 1911), 840–41.

33. E.g., Captain Henry R. Brinkerhoff, USA, "A Plea for the Increase of the Army," *United Service*, N.S., XIV (December 1895), 496–98; Lieutenant Colonel Harry C. Egbert, USA, "Is an Increase of the Regular Army Necessary?," *United Service*, N.S., XVI (November 1896), 393–95; Wilson, "The Army," *JMSIUS*, XVIII, 504 (28).

34. Millis, *Arms and Men*, p. 147.

35. *ARWD* (1880), I, xviii–xx; *ARWD* (1881), I, 16–17; *ARWD* (1885), I,

25–26; *ARWD* (1889), I, 17–19; *ARND* (1881), pp. 3–6; *ARND* (1882), I, 5–7; *ARND* (1888), pp. iii–iv; *ARND* (1889), I, 3–6, 10–14.

36. Arthur, December 6, 1881, and December 1, 1884, annual messages to Congress, in James D. Richardson, *A Compilation of the Messages and Papers of the Presidents, 1789–1890* (11 vols; Washington: Bureau of National Literature and Art, 1908), VIII, 41, 51–52, and VIII, 248; Cleveland, December 8, 1885, and December 6, 1886, annual messages to Congress, in ibid., VIII, 351, and VIII, 514.

37. Tilden to New York governor David B. Hill, March 28, 1886, in John Bigelow, ed., *Letters and Literary Memorials of Samuel J. Tilden* (2 vols; New York: Harper & Brothers, 1908), II, 715–17.

38. McAdoo, February 28, 1885, *Cong. Rec.*, XVI, 2310; Curtin, February 28, 1885, ibid., 2316.

39. "The Monroe Doctrine and the Isthmian Canal," *N. Amer. Rev.*, CXXX (May 1880), 499.

40. *Atlantic*, LIII (June 1884), 860; Kasson, "The Monroe Doctrine in 1881," *N. Amer. Rev.*, CXXXIII (December 1881), 523–33.

41. John A. S. Grenville and George Berkeley Young, *Politics, Strategy, and American Diplomacy: Studies in Foreign Policy, 1873–1917* (New Haven: Yale University Press, 1966), pp. xi–xviii, 76–77, 83.

42. Kenneth J. Hagan, *American Gunboat Diplomacy and the Old Navy, 1877–1889* (Westport: Greenwood Press, 1973), p. 191; Walter LaFeber, *The New Empire: An Interpretation of American Expansion, 1860–1898* (Ithaca: Cornell University Press, 1963), pp. 60, 88–93.

43. "War with Chili [*sic*]," *A&N Journal*, XXIX (January 30, 1892), 392.

44. "The Hawaiian Annexation," *A&N Journal*, XXXIV (June 26, 1897), 803.

45. Shufeldt to Moll, February 16, 1880, Shufeldt Papers, NHF, General Correspondence, cont. 16; Taylor, "The Nicaraguan Canal," *A&N Journal*, XXIV (October 16, 1886), 225 [Taylor's italics].

46. LaFeber, *New Empire*, p. 89. *The Interest of America in Sea Power, Present and Future* (Boston: Little, Brown, 1897) reprints Mahan's essays, whose quoted passages appear on pages 21–22, 221. For contrast, see James A. Field, Jr., "American Imperialism: The Worst Chapter in Almost Any Book," *American Historical Review*, LXXXIII (June 1978), 644–68, 679–83.

47. Mahan, *Interest of America*, pp. 221–22, 238–39.

48. Robert Seager, *Alfred Thayer Mahan: The Man and His Letters* (Annapolis: Naval Institute Press, 1977), pp. 353, 391; Mahan to John S. Barnes, July 21, 1898, reprinted in Seager and Doris D. Maguire, *Letters and Papers of Alfred Thayer Mahan* (3 vols; Annapolis: Naval Institute Press, 1975), II, 566.

49. Mahan, *Interest of America*, pp. 229–30, 243, 254.

50. Mahan to the editor of the *New York Times*, June 30, 1893, reprinted in Seager and Maguire, *Mahan*, II, 92–93.

51. Brown, "The Korean Expedition of '71," *United Service*, 3rd Ser., I (January 1902), 74; "Record of Sheridan's Command," *A&N Journal*, XX (October 21, 1882), 262; "Trade as the Hand-Maid of Peace," *A&N Journal*, XXXVIII (April 20, 1901), 820; *A&N Journal*, XLI (October 31, 1903), 208; James A. Field, Jr., *America and the Mediterranean World, 1776-1882* (Princeton: Princeton University Press, 1969), preface and chap. 1.

52. Sims to his family, January 29, 1895, Sims Papers, NHF, Personal Correspondence, cont. 3.

53. Porter, *ARND* (1883), I, 388, and *ARND* (1885), I, 288; Hagan, *Gunboat Diplomacy*, pp. 19–20, 190; "Our Coaling Stations," *A&N Journal*, XXXVI (February 4, 1899), 536; Seward W. Livermore, "American Naval-Base Policy in the Far East, 1850–1914," *Pacific Historical Review*, XIII (June 1944), 114–16.

54. Sherman to John Sherman, September 6, 1887, in Rachel S. Thorndike, ed., *The Sherman Letters: Correspondence between General and Senator Sherman from 1837 to 1891* (New York: Charles Scribner's Sons, 1894), p. 377; Graham A. Cosmas, *An Army for Empire: The United States Army in the Spanish-American War* (Columbia: University of Missouri Press, 1971), pp. 41, 43–44.

55. Dewey, *Autobiography*, p. 185; Rear Admiral Bradley A. Fiske, USN, *From Midshipman to Rear Admiral* (New York: Century, 1919), pp. 239–41; Frederick Palmer, *With My Own Eyes: A Personal Story of Battle Years* (Indianapolis: Bobbs-Merrill, 1933), p. 110.

56. Russell F. Weigley, *Towards an American Army: Military Thought from Washington to Marshall* (New York: Columbia University Press, 1962), p. 147; Bliss to his wife, c. August, 1897, quoted in Frederick Palmer, *Bliss, Peacemaker—The Life and Letters of General Tasker H. Bliss* (New York: Dodd, Mead, 1934), p. 40; Scott, *Some Memories of a Soldier* (New York: Century, 1928), p. 218.

57. Michie address at New York City's Steinway Hall, February 15, 1883, reprinted in "Our National Danger," *A&N Journal*, XX (February 24, 1883), 671.

58. Commodore G. Melville, USN, "Our Future on the Pacific—What We Have There to Hold and Win," *N. Amer. Rev.*, CLXVI (March 1898), 284; Captain Alfred T. Mahan, USN, quoted in "The United States Looking Ahead," *A&N Journal*, XXXV (January 29, 1898), 408; Rear Admiral Stephen B. Luce, USN, to Senator Henry Cabot Lodge, June 25, 1897, Luce Papers, LOC, General Correspondence cont. 10; Lt. Gen. John M. Schofield, USA, to Hiram Barney [confidential], February 27, 1897, Schofield Papers, LOC, Letters Sent, cont. 58.

Chapter 4: The Response to Imperialism, pp. 65–83

1. Lieutenant General Nelson A. Miles, USA, *ARWD* (1899), I, part 3, 7.
2. "The Naval Review of 1906," *A&N Journal*, XLIV (September 8, 1906), 40.
3. *A&N Journal*, XL (August 29, 1903), 1307.
4. "The General Staff System," *A&N Journal*, XLIV (October 13, 1906), 179; Graham A. Cosmas. *An Army for Empire: The United States Army in the Spanish-American War* (Columbia: University of Missouri Press, 1971), pp. 195–97, 245–94. See also: *ARWD* (1899), I, part 1, 49–50; *ARWD* (1902), I, 42–46; Russell F. Weigley, *History of the United States Army* (New York: Macmillan, 1967), pp. 308, 314–20.
5. Taylor to Rear Admiral Stephen B. Luce, April 8, 1902, Luce Papers, LOC, General Correspondence, cont. 11.
6. Daniel J. Costello, "Planning for War: A History of the General Board of the Navy, 1900–1914" (Ph.D. dissertation, Fletcher School of Law and Diplomacy, 1968), *passim*.
7. Reichmann, "In Pace Para Bellum," *Inf. J.*, II (January 1906), 5; *A&N Journal*, XLI (September 5, 1903), 3.
8. "Public Opinion and the Army," *A&N Journal*, XLIV (February 16, 1907), 678; "The President's Message," *A&N Journal*, XLII (December 10, 1904), 372.
9. Entry for October 8, 1902, Diary No. 2, Bullard Papers, LOC, Diaries, cont. 1.
10. Fiske, "Manifest Destiny," *Harper's*, LXX (March 1885), 578–90; Burgess, *Political Science and Comparative Constitutional Law* (2 vols.; Boston: Ginn, 1890–91), I, 3–4, 39–47, 85–86; Strong, *Our Country: Its Possible Future and Its Present Crisis* (Harvard Library ed.; Cambridge: Belknap Press of Harvard University Press, 1963), pp. 200–18.
11. Strong, *Expansion Under New World-Conditions* (New York: Baker & Taylor, 1900), pp. 45–64, 72–162, 185–213, 238–46, 253–82.
12. Conant, *The United States in the Orient* (Boston: Houghton Mifflin, 1900).
13. Adams, *The Law of Civilization and Decay* (2nd ed.; New York: Macmillan, 1897), pp. vi–ix, 321–83.
14. Adams, *America's Economic Supremacy* (New York: Macmillan, 1900), pp. v–vii, 26–53, 83–84, *The New Empire* (New York: Macmillan, 1903), pp. xi–xxxv, 208–11, and "War as the Ultimate Form of Economic Competition," July 30–31, 1903, lectures at the Naval War College, *PUSNI*, XXIX (December 1903), 829–81.
15. *A&N Journal*, XXXIX (February 15, 1902), 599; Richard D. Challener, *Admirals, Generals, and American Foreign Policy, 1898–1914* (Princeton:

Princeton University Press, 1973), pp. 17–19, 218–25; Ronald H. Spector " 'The Professors of War,' The Naval War College and the Modern American Navy" (Ph.D. dissertation, Yale University, 1967), pp. 202–11.

16. Seward W. Livermore, "American Naval-Base Policy in the Far East, 1850–1914," *Pacific Historical Review*, XIII (June 1944), 116–30; Costello, "Planning for War," pp. 156–58, 198–201; Challener, *Admirals and Generals*, pp. 6–7, 37–38, 66, 178–95.

17. Chaffee to Corbin, August 15, 28, and 29, and December 3, 1900, RG 94, AGO File No. 329412; Chaffee to Corbin, c. 1904, Corbin Papers, LOC, Correspondence, cont. 1; Challener, *Admirals and Generals*, pp. 179, 184.

18. Melville, "The Important Elements in Naval Conflicts," *Annals*, XXVI (July 1905), 123–36; Dewey to Long, November 12, 1901, in Richard W. Turk, "Strategy and Foreign Policy: The United States Navy in the Caribbean, 1865–1913" (Ph.D. dissertation, Fletcher School of Law and Diplomacy, 1968), p. 207; Glassford, "The Selection of Suitable Military Stations in the West Indies," *JMSIUS*, XXX (January 1902), 86; Hermann Hagedorn, *Leonard Wood: A Biography* (2 vols.; New York: Harper & Brothers, 1913), I, 371; David F. Healy, *The United States and Cuba, 1898-1902: Generals, Politicians, and the Search for Policy* (Madison: University of Wisconsin Press, 1963), pp. 90–97.

19. Goodrich, "Discussion," *PUSNI*, XXX (June 1904), 411; Captain William H. Beehler, USN, "Discussion," *PUSNI*, XXXI (March 1905), 188; Fiske, "American Naval Policy," 1905 Prize Essay, *PUSNI*, XXXI (March 1905), 6–7, 10; Fullinwider, "The Fleet and Its Personnel," 1904 Prize Essay, *PUSNI*, XXX (March 1904), 2; Hobson, "America Must Be Mistress of the Seas," *N. Amer. Rev.*, CLXXV (October 1902), 552–54, 557.

20. RG 165, AWC Serial Numbers 5, 7,11, 24, 56, and 110; Major Augustus B. Blocksom, USA, "A Retrospect and Prospect of War," *JMSIUS*, XXXV (September–October 1904), 225; Commander Harry S. Knapp, USN, "The Cooperation of the Army and Navy," May 1907 lecture series at the Army War College, RG 165, AWC Serial No. 42.

21. "The Mastery of the Pacific," *A&N Journal*, XXXIX (March 22, 1902), 724; Stockton to Luce, June 5, 1898, and Luce to Lodge, June 7, 1898, Luce Papers, LOC, General Correspondence, cont. 10; Allen to Taft, February 4, 1904, Allen Papers, LOC, General Correspondence, cont. 8; Young, speech to Cleveland Chamber of Commerce, reprinted in "Military Needs in the Orient," *A&N Journal*, XL (December 27, 1902), 411; Dewey, interview printed in *A&N Journal*, XLV (September 28, 1907), 83.

22. Fiske, "American Naval Policy," *PUSNI*, XXXI, 9.

23. Miles to Alger, May 18, 1898, in U.S., War Department, Adjutant General's Department, *Correspondence Relating to the War with Spain . . .* (2 vols.; Washington: Government Printing Office, 1902), II, 649; Virginia W. Johnson, *The Unregimented General: A Biography of Nelson A. Miles* (Boston: Houghton Mifflin, 1962), pp. 271 and 353; Miles's 1906 cable to editor, *A&N Journal*, XLIV (September 15, 1906), 55; Miles's statement to Lieutenant Henry T. Allen, diary entry for May 29, 1898, Allen Papers, LOC, Diaries, cont. 1.

24. Schofield, transcript of speech to 1897 Coast Defense Convention, Schofield papers, LOC, Speech, Article and Book File, cont. 95.

25. Ammen to Dewey, May 13, 1898, Dewey Papers, LOC, General Correspondence, cont. 4; Palmer, *With My Own Eyes: A Personal Story of Battle Years* (Indianapolis: Bobbs-Merrill, 1933), p. 110; Dean C. Worcester, "General Lawton's Work in the Philippines," *McClure's Magazine*, XV (May 1900), 21; Story, "Introduction" to the 1909 edition of Homer Lea's *The Valor of Ignorance* (New York: Harper & Brothers, 1942), p. xlviii; Parker, *The Old Army: Memories, 1872-1918* (Philadelphia: Dorrance, 1929), pp. 361–67.

26. "Those Horrid Philippines," *A&N Journal*, XXXVII (February 17, 1900), 581; "From Our Philippine Correspondent," *A&N Journal*, XXXVI (February 25, 1899), 601; "Sick of the Philippines," *A&N Journal*, XLII (March 4, 1905), 712.

27. Bullard, "Cardinal Vices of the American Soldier," *JMSIUS*, XXXVI (January–February 1905), 107; letters from "Candor" and "Critic" in "Cardinal Vices of the American Soldier," *A&N Journal*, XLII (February 11, 1905), 628, and (March 4, 1905), 711–12, respectively.

28. Bryan, August 18, 1900, speech in Indianapolis, reprinted in Ray Ginger, ed., *William Jennings Bryan: Selections* (Indianapolis: Bobbs-Merrill, 1967), p. 65; Schurz, "The Anglo-American Friendship," *Atlantic*, LXXXII (October 1898), 439; Jordan, speech reprinted as "Lest We Forget" in his *Imperial Democracy* (New York: D. Appleton, 1899), p. 5.

29. Schurz, "Militarism and Democracy" in "The Foreign Policy of the United States: Political and Commercial," *Supplement to the Annals* (May 1899), 90; Parker, "What Shall We Do with the Philippines?" *Forum*, XXXII (February 1902), 667; Beach, "The Pioneer of America's Pacific Empire: David Porter," *PUSNI*, XXXIV (June 1908), 551.

30. David F. Healy, *US Expansionism: The Imperialist Urge in the 1890's* (Madison: University of Wisconsin Press, 1970), pp. 234–44.

31. Parker, "Philippines?," *Forum*, XXXII, p. 667; Beach, "Pioneer," *PUSNI*, XXXIV, 551; Schurz, "Anglo-American Friendship," *Atlantic*, LXXXII, p. 436.

32. Schurz, "Militarism and Democracy," *Annals*, p. 82.

33. Jordan, "The Human Harvest," *Proceedings of the American Philosophical Society*, XLV (January–April 1906), 68–69.

34. William E. Leuchtenburg, "Progressivism and Imperialism: The Progressive Movement and American Foreign Policy, 1898–1916," *Mississippi Valley Historical Review*, XXXIX (December 1952), 483–504.

35. Allen to his wife, July 12, 1898, Allen Papers, LOC, Correspondence, cont. 6; "A" to the editor, "Condition of the Philippines," *A&N Journal*, XXXVIII (September 9, 1900), 109.

36. Sperry to Rear Admiral Arent S. Crowninshield, chief of the Bureau of Navigation, February 1, 1900, Sperry Papers, LOC, General Correspondence, cont. 7; Bullard, manuscript entitled "Cubans," quoted in Allan Millett, *The Politics of Intervention: The Military Occupation of Cuba, 1906–1909* (Columbus: Ohio State University Press, 1968), p. 28.

37. Bliss, speech while governor of Moro Province, Philippines, c. 1906, Bliss Papers, LOC, New Acquisitions, cont. 6; Gates, *Schoolbooks and Krags: The United States Army in the Philippines, 1898–1902* (Westport: Greenwood Press, 1973), p. 67; Scott, *Some Memories of a Soldier* (New York: Century, 1928), pp. 233–34; Chaffee, quoted in *A&N Journal*, XL (November 22, 1902), 272; Bell to Major General Henry C. Corbin, USA, May 17, 1901, Corbin Papers, LOC, Correspondence, cont. 1A.

38. Chambers to Admiral George Dewey, USN, February 6, 1906, Dewey Papers, LOC, General Correspondence, cont. 22; Melville, "The United States as a World Power," *A&N Journal*, XLII (April 15, 1905), 884; Wood to J. St. Loe Strachey, January 6, 1904, reprinted in Hagedorn, *Wood*, II, 14–15; "Duty and the Dollar Mark," *A&N Journal*, XXXIX (May 17, 1902), 932; "In the Philippines to Stay," *A&N Journal*, XXXIX (February 1, 1902), 534; "How to Obtain the Philippines," *A&N Journal*, XXXVI (September 24, 1898), 89; "A Protectorate for the Philippines," *A&N Journal*, XXXVIII (March 30, 1901), 748.

39. "How to Obtain the Philippines," *A&N Journal*, XXXVI (September 24, 1898), 89; "Good in Imperialism," *A&N Journal*, XXXVI (April 22, 1898), 801; "European Hostility to America," *A&N Journal*, XXXIX (November 2, 1901), 210.

40. Bullard, quoted in Millett, *Intervention*, pp. 28 and 254; Sperry to his son, December 12, 1904, April 22, 1905, and October 9, 1906, Sperry Papers, LOC, Family Correspondence, cont. 5; Walker, "Notes on Cuban Ports," *PUSNI*, XXVI (June 1900), 339. See also Millett, *Intervention*, pp. 262–63.

41. Sperry to his son, December 24, 1904 [Sperry's italics], Sperry Papers, LOC, Family Correspondence, cont. 5; *A&N Journal*, XLII (January 28, 1905), 567.

42. Millett, *Intervention*, pp. 262–63.

43. *A&N Journal*, XLIV (May 18, 1907), 1031; *A&N Journal*, XLV (June 13, 1908), 1119; Sperry to his son, August 3, 1907, Sperry Papers, LOC, Family Correspondence, cont. 5.

Chapter 5: The Burdens of Empire, pp. 84–101

1. "Editorial Department," *Inf. J.*, VIII (January–February 1912), 580; Sims to his sister, February 13, 1901, Sims Papers, NHF, Personal Correspondence, cont. 4.
2. Dulles, *The Imperial Years* (New York: Thomas Y. Crowell, 1956), pp. 302–5, 309–312.
3. "Relations of the Powers in China," *A&N Journal*, XXXVII (July 7, 1900), 1064; RG 165, WCD File Nos. 6178–23, 6178–25, 6178–34, 6178–71; Richard D. Challener, *Admirals, Generals, and American Foreign Policy, 1898–1914* (Princeton: Princeton University Press, 1973), pp. 285–86; Captain James H. Reeves, USA, to Captain Frank R. McCoy, USA, June 30, 1912, and Bowley to McCoy, April 29, 1913, McCoy Papers, LOC, General Correspondence, cont. 13.
4. Challener, *Admirals and Generals*, pp. 326, 332; Captain S. A. Stanton, USN, memorandum to Joint Board, October 19, 1909, and Joint Board memorandum dated November 1, 1909, Bliss Papers, LOC, First Period, Correspondence, vol. 100; War Department, Philippine Division, "Proceedings, 1915," RG 165, WCD File No. 4853–54; Brigadier General Hunter Liggett, USA, to Major John McA. Palmer, USA, September 25, 1916, Palmer Papers, LOC, Chronological File.
5. Sperry to his son, April 22, 1905, Sperry Papers, LOC, Family Correspondence, cont. 5; "The Situation in Venezuela," *A&N Journal*, XLII (March 25, 1905), 807; "Editorial Department," *Inf. J.*, IX (March–April 1913), 711; Gillette, "Mexico: Its People and Its Problem," *Annals*, LIV (July 1914), 202.
6. Captain William S. Sims, USN, to Captain Ridley McLean, USN, April 16, 1914, Sims Papers, NHF, Special Correspondence, cont. 71; Brigadier General Tasker H. Bliss to Chief of Staff W. W. Wotherspoon, c. 1913, RG 165, WCD File No. 6474–347.
7. Fiske diary entry for September 26, 1914, reprinted in his *From Midshipman to Rear Admiral* (New York: Century, 1919), p. 551.
8. Wagner, "The Fort Riley Maneuvers," *JMSIUS*, XXXII (January–February 1903), 70.
9. Lieutenant Colonel Alfred Sharpe, USA, "The Present Military Education System of the United States," *United Service*, 3rd Ser., VII (April 1905), 402; *ARWD* (1905), I, 31; Representative Hull as quoted in "Army Legislation in Prospect," *A&N Journal*, XLII (December 3, 1904), 342–43.

10. Bjornstad, "The Military Necessities of the United States and the Best Provisions for Meeting Them," 1907 Gold Medal Essay, *JMSIUS*, XLII (May–June 1908), 360; *ARWD* (1906), I, 552–53.

11. *ARWD* (1907), I, 192–93, 195; *ARWD* (1908), I, 356.

12. Taft, *ARWD* (1904), I, 15; Roosevelt, U.S., Congress, Senate, *Coast Defenses of the United States and the Insular Possessions*, S. Doc. 248, 59th Cong., 1st sess., 1906, p. 4.

13. *ARWD* (1909), II, 267–69; RG 165, WCD File Nos. in the 6000 to 9000 series.

14. Rear Admiral Caspar F. Goodrich, "Discussion," *PUSNI*, XXX (June 1904), 411; Ronald H. Spector, " 'Professors of War,' The Naval War College and the Modern American Navy" (Ph.D. dissertation, Yale University, 1967), pp. 202–11; Daniel J. Costello, "Planning for War: A History of the General Board of the Navy, 1900–1914" (Ph.D. dissertation, Fletcher School of Law and Diplomacy, 1968), pp. 27ff.

15. *A&N Journal*, XLI (August 6, 1904), 1267; "Editorial Notes," *United Service*, 3rd Ser., VI (September 1904), 371; Alger, "Discussion," *PUSNI*, XXXI (March 1905), 180–81.

16. Sampson, "The United States Navy," *Independent*, LI (June 8, 1899), 1533; Commodore William H. Beehler, USN, "The Navy and Coast Defense," 1909 Honorable Mention Essay, *PUSNI*, XXXV (June 1909), 379 [Beehler's italics].

17. Stockton, "Discussion," *PUSNI*, XXXI (March 1905), 194–95, and "Discussion," *PUSNI*, XXIV (March 1898), 128.

18. Wainwright, "Our Naval Power," 1898 Honorable Mention Essay, *PUSNI*, XXIV (March 1898), 57–59.

19. Admiral George Dewey to Secretary of the Navy, March 28, 1913, GB #445, reprinted in *ARND* (1913), pp. 30ff.

20. Converse, *ARND* (1905), I, 388, and *ARND* (1906), pp. 403–5; Costello, "Planning for War," pp. 287–88.

21. Southerland, *ARND* (1900), p. 92; "For a Naval Reserve," *A&N Journal*, XXXVI (December 10, 1898), 356.

22. Challener, *Admirals and Generals*, pp. 225, 227.

23. March, Report No. 6 and text of 1905 Military Academy speech, March Papers, LOC, General Correspondence, cont. 9 [March's italics]; Beehler, "Discussion," *PUSNI*, XXXI (March 1905), 187; Wood to Roosevelt, December 13, 1905, quoted in Hermann Hagedorn, *Leonard Wood: A Biography* (2 vols.; New York: Harper & Brothers, 1931), II, 70.

24. Bell to Rear Admiral George A. Converse, USN, chief of the Bureau of Navigation, January 9, 1907, RG 165, AWC Serial No. 43.

25. March, text of 1905 Military Academy address, March Papers, LOC, General Correspondence, cont. 9; "Miscellaneous Correspondence, Re-

ports, etc., in Regard to the Relative Advantages of Subic and Manila as a Naval Base in the Philippines," c. January 1910, RG 165, AWC Serial No. 43; RG 165, WCD File No. 4853.

26. Louis Morton, "War Plan ORANGE: Evolution of a Strategy," *World Politics*, XI (January 1959), 221–50.

27. Crane, "Our Military Policy," *Inf. J.*, IV (January and March 1908), 565.

28. General Board, quoted in Seward W. Livermore, "American Naval-Base Policy in the Far East, 1850–1914," *Pacific Historical Review*, XIII (June 1944), 128.

29. Challener, *Admirals and Generals*, pp. 37–45, 193–94; "Memorandum Submitted by Rear Admiral Ingersoll to the Joint Board at Its Meeting, October 19, 1909," Bliss papers, LOC, First Period, Correspondence, vol. 100; Major General Leonard Wood to adjutant general, December 23, 1907, RG 165, WCD File No. 4853-2.

30. Holger H. Herwig, *Politics of Frustration: The United States in German Naval Planning, 1889-1941* (Boston: Little Brown, 1976), pp. 13–39.

31. *A&N Journal*, XXXIX (June 21, 1902), 1059; Rear Admiral Henry C. Taylor to Secretary of the Navy Moody, June 6, 1902, and Lieutenant Commander Samuel M. B. Diehl to Moody, December 16, 1902, RG 45, Entry 464, box 3; Challener, *Admirals and Generals*, pp. 111–19.

32. *A&N Journal*, XL (October 4, 1902), 105; "Venezuelan Situation," *A&N Journal*, XL (January 24, 1903), 503; "Germany's American Squadron," *A&N Journal*, XL (October 18, 1902), 161; "Germany in the West Indies," *A&N Journal*, XLII (June 10, 1905), 1106; *A&N Journal*, XL (September 13, 1902), 27.

33. Herwig, *Politics of Frustration*, pp. 42–54, 57–66, 85–92; John A. S. Grenville and George B. Young, *Politics, Strategy, and American Diplomacy: Studies in Foreign Policy, 1873-1917* (New Haven: Yale University Press, 1966), pp. 305–7.

34. Richard W. Turk, "Strategy and Foreign Policy: The United States Navy in the Caribbean, 1865–1913" (Ph.D. dissertation, Fletcher School of Law and Diplomacy, 1968), pp. 169–76; Costello, "Planning for War," p. 333; Challener, *Admirals and Generals*, pp. 37–45.

35. Turk, "Strategy and Foreign Policy," pp. 11–13.

36. Brigadier General W. W. Wotherspoon, president of the Land Defense Board, to Major General J. Franklin Bell, Chief of Staff, November 24, 1908, RG 165, WCD File No. 6947-1; War Department, General Staff, "Is the Present Force of Artillery in Proper Proportion to the Force of the Two Other Branches of the Service?," *Inf. J.*, II (July 1905), 100; Major John P. Wisser, USA, quoted in *A&N Journal*, XLII (January 7, 1905), 479; "Board on Army Reorganization," *A&N Journal*, XLV (April 4, 1908), 826.

37. Croly, *The Promise of American Life* (American Heritage Series ed.; Indianapolis: Bobbs-Merrill, 1965), pp. 309, 312.
38. Clara E. Schieber, *The Transformation of American Sentiment towards Germany, 1870-1914* (Boston: Cornhill, 1923), pp. xiii, 161, 178-79; Eleanor Tupper and George E. McReynolds, *Japan in American Public Opinion* (New York: Macmillan, 1937), pp. 2-5, 9-15, 17, 19-45.
39. Dulles, *The Imperial Years*, pp. 302-5, 309-12.
40. Croly, *The Promise of American Life*, pp. 310-12.
41. Ibid., pp. 291, 295-96, 299, 302.
42. Ibid., p. 309.
43. Clare Booth, "The Valor of Homer Lea," pp. ix-xxxviii, in the reissue of Lea's *The Valor of Ignorance* (New York: Harper & Brothers, 1942).
44. Tarlton, "Internationalism, War and Politics in American Thought, 1898-1920" (Ph.D. dissertation, University of California at Los Angeles, 1964), pp. 110-29; Lea, *Valor of Ignorance*, pp. 7-18, 22-28, *passim*.
45. Ibid., pp. 19-22.
46. Ibid., pp. 22-40, 61-70, 166-220.

Chapter 6: The Quest for Efficiency, pp. 105-27

1. General Staff, "Statement of a Proper Military Policy for the United States," *ARWD* (1915), I, 114-15; Evans, "National Enlistment," *Inf. J.*, VIII (July-August 1911), 4. William A. Ganoe, *The History of the United States Army* (New York: D. Appleton, 1936), p. 441, was among the first to call attention to the progressivism of military officers.
2. Hays, *Conservation and the Gospel of Efficiency: The Progressive Conservation Movement, 1890-1920* (new ed.; New York: Atheneum, 1972), preface to Atheneum edition and pp. 265-71; Gates, *Schoolbooks and Krags: The United States Army in the Philippines, 1898-1902* (Westport: Greenwood Press, 1973), pp. 54-69. On the military in Cuba, see Howard Gillette, Jr., "The Military Occupation of Cuba, 1899-1902: Workshop for American Progressivism," *American Quarterly*, XXV (October 1973), pp. 410-25, and Allan R. Millett, *The Politics of Intervention: The Military Occupation of Cuba, 1906-1909* (Columbus: Ohio State University Press, 1968), pp. 1-16, 139, 191, 212-14, and 262-63.
3. "On Varied Ground," *Inf. J.*, VIII (November-December 1911), 429; Boughton to editor, June 18, 1911, reprinted in "Military Notes" *Cav. J.*, XXII (July 1911), 137-38.
4. General Staff, "Organization of the Land Forces of the United States," *ARWD* (1912), I, 126.
5. GS, "Statement," *ARWD* (1915), I, 114, 116.

6. Reilly, "The Russo-Japanese War," *JMSIUS*, LII (January–February 1913), 58; Bliss memorandum, c. 1915, Bliss Papers, LOC, First Period, Correspondence, vol. 196; Bell to Secretary of War Dickinson, April 20, 1910, RG 165, AWC Serial No. 168, Appendix I.

7. Wallace, "Our Military Decline," *Inf. J.*, IX (March–April 1913), 632–33; McAndrew, "The Monroe Doctrine," *Inf. J.*, VIII (July–August 1911), 26.

8. Brown, "A Regular Army Reserve," *JMSIUS*, XLV (September–October 1909), 265; Crawford, "Militarism," *Inf. J.*, VII (November 1910), 369.

9. Bell to Secretary of War Dickinson, April 20, 1910, RG 165, AWC Serial No. 168, Appendix I.

10. Martha A. Derthick, *The National Guard in Politics* (Cambridge: Harvard University Press, 1965), pp. 27–28; Russell F. Weigley, *History of the United States Army* (New York: Macmillan, 1967), pp. 321–24; *ARWD* (1912), I, 120, 147–50.

11. Weigley, *History of Army*, pp. 277–81; "Editorial Notes," *United Service*, 3d Ser., VI (November 1904), 629; "Evolution of the National Guard," *A&N Journal*, XLII (September 19, 1904), 37; Pierce, "A Militiaman's View of the Manassas Maneuvers," *Inf. J.*, II (July 1905), 35–36.

12. *ARWD* (1908), I, 37; "What Are We to Expect of the Militia?," *A&N Journal*, XLV (March 21, 1908), 769; Weaver to editor, March 18, 1908, reprinted as "Proposed Amendment to Dick Law," *A&N Journal*, XLV (March 28, 1908), 790.

13. Bliss to Brigadier General John J. Pershing, USA, February 8, 1916, and Bliss to William N. Dykman [New York] Mayor's Committee on National Defense, February 8, 1917, Bliss Papers, LOC, First Period, Correspondence, vols. 198 and 209, respectively.

14. Bliss report to the adjutant general, "Inspection of the Organized Militia along the Mexican Border," August 11, 1916, Bliss Papers, LOC, First Period, Correspondence, vol. 204.

15. Walter Millis, *Arms and Men: A Study in American Military History* (New York: G. P. Putnam's Sons, 1956), pp. 230–31; James W. Pohl, "The General Staff and American Military Policy: The Formative Period, 1898–1917" (Ph.D. dissertation, University of Texas, 1967), pp. 371–82.

16. William H. Riker, *Soldiers of the States: The Role of the National Guard in American Democracy* (Washington: Public Affairs Press, 1957), pp. 67–74; Derthick, *National Guard*, pp. 28–32.

17. Moseley, "National Liability for Training and Service," *Cav. J.*, XXVII (January 1917), 421; Palmer, *An Army of the People: The Constitution of an Effective Force of Trained Citizens* (New York: G. P. Putnam's Sons, 1916), p. 4 [Palmer's italics], and "The Militia Pay Bill," *Inf. J.*, XI (November–December 1914), 352; "Editorial Department," *Inf. J.*, VIII (May–June 1912), 861–62; Captain William A. Mitchell, USA, "Military

Organization of the United States," *Inf. J.*, X (November–December 1913), 350–92.

18. Chief of Staff J. Franklin Bell, *ARWD* (1901), I, 192–93; Chief of Staff William W. Wotherspoon, *ARWD* (1914), I, 131–33.

19. GS, "Land Forces," *ARWD* (1912), I, 76.

20. "A National Reserve," *A&N Journal*, XLIII (September 23, 1905), 107; Chief of Staff J. Franklin Bell, *ARWD* (1907), I, 190, and *ARWD* (1909), I, 216; Chief of Staff Leonard Wood, *ARWD* (1911), I, 151.

21. Bell, *ARWD* (1907), I, 189–90; Bell to Secretary of War Dickinson, April 20, 1910, RG 165, AWC Serial No. 168, Appendix I.

22. GS, "Land Forces," *ARWD* (1912), I, 96.

23. Stimson Diaries, Yale University, reel 1, II, 65–66; Wood, *ARWD* (1911), I, 152; Stimson, *ARWD* (1911), I, 21.

24. Stimson, *ARWD* (1912), I, 20; Wood, *ARWD* (1912), I, 247; Reichmann, "Our Reserve System," *Inf. J.*, IX (March–April 1913), 699.

25. GS, "Statement," *ARWD* (1915), I, 129–30; Weigley, *History of Army*, pp. 344–45.

26. Weigley, *History of Army*, pp. 344–48; Bliss to Major General Thomas H. Barry, February 8, 1916, Bliss Papers, LOC, First Period, Correspondence, vol. 198; *ARWD* (1916), I, 156–67.

27. Weigley, *History of Army*, pp. 344–48; Garrison, *ARWD* (1913), I, 19–21. On the camps see John G. Clifford, *The Citizen Soldiers: The Plattsburg Training Camp Movement, 1913-1920* (Lexington: University Press of Kentucky, 1972).

28. Clifford, *Citizen Soldiers*, pp. 195–202; "The Plattsburg Idea," *New Republic*, IV (October 9, 1915), 247–49.

29. Stewart, "The Army as a Factor in the Upbuilding of Society," *JMSIUS*, XXXVI (May–June 1905), 391; Palmer to Grenville Clark, December 24, 1916, Palmer Papers, LOC, Chronological File; Scott, *Some Memories of a Soldier* (New York: Century, 1928), pp. 445, 560–61; Wood, "Status of the Military Department in the Land-Grant Colleges," *Cav. J.*, XXIV (March 1914), 944; "Eugenics versus Euthenics," *Cav. J.*, XXIII (November 1912), 546–47.

30. Brigadier General John W. Clous, USA, "Address Before the Army Relief Society . . . ," *Inf. J.*, IV (May 1908), 835–40; "Militarism Ceasing to Be a Bugaboo," *Inf. J.*, V (January 1909), 621–22; "Editorial Department," *Inf. J.*, XI (September–October 1914), 291–92; "Militarism and Commerce," *A&N Journal*, XXXVIII (October 13, 1900), 156; "Compulsory Military Service," *A&N Journal*, XLI (August 20, 1904), 1327.

31. Scott, U.S., Congress, Senate, Committee on Military Affairs, *Universal Military Training, Hearings* before a subcommittee of the Committee on Military Affairs, Senate, on S. 1695, 64th Cong., 2d sess., 1917, pp. 93, 96.

32. Major General Leonard Wood, USA, testimony before U.S., Congress,

House, Committee on Military Affairs, *To Increase the Efficiency of the Military Establishment of the United States, Hearings* before the Committee on Military Affairs, House of Representatives, on the bill, 64th Cong., 1st sess., 1916, II, 737; Pohl, "General Staff," pp. 362–82; Major General Hugh L. Scott, USA, *ARWD* (1916), I, 157–62, 191; John W. Chambers II, "Conscripting for Colossus: The Adoption of the Draft in the United States in World War I" (Ph.D. dissertation, Columbia University, 1973), pp. 141–43.

33. J. McA. P. memorandum, c. early 1916, Palmer Papers, LOC, Chronological File.

34. Harold T. Wieand, "The History of the Development of the United States Naval Reserve, 1889–1941" (Ph.D. dissertation, University of Pittsburgh, 1953), p. 96; Jim Dan Hill, *The Minute Man in Peace and War: A History of the National Guard* (Harrisburg: Stackpole, 1964), pp. 141–44.

35. Peter Karsten, *The Naval Aristocracy: The Golden Age of Annapolis and the Emergence of Modern American Navalism* (New York: The Free Press, 1972), pp. 207–8; Lieutenant Commander John P. Jackson, USN, "A Plea for Universal Service," *PUSNI*, XLIII (February 1917), 309–11.

36. Riggs, "Wanted: A Naval Militia Mission," *PUSNI*, XLII (March–April 1916), 418; Sperry, manuscript entitled "The Cruise of the United States Fleet," c. 1910, Sperry Papers, LOC, Speech, Article and Lecture File; *ARND* (1911), pp. 35–36.

37. Wieand, "Naval Reserve," pp. 44–77; *ARND* (1898), pp. 53, 103, 143–44, 324–25.

38. Wieand, "Naval Reserve," pp. 97–98; Hill, *Minute Man*, pp. 141–44.

39. Fiske to Secretary of the Navy Daniels, November 9, 1914, reprinted in Fiske's *From Midshipman to Rear-Admiral* (New York: Century, 1919), pp. 557–58; Lieutenant Commander Walter B. Tardy, USN, "The First Naval Training Cruise: Its Accomplishment and Portent," *PUSNI*, XLIII (March 1917), 505–57.

40. Stirling, "Organization for Navy Department Administration," *PUSNI*, XXIX (June 1913), 442.

41. Morison, *Admiral Sims and the Modern American Navy* (Boston: Houghton Mifflin, 1942), pp. 37–147, 156–215.

42. Ibid., pp. 140–41.

43. Sims to Rear Admiral Stephen B. Luce, December 13, 1909, Luce Papers, LOC, General Correspondence, cont. 13; Taylor, "Memorandum on General Staff for the U.S. Navy," *PUSNI*, XXVI (September 1900), 444.

44. Cotten, "Naval Efficiency and Command of the Sea," *PUSNI*, XXXIX (September 1913), 981; Taylor to Luce, "Memorandum," February 24, 1900 [Taylor's italics], Luce Papers, LOC, General Correspondence, cont. 11.

45. *ARND* (1909), pp. 8–9; *ARND* (1912), p. 6.

46. Costello, "Planning for War: A History of the General Board of the Navy, 1900–1914" (Ph.D. dissertation, Fletcher School of Law and Diplomacy, 1968), pp. 94, 98–99.

47. Harold Sprout and Margaret Sprout, *The Rise of American Naval Power, 1776–1918* (Princeton: Princeton University Press, 1939), pp. 315–16; Morison, *Sims*, pp. 315–17; Fiske, *Midshipman to Admiral*, chap. 36.

48. Jack C. Lane, *Armed Progressive: General Leonard Wood* (San Rafael: Presidio Press, 1978), pp. 156–67; Weigley, *History of Army*, pp. 329–33; Mabel E. Deutrich, *Struggle for Supremacy: The Career of General Fred C. Ainsworth* (Washington: Public Affairs Press, 1962), chap. 8; Henry L. Stimson and McGeorge Bundy, *On Active Service in Peace and War* (New York: Harper & Brothers, 1948), pp. 32–38.

49. Harbord to Wood, July 18, 1913, Harbord Papers, LOC, Private Letters, vol. V.

50. Sprout and Sprout, *Rise*, pp. 290–94; Weigley, *History of Army*, pp. 333–35.

51. Robert D. Cuff, *The War Industries Board: Business-Government Relations during World War I* (Baltimore: Johns Hopkins University Press, 1973), pp. 13–42; *Statutes at Large*, XXXIX, pt. 1, 649–50.

52. Morton, "Interservice Co-operation and Political-Military Collaboration, 1900–38," in *Total War and Cold War: Problems in Civilian Control of the Military*, ed. by Harry L. Coles (Columbus: Ohio State University Press, 1962), p. 136; "A Council of National Defense," *Inf. J.*, X (May–June 1914). 948–51.

53. Luce to Tracy, March 18, 1892, Luce Papers, LOC, General Correspondence, cont. 9; "Our Greatest Need," *Inf. J.*, IV (July 1907), 156–58; *Cong. Rec.*, XLVI, pt. 1, 323, pt. 2, 1966, XLVII, pt. 1, 27, XLIX, pt. 2, 1811, pt. 4, 3294, L, pt. 1, 89; U.S., Congress, House, *Council of National Defense*, H. Report 584, 62d Cong., 2d sess., 1912.

54. Dewey, *ARND* (1913), p. 32; Harbord to Major General Leonard Wood, USA, April 16, 1910, Harbord Papers, LOC, Private Letters, vol. III.

55. McKean, Army War College lecture, reprinted as "Policy," *Inf. J.*, IX (January–February 1913), 473–85.

56. Hill to Brigadier General William W. Wotherspoon, USA, April 10, 1911, quoted in Richard D. Challener, *Admirals, Generals, and American Foreign Policy, 1898–1914* (Princeton: Princeton University Press, 1973), p. 268.

57. GS, "Land Forces," *ARWD* (1912), I, 127; GS, "Statement," *ARWD* (1915), I, 115–16.

58. "Council," *Inf. J.*, X, 951.

59. Cuff, *WIB*, pp. 69–82, 115–22.

60. Gates, *Schoolbooks and Krags*, chap. 2.

61. Palmer, "Militia Pay," *Inf. J.*, XI, 337.

CHAPTER 7: The Armed Services and American Society, pp. 128–50

1. Arthur A. Ekirch, Jr., *The Civilian and the Military: A History of the American Antimilitarist Tradition* (New York: Oxford University Press, 1956), has described the evolution of antimilitary thought in America.

2. Eisenhower's "Farewell Radio and Television Address to the American People," January 17, 1961, is reprinted in U.S., President, *Public Papers of the President of the United States: Dwight D. Eisenhower, 1960–61* (Washington: U.S. Government Printing Office, 1961), p. 1038; Peter Karsten, *The Naval Aristocracy: The Golden Age of Annapolis and the Emergence of Modern American Navalism* (New York: The Free Press, 1972), p. 174; Fred J. Cook, *The Warfare State* (New York: Collier Books, 1962); Paul A. C. Koistinen, "The 'Industrial-Military Complex' in Historical Perspective: World War I," *Business History Review*, XLI (Winter 1967), 378–403, and "The 'Industrial-Military Complex' in Historical Perspective: The Inter-War Years," *Journal of American History*, LVI (March 1970), 819–39.

3. E.g., Gabriel Kolko, *The Roots of American Foreign Policy: An Analysis of Power and Purpose* (Boston: Beacon Press, 1969), and *The Triumph of Conservatism: A Re-interpretation of American History, 1900–1916* (Glencoe: Free Press, 1963).

4. Russell F. Weigley, *History of the United States Army* (New York: Macmillan, 1967), p. 265; Samuel P. Huntington, *The Soldier and the State: The Theory and Politics of Civil-Military Relations* (Cambridge: Belknap Press of Harvard University Press, 1957), p. 227.

5. Richard C. Brown, "Social Attitudes of American Generals, 1898–1940" (Ph.D. dissertation, University of Wisconsin, 1951), pp. 1–16, 34, 38–39; Morris Janowitz, *The Professional Soldier: A Social and Political Portrait* (Glencoe: Free Press, 1960), p. 100; Karsten, *Naval Aristocracy*, p. 10.

6. "Service Members of Civil Clubs," *A&N Journal*, XXXIX (February 15, 1902), 590; Colonel T. Bentley Mott, USA, *Twenty Years as Military Attaché* (New York: Oxford University Press, 1937), p. 49.

7. Andrew J. Bacevich, Jr., "Family Matters: American Civilian and Military Elites in the Progressive Era" (typewritten manuscript lent by the author, West Point, New York, 1979).

8. *A&N Journal*, XXVIII (January 3, 1891), 317.

9. *Annals*, XXVI (1905); "Editorial Department," *Inf. J.*, IX (January–February 1913), 543; Rear Admiral French E. Chadwick, USN, "Sea Power: The Decisive Factor in Our Struggle for Independence," *Annual Report of the American Historical Association for the Year 1915* (Washington: American Historical Association, 1917), pp. 171–89.

10. "Editorial Department," *Inf. J.*, XII (February 1916), 741-42; W. D.

Puleston, *Mahan: The Life and Work of Captain Alfred Thayer Mahan* (New Haven: Yale University Press, 1939), pp. 90–92; Roosevelt, "The Influence of Sea Power Upon History," *Atlantic* LXVI (October 1890), 563–67; Strong, *Expansion Under New World-Conditions* (New York: Baker & Taylor, 1900), p. 10; Lea, *The Valor of Ignorance* (reissued ed.; New York: Harper and Brothers, 1942); Huidekoper, *The Military Unpreparedness of the United States: A History of the American Land Forces from Colonial Times until June 1, 1915* (New York: Macmillan, 1915), pp. xiii–xvi.

11. Sharpe, "Military Training in Colleges," *JMSIUS*, VIII (December 1887), 405. See also Lieutenant Colonel Joseph P. Sanger to the War College [Ludlow] Board, September 12, 1900, RG 94, AGO File No. 311224.

12. John G. Clifford, *The Citizen Soldiers: The Plattsburg Training Camp Movement, 1913-1920* (Lexington: University Press of Kentucky, 1972), pp. 11–25; Wood to Major General Thomas H. Barry, quoted in Hermann Hagedorn, *Leonard Wood: A Biography* (2 vols.; New York: Harper and Brothers, 1931), II, 131.

13. Clifford, *Citizen Soldiers*, pp. 66–68, 72, 81–82, 87–115, 155, 182–84.

14. *PUSNI*, XIII (1887), 1–126; "The Railroads and National Defense," *JMSIUS*, LVIII (March-April 1916), 207–32; Barclay Parsons to Brigadier General Tasker H. Bliss, August 2, 1915, Bliss to Parsons, August 6, 1915, and Parsons to Congressman James Hay, November 24, 1915, Bliss Papers, LOC, First Period, Correspondence, vols. 192 and 195.

15. Karsten, *Naval Aristocracy*, p. 176; Evans, *A Sailor's Log: Recollections of Forty Years of Naval Life* (New York: D. Appleton, 1901), p. 234.

16. John P. Finnegan, *Against the Specter of a Dragon: The Campaign for American Military Preparedness, 1914-1917* (Westport: Greenwood Press, 1974), pp. 177–83; Jack C. Lane, *Armed Progressive: General Leonard Wood* (San Rafael: Presidio Press, 1978), pp. 200–1; Chase C. Mooney and Martha E. Layman, "Some Phases of the Compulsory Military Training Movement, 1914–1920," *Mississippi Valley Historical Review*, XXXVIII (March 1952), 633–56.

17. Luce to Aldrich, March 15, 1889, quoted in Ronald H. Spector, " 'Professors of War,' The Naval War College and the Modern American Navy" (Ph.D. dissertation, Yale University, 1967), p. 98; typescript of Luce's remarks at the Naval War College Conference, June 2, 1906, Luce Papers, LOC, Subject File, cont. 19; Taylor, *ARND* (1895), pp. 168–69.

18. Lieutenant Colonel Henry C. Hodges, USA, secretary to the General Staff, to chief, War College Division, November 25, 1912, RG 165, WCD File No. 7426–2.

19. Daniel J. Costello, "Planning for War: A History of the General Board of the Navy, 1900-1914" (Ph.D. dissertation, Fletcher School of Law and Diplomacy, 1968), pp. 72–74, 82–83, 87, 99; Fiske, *From Midshipman to*

Rear Admiral (New York: Century, 1919), pp. 567–69; Fleet Admiral Ernest J. King, USN, and Commander Walter M. Whitehill, USNR, *Fleet Admiral King: A Naval Record* (New York: W. W. Norton, 1952), p. 103; Richard W. Sheldon, "Richmond Pearson Hobson: The Military Hero as Reformer during the Progressive Era" (Ph.D. dissertation, University of Arizona, 1970), p. 182.

20. Miles to Schofield, October 31, 1889, Schofield Papers, LOC, Letters Received, Special Correspondence, cont. 41; *A&N Journal*, XXXIV (January 30, 1897); 386, and XXXV (November 6, 1897), 170.

21. Miles, quoted in *San Francisco Evening Bulletin,* October 28, 1889, clipping found in Schofield Papers, LOC, Letters Received, Special Correspondence, cont. 41; Schofield to Snow, December 16, 1886, Schofield Papers, LOC, Letters Sent, cont. 52; Griffin's paper published in *JMSIUS*, VII (December 1886), 405–65.

22. Wainwright, "Our Merchant Marine: The Causes of Its Decline, and the Means to Be Taken for Its Revival," 1882 Honorable Mention Essay, *PUSNI*, VIII (1882), 147; Field S. Pendleton, Atlantic Carriers Association, to Luce, May 15, 1902, Leighton C. Powell Robinson, Shipowners' Association of the Pacific Coast, to Luce, December 1, 1904, Luce to Winthrop L. Marvin, secretary to the Merchant Marine Commission, May 20 and 24, 1904, Luce to Senator Jacob Gallinger, chairman of the Merchant Marine Commission, November 17, 1904, and Luce to William McCarroll, New York Board of Trade, April 13, 1907, all in Luce Papers, LOC, General Correspondence, conts. 11 and 12.

23. "Army's Need of Merchant Ships in War," *A&N Journal*, XLIII (January 20, 1906), 581–82.

24. Allard, "The Influence of the United States Navy upon the American Steel Industry, 1880–1900" (M.A. thesis, Georgetown University, 1959).

25. Ibid., pp. 5–14, 38–48.

26. Evans, *Sailor's Log*, p. 237; Allard, "Influence of the Navy," pp. 15–38.

27. Ibid., pp. 36–38, 109–11.

28. Donald W. Mitchell, *History of the Modern American Navy from 1883 through Pearl Harbor* (New York: Knopf, 1946), p. 19; Allard, "Influence of the Navy," pp. 38–43, 64–80.

29. Ibid., pp. 44–64, 80–85.

30. Ibid., pp. 89–102, 104.

31. Ibid., p. 114.

32. Ibid., pp. 112, 114, 117; "The Question of Armor Plate," *A&N Journal*, XXXVII (April 7, 1900), 471; John F. Meigs, ex-USN and engineer of ordnance for Bethlehem Steel Company, to Rear Admiral Stephen B. Luce, USN, Nov. 26, 1906, Luce Papers, LOC, Gen. Corres., cont. 12.

33. "Report of the Gun Foundry Board," *ARND* (1884), I, 298; Allard, "Influence of the Navy," pp. 116–27; Commander Richardson Clover, chief of naval intelligence, to Lieutenant Commander William H. Beehler, April 26, 1899, RG 38, Entry 102.

34. "Report of the [Endicott] Board on Fortifications or Other Defenses," *ARWD* (1886), II, pt. 1, app. 3, 520; "Report of the [Naval Advisory] Board," *ARND* (1881), p. 31; "Report of GFB," *ARND* (1884), I, 299–302; "Report of the Board of Engineers for Fortifications," *ARWD* (1883), II, pt. 1, 52.

35. "Public and Private Ordnance Work," *A&N Journal*, XIX (October 15, 1881), 234; "The Proposed Armor Plate Factory," *A&N Journal*, XXXVII (June 2, 1900), 944; "Coast Defence," *A&N Journal*, XVIII (October 9, 1880), 186; "The Naval Advisory Board," *A&N Journal*, XVIII (July 16, 1881), 1050.

36. "Report of GFB," *ARND* (1884), I, 298–302. See also "Report of Endicott Board," *ARWD* (1886), II, pt. 1, app. 3, 520–22.

37. Carnegie's March 9, 1887, complaint to Secretary of the Navy Whitney is quoted in Allard, "Influence of the Navy," p. 72.

38. Bryant, *The Sea and the States* (New York: Thomas Y. Crowell, 1947), p. 348; Tillman is quoted in Costello, "Planning for War," p. 180; Leon B. Richardson, *William E. Chandler: Republican* (New York: Dodd, Mead & Company, 1940), pp. 287–89, 305, 308–12.

39. Stewart, "The Fog of War—In Peace," *Inf. J.*, XII (July–August 1915), 14; James W. Pohl, "The General Staff and American Military Policy: The Formative Period, 1898–1917" (Ph.D. dissertation, University of Texas, 1967), pp. 184–86.

40. Costello, "Planning for War," pp. 178–83, 322–23; Secretary of the Navy Chandler, *ARND* (1883), I, 17.

41. Hagedorn, *Wood*, II, 115; "Better Prospects for the Army," *A&N Journal*, LI (August 29, 1914), 1668.

42. Karsten, *Naval Aristocracy*, p. 187; Mahan to Ashe, August 10, 1888, quoted in ibid., p. 189; Howard to J. Gruesel, November 6, 1896, and Howard to Charles H. Howard, October 27, 1888, quoted in John A. Carpenter, *Sword and Olive Branch: Oliver Otis Howard* (Pittsburgh: University of Pittsburgh Press, 1964), pp. 291 and 285; Michaelis, "The Military Necessities of the United States, and the Best Provisions for Meeting Them," 1883 Honorable Mention Essay, *JMSIUS*, V (1884), 288; Sims to his parents, July 21, 1894, Sims Papers, NHF, Personal Correspondence, cont. 3.

43. Sperry to his son, January 14, 1905, Sperry Papers, LOC, Family Correspondence, cont. 5; army major quoted in Huntington, *Soldier and the*

State, p. 259; Field, "Our Coast Defenses," *United Service*, N.S., III (January 1890), 2; "Representation That Does Not Represent," *A&N Journal*, XXI (October 6, 1883), 191.

44. Huntington, *Soldier and the State*, pp. 222–25.

45. C. Roland Marchand, *The American Peace Movement and Social Reform, 1898-1918* (Princeton: Princeton University Press, 1972), pp. xi–xiii.

46. Karsten, *Naval Aristocracy*, p. 192.

47. Janowitz, *Professional Soldier*, p. vii; "On Varied Ground," *Inf. J.*, VIII (May–June 1912), 880.

48. Price, "The Necessity for Closer Relations between the Army and the People, and the Best Method to Accomplish the Result," 1885 Prize Essay, *JMSIUS*, VI (December 1885), 324–25.

49. "A Navy General Staff," *A&N Journal*, XLI (January 16, 1904), 517; Admiral George Dewey to secretary of the navy, March 28, 1913, G.B. No. 445, reprinted in *ARND* (1913), p. 33; Lieutenant Colonel Henry C. Hodges, Jr., to chief, War College Division, November 21, 1912, RG 165, WCD File No. 7426–1.

50. "The German Navy League," *A&N Journal*, XXXIX (November 9, 1901), 227; Lieutenant Commander Roy C. Smith, USN, "The Navy's Greatest Need," *N. Amer. Rev.*, CLXXV (September 1902), 398; "The Navy's Greatest Need," *A&N Journal*, XL (September 13, 1902), 37; "United States Navy League," *A&N Journal*, XL (February 7, 1903), 552–53; Lieutenant Commander John H. Gibbons, USN, "Navy Leagues," *N. Amer. Rev.*, CLXXVI (May 1903), 761–64; "The British National Service League," *A&N Journal*, XLII (March 18, 1905), 779; Captain James G. Harbord, USA, to Major General Leonard Wood, USA, October 29, 1911, Harbord Papers, LOC, Private Letters, vol. IV; Commander Reginald R. Belknap, USN, to his wife, March 2, 1916, R. R. Belknap Papers, NHF, General Correspondence, cont. 11; Colonel George Van Horn Moseley, USA, to H. H. Gross, President of the Universal Military Training League, August 23, 1916, Moseley Papers, LOC, Letters, cont. 5; Major General Tasker H. Bliss, USA, to Willard Straight, [New York] Mayor's Committee on National Defense, January 18, 1917, Bliss Papers, LOC, First Period, Correspondence, vol. 208; Clifford, *Citizen Soldiers*, pp. 205–7, 209–10. See also Armin Rappaport's *The Navy League of the United States* (Detroit: Wayne State University Press, 1962).

51. Miles, *ARWD* (1890), I, 158; Simpson, "Wants of the Navy—Cannon," *United Service*, II (May 1880), 647–48.

52. Wagner, "The Military and Naval Policy of the United States," *JMSIUS*, VII (December 1886), 397; Webb, "The Military Service Institution; What It Is Doing; What It May Do; Its Relations to the National Guard," *JMSIUS*, V (March 1884), 3; "A Question of Cooks—Or Broth," *Inf. J.*, V (May 1909), 980.

53. Wood speech to the Land-Grant College Engineering Organization, re-printed as "The Status of the Military Department in the Land-Grant Colleges," *Cav. J.*, XXIV (March 1914), 945; Wood to Harbord, April 19, 1915, Harbord Papers, LOC, Private Letters, vol. V; McCoy to Wood, November 3, 1916, McCoy Papers, LOC, General Correspondence, cont. 14; John P. Finnegan, "Military Preparedness in the Progressive Era, 1911–1917" (Ph.D. dissertation, University of Wisconsin, 1969), pp. 94–120.

54. Wood diary, entry for September 1, 1916, Wood Papers, LOC, Diary, cont. 8; Major General Tasker H. Bliss, USA, to Major General Hugh L. Scott, USA, March 6, 1916, Bliss Papers, LOC, First Period, Correspondence, vol. 198.

55. Andrews, *Fundamentals of Military Service* (Philadelphia: J. B. Lippincott, 1916); Palmer, *An Army of the People: The Constitution of a Force of Trained Citizens* (New York: G. P. Putnam's Sons, 1916); Reilly, *Why Preparedness: The Observations of an American Army Officer in Europe, 1914–1915* (Chicago: Daughaday, 1916); Greene, *The Present Military Situation in the United States* (New York: Charles Scribner's Sons, 1915); Carter, *The American Army* (Indianapolis: Bobbs-Merrill, 1915); Wood, *Our Military History: Its Facts and Fallacies* (Chicago: Reilly & Britton, 1916) and *The Military Obligation of Citizenship* (Princeton: Princeton University Press, 1915).

Chapter 8: The Response to War, pp. 151–76

1. Luce to Los Angeles Public Library, c. 1909, reprinted in Rear Admiral Albert Gleaves, USN, *Life and Letters of Rear Admiral Stephen B. Luce* (New York: G. P. Putnam's Sons, 1925), pp. 297–98.

2. Robert E. Osgood, *Ideals and Self-Interest in America's Foreign Relations: The Great Transformation of the Twentieth Century* (Chicago: University of Chicago Press, 1953), pp. 17–23; Samuel P. Huntington, *The Soldier and the State: The Theory and Politics of Civil-Military Relations* (Cambridge: Belknap Press of Harvard University Press, 1957), pp. 143ff, 222ff.

3. Allen, typescript of 1916 speech, Allen Papers, LOC, Correspondence, cont. 6; Reilly, "The Russo-Japanese War," *JMSIUS*, LII (January–February 1913), 56; Hickok, "Peace; Or Patriotism and Preparedness *versus* Platitude and Parsimony," *JMSIUS* LIX (November–December 1916), 396; McKean, "Policy," reprint of 1912 lecture, *Cav. J.*, XXIII (January 1913), 621; GS, "Organization of the Land Forces of the United States," *ARWD* (1912), I, 127; Schwan, "The Coming General Staff—Its Importance as a Factor in the Military System of the Country," *JMSIUS*,

XXXIII (July–August 1903), 2; Reichmann, "In Pace Para Bellum," *Inf. J.*, II (January 1906), 3–4.

4. Reichmann, "In Pace Para Bellum," *Inf. J.*, II, 3.

5. Clarkson, *Industrial America in the World War: The Strategy Behind the Line, 1917–1918* (Boston: Houghton Mifflin, 1923), p. 111; Weigley, *The American Way of War: A History of United States Military Strategy and Policy* (New York: Macmillan, 1973), pp. 207, 209.

6. Wood, introduction to Henry J. Reilly's *Why Preparedness: The Observations of an American Army Officer in Europe, 1914–1915* (Chicago: Daughaday, 1916), p. vii; Bliss memoranda for the chief of staff, March 26, 1917, and December 10, 1915, Bliss Papers, LOC, First Period, Correspondence, vols. 210 and 196, respectively.

7. *A&N Journal*, XXVI (December 29, 1888), 351; Rhodes, "The Experience of Our Army since the Outbreak of War with Spain . . . ," 1904 Gold Medal Essay, *JMSIUS*, XXXVI (March–April 1905), 209; Bliss, paper read at annual meeting and reprinted as "Mobilization and Maneuvers" in *JMSIUS*, L (March–April 1912), 176.

8. Davis, "Transportation of Military Commands by Rail," *Inf. J.*, VII (January 1911), 572–76, 584; Sharpe, *ARWD* (1916), I, 375.

9. Sharpe, *ARWD* (1916), I, 374–75, 377; Benson, *ARND* (1916), p. 87.

10. Rhodes, "Experience," *JMSIUS*, XXXVI, 208; War College Division, "Personnel versus Materiel in Plans for National Defense," *JMSIUS*, LVIII (May–June 1916), 389–400.

11. Crozier testimony, U.S. Congress, Senate, Committee on Military Affairs, *Army Appropriation Bill, Hearings* before a subcommittee of the Committee on Military Affairs, Senate, on H.R. 13453, 63rd Cong., 2d sess., 1914, pp. 73–82; Taylor, "America and the Next War," *JMSIUS*, LX (May–June 1917), 355–56; Moore, "The Supply of an Army," *Arty. J.*, XLVII (January–February 1917), 40.

12. Gillen, "The Mobilization and Supply of Army Material," *JMSIUS*, LVII (November–December 1915), 379–86; U.S., War Department, War College Division, *Mobilization of Industries and Utilization of the Commercial and Industrial Resources of the Country for War Purposes in Emergency*, WCD 8121–45, Doc. No. 517 (Washington: Government Printing Office, 1916), pp. 9–12.

13. GS, "Statement of a Proper Military Policy for the United States," *ARWD* (1915), I, 131; Wood, *Our Military History: Its Facts and Fallacies* (Chicago: Reilly & Britton, 1916), pp. 185–86.

14. Edward M. Coffman, *The War to End All Wars: The American Military Experience in World War I* (New York: Oxford University Press, 1968), pp. 29–42, 49–50; Russell F. Weigley, *History of the United States Army* (New York: Macmillan, 1967), pp. 360–69.

15. March, *ARWD* (1919), I, 238; Pershing, *My Experiences in the World War*

(2 vols.; New York: Frederick A. Stokes, 1931), I, 16; Johnson, *The Blue Eagle from Egg to Earth* (Garden City: Doubleday, Doran, 1935), p. 90; Weigley, *History of Army,* p. 352.

16. Sims and Laning as quoted in Lieutenant Tracy B. Kittredge, USNR, *Naval Lessons of the Great War* (Garden City: Doubleday, Page, 1921), pp. 101, 162; Harold Sprout and Margaret Sprout, *The Rise of American Naval Power, 1776-1918* (Princeton: Princeton University Press, 1939), pp. 342-43.

17. Johnson, *Blue Eagle*, pp. 86-87, 90-93; March, *ARWD* (1919), I, 245, 341-42, and *The Nation at War* (Garden City: Doubleday, Doran, 1932), pp. 45-46, 163-65; Quartermaster General Henry G. Sharpe, USA, *The Quartermaster Corps in the Year 1917 in the World War* (New York: Century, 1921), pp. 7-9; Edward M. Coffman, *War to End Wars*, pp. 31-34, 166-67; Kittredge, *Naval Lessons*, p. 162; Robert D. Cuff, *The War Industries Board: Business-Government Relations during World War I* (Baltimore: Johns Hopkins University Press, 1973), pp. 62-63.

18. Scott as quoted in Coffman, *War to End Wars*, p. 52; Daniel R. Beaver, *Newton D. Baker and the American War Effort, 1917-1919* (Lincoln: University of Nebraska Press, 1966), p. 93.

19. Beaver, *Baker*, pp. 52, 54, 61, 71, 93; Coffman, *War to End Wars*, pp. 87-90; Cuff, *WIB*, pp. 63-64.

20. Coffman, *War to End Wars*, pp. 162-64, 166-67; Beaver, *Baker,* pp. 80, 93-98, 108-9; Cuff, *WIB*, pp. 62-64.

21. Editor, "A Larger Army," *Cav. J.*, XXV (January 1915), 560; Lieutenant Kinzie B. Edmunds, USA, "The Regular Army and the Reserves," *Cav. J.*, XXV (January 1915), 480; "Editorial Department," *Inf. J.*, XIII (September-October 1916), 231; Rear Admiral Colby M. Chester, USN, to Rear Admiral William S. Benson, USN, July 2, 1917, and to Rear Admiral Stephen B. Luce, USN, July 14, 1917, Luce Papers, LOC, General Correspondence, cont. 13; "Editor's Table," *Cav. J.*, XXVI (January 1916), 494.

22. Scott to Major General Leonard Wood, USA, April 9, 1917, Scott Papers, LOC, General Correspondence, cont. 28; Admiral George Dewey, on behalf of the General Board, to secretary of the navy, G.B. No. 445, March 28, 1913, reprinted in *ARND* (1913), p. 30.

23. Unidentified letter to the editor, *Cav. J.*, XXV (April 1915), 747; Sims to his wife, November 4, 1914, Sims Papers, NHF, Personal Correspondence, cont. 7; Ryan to Major General Hugh L. Scott, USA, May 31, 1915, Scott Papers, LOC, General Correspondence, cont. 18; Langhorne to Major General Tasker H. Bliss, USA, March 1, 1917, Bliss Papers, LOC, First Period, Correspondence, vol. 210.

24. "Editorial Department," *Inf. J.*, XIII (July-August 1916), 86.

25. "An Awakened Congress," *A&N Journal*, LII (September 5, 1914), 16.

26. Allen to secretary of war, October 12 and 21, 1914, and Allen to his wife, August 6, 1914, Allen Papers, LOC, General Correspondence, cont. 10; Knight to secretary of the navy, G.B. No. 420–1, August 1, 1914, Dewey Papers, LOC, General Correspondence, cont. 43.

27. Bennett, "From Harbor Defense to Coast Defense," *Arty. J.*, XLIV (September–October 1915), 159; Captain Howard L. Landers, USA, "Initial Strategy on Our North Atlantic Frontier—A Study in the Preparation of War Plans to Meet Certain Conditions," 1916 Second Prize Essay, *Arty. J.*, LXVII (May–June 1917), 276–77; Jackson, "Preparedness—A Vital Necessity," *PUSNI*, XLII (September–October 1916), 1564; Scott testimony, U.S., Congress, Committee on Military Affairs, *Universal Military Training, Hearings* before a subcommittee of the Committee on Military Affairs, Senate, on S. 1695, 64th Cong., 2d sess., 1917, pp. 96–98.

28. Scott and Moseley testimony, U.S., Congress, *UMT*, pp. 96–98 and 306, respectively; Blakeslee to Captain Albert Gleaves, USN, October 4, 1914, Gleaves Papers, NHF, General Correspondence, cont. 8.

29. Greene, *The Present Military Situation in the United States* (New York: Charles Scribner's Sons, 1915), pp. 17–48, 65–86; GS, "Statement," *ARWD* (1915), I, 116–18; Sims to his wife, November 20, 1914, NHF, Personal Correspondence, cont. 7.

30. Admiral George Dewey to secretary of the navy, G.B. No. 240–2, July 30, 1915, reprinted in *ARND* (1915), p. 73; GS, "Statement," *ARWD* (1915), I, 129–33; Finnegan, "Military Preparedness in the Progressive Era, 1911–1917" (Ph.D. dissertation, University of Wisconsin, 1969), p. 262.

31. Louis Morton, "War Plan ORANGE: Evolution of a Strategy," *World Politics*, XI (January 1959), 221–50; WCD, "War Plan *Orange* . . . ," May 19, 1913, RG 165, WCD File No. 7820–13; WCD, "Plan for War with Japan," April 13, 1915, RG 165, WCD File No. 7820–16.

32. U.S., Department of the Army, *History of Military Mobilization in the United States Army, 1775–1945*, by Lieutenant Colonel Marvin A. Kreidberg, USA, and Lieutenant Merton G. Henry, USA, DA Pamphlet No. 20–212 (Washington: Government Printing Office, 1955), pp. 236–39; WCD, "Plans for War with Germany," July, 1915, RG 165, WCD File No. 9433.

33. Wood, Aleshire, and Crozier testimony, U.S., Congress, *To Increase the Efficiency of the Military Establishment of the United States, Hearings* before the Committee on Military Affairs, House of Representatives, on the bill, 64th Cong., 1st sess., 1916, I, 262ff, 281–85, 522–24, II, 777.

34. Maxim, *Defenseless America* (New York: Hearst's International Library, 1915), pp. 71–72. For the civilians' preparedness argument as found in the sixty-some titles on national defense issued between the outbreak of war

and early 1917, see Finnegan, "Military Preparedness," p. 158 and *passim*.

35. Beer, "America's International Responsibilities and Foreign Policy," *Annals*, LXVI (July 1916), 84.

36. Finnegan, "Military Preparedness," pp. v, 323.

37. Ibid., p. 323.

38. U.S., War Department, War College Division, *The General Staffs of Certain Belligerent Powers*, WCD 9286-2, Doc. No. 514 (Washington: Government Printing Office, 1916), *passim*.

39. Major General Hugh L. Scott, USA, *ARWD* (1916), I, 167–68, and *ARWD* (1917), I, 128; General Peyton C. March, USA, *ARWD* (1918), I, 149; James W. Pohl, "The General Staff and American Military Policy: The Formative Period, 1898–1917" (Ph.D. dissertation, University of Texas, 1967), pp. 355–56; Coffman, *War to End Wars*, pp. 23–24; Major General Johnson Hagood, USA, *The Services of Supply: A Memoir of the Great War* (Boston: Houghton Mifflin, 1927), pp. 22–23; Major General William J. Snow, USA, *Signposts of Experience: World War Memoirs* (Washington: United States Field Artillery Association, 1941), pp. 20–21.

40. Benson testimony, U.S., Congress, Senate, Committee on Naval Affairs, *Naval Investigation, Hearings* before a subcommittee of the Committee on Naval Affairs, Senate, 66th Cong., 2d sess., 1920, II, 1894; Sprout and Sprout, *Rise*, p. 315; Kittredge, *Naval Lessons*, pp. 210–37; Rear Admiral Bradley A. Fiske, USN, *From Midshipman to Rear Admiral* (New York: Century, 1919), *passim*, pp. 526–619.

41. Weigley, *History of Army*, p. 353; Fiske, *Midshipman to Rear Admiral*, pp. 535–36; Kreidberg, *Military Mobilization*, pp. 196–201.

42. John A. S. Grenville and George B. Young, *Politics, Strategy, and American Diplomacy: Studies in Foreign Policy, 1873–1917* (New Haven: Yale University Press, 1966), p. 322; Arthur S. Link, *Woodrow Wilson and the Progressive Era* (Torchbook ed.; New York: Harper & Row, 1954), pp. 86–87.

43. Hermann Hagedorn, *Leonard Wood: A Biography* (2 vols.; New York: Harper & Brothers, 1931), II, 144.

44. Bliss memorandum reprinted in Frederick Palmer, *Bliss, Peacemaker—The Life and Letters of Tasker H. Bliss* (New York: Dodd, Mead, 1934), pp. 106–7 [Bliss's italics].

45. James MacG. Burns, *Roosevelt: The Lion and the Fox* (New York: Harcourt, Brace, 1956), p. 63.

46. Frederick Palmer, *Newton D. Baker: America at War* (2 vols.; New York: Dodd, Mead, 1931), I, 58–59; Kittredge, *Naval Lessons*, pp. 451, 452; Mott, *Twenty Years as a Military Attaché* (New York: Oxford University Press, 1937), p. 340.

47. Grenville and Young, *Politics and Diplomacy*, p. 294; Hagedorn, *Wood*, II, 136, 139.

48. Scott to David Hunter Scott, February 15, 1917, and March 24, 1917, Scott to his daughters, April 11, 1917, and Scott to Pershing, April 11, 1917, Scott Papers, LOC, Family Correspondence, cont. 5, and General Correspondence, cont. 28.

49. Sims's criticisms as reprinted in Kittredge, *Naval Lessons*, pp. 86–88, 101.

50. Greene, *Present Military Situation*, pp. 9, 15–16; Liggett, *A. E. F.: Ten Years Ago in France* (New York: Dodd, Mead, 1928), p. 1; Bullard and Earl Reeves, *American Soldiers Also Fought* (New York: Maurice H. Louis, 1939), p. 1; Allen to his wife, August 6, 1914, Allen Papers, LOC, General Correspondence, cont. 10.

51. Bliss to Colonel Fred Bennitt, May 22, 1915, Bliss Papers, LOC, First Period, Correspondence, vol. 190; Sims to his wife, August 5, 1914, Sims Papers, NHF, Personal Correspondence, cont. 7; Rodgers to Commander Reginald R. Belknap, USN, May 1, 1915, R. R. Belknap Papers, NHF, General Correspondence.

52. "Editorial Department," *Inf. J.*, XI (September–October 1914), 293.

53. Harbord, *The American Army in France, 1917-1919* (Boston: Little, Brown, 1936), p. 21; Palmer, *America in Arms: The Experience of the United States with Military Organization* (New Haven: Yale University Press, 1941), p. 150.

54. WCD, "Personnel versus Materiel in Plans for National Defense," *JMSIUS*, LVIII (May–June 1916), 400.

55. Gleaves diary, August 4, 1914, Gleaves Papers, NHF, Diaries, Journals, and Notebooks, cont. 3; Sims to wife, November 2, 1914, and August 4, 1915, Sims Papers, NHF, Personal Correspondence, conts. 7 and 8; Rodgers to Commander Reginald R. Belknap, USN, May 1, 1915, R. R. Belknap Papers, NHF, General Correspondence, cont. 10; E. David Cronin, ed., *The Cabinet Diaries of Josephus Daniels, 1913-1921* (Lincoln: University of Nebraska Press, 1963), p. 133.

56. Martin quoted in Coffman, *War to End Wars*, p. 8; Wilson note quoted in Johnson, *Blue Eagle*, p. 81.

57. Sims quoted in Kittredge, *Naval Lessons*, p. 83; Sims and Burton J. Hendrick, *The Victory at Sea* (Garden City: Doubleday, Page, 1921), pp. 6–7; Coffman, *War to End Wars*, pp. 91–105.

58. Beaver, *Baker*, p. 39; Johnson, *Blue Eagle*, pp. 81–82.

59. Harbord, *American Army*, p. 60.

60. Bliss and chief, War College Division, quoted in Kriedberg, *Military Mobilization*, pp. 238, 297; Bliss to secretary of war, May 25, 1917, Bliss Papers, LOC, New Acquisitions, cont. 1.

61. Kriedberg, *Military Mobilization*, pp. 298–309; Beaver, *Baker*, pp. 46–47, 111, 116–20; General Peyton C. March, USA, *ARWD* (1919), I, 239–40.

Chapter 9: The Afterclap of the First World War, pp. 177–94

1. Harbord, *The American Army in France, 1917-1919* (Boston: Little, Brown, 1936), pp. 556-57; Kittredge, *Naval Lessons of the Great War* (Garden City: Doubleday, Page, 1921), p. 5.
2. "Editorial Department," *Inf. J.*, XV (February 1919), 682
3. March testimony, U.S., Congress, House, Committee on Military Affairs, *Army Reorganization, Hearings* before the Committee on Military Affairs, House of Representatives, on H.R. 8287, 8068, 7925, and 8870, 66th Cong., 1st sess., 1919, p. 38, and *ARWD* (1919), I, 474; *ARND* (1922), p. 3; McGlachlin and McLean quoted in George S. Pappas, *Prudens Futuri: The U.S. Army War College, 1901-1967* (Carlisle Barracks: Alumni Association, U.S. Army War College, n.d.), pp. 115 and 116-117. See also ibid., pp. 89-117, and Elting E. Morison, *Admiral Sims and the Modern American Navy* (Boston: Houghton Mifflin, 1942), pp. 473-75.
4. "Editorial Department," *Inf. J.*, XVII (July 1920), 73-74; March, *ARWD* (1919), I, 471, and *ARWD* (1920), I, 232; Russell F. Weigley, *The American Way of War: A History of United States Military Strategy and Policy* (New York: Macmillan, 1973), p. 209.
5. March, *ARWD* (1919), I, 475; Denby, *ARND* (1922), p. 3.
6. Bliss to Mark Sullivan, January 11, 1923, and to Miss Lape, May 31, 1927, Bliss Papers, LOC, New Acquisitions, cont. 1; Francis B. Lowry, "The Generals, the Armistice, and the Treaty of Versailles, 1919" (Ph.D. dissertation, Duke University, 1963), pp. 208-9, 311.
7. Stockton, "The Army We Need," *N. Amer. Rev.*, CCX (November 1920), 646.
8. Moseley to Lieutenant Waldo Adler, December 10, 1918, to Major General John F. O'Ryan, March 1, 1919, and to Major General Robert E. Wood, March 3, 1919, Moseley Papers, LOC, Letterbooks, cont. 3.
9. Robert K. Griffith, Jr., "The Volunteer Army and American Society, 1919 to 1940" (Ph.D. dissertation, Brown University, 1979), pp. 21-33, 36-41; Russell F. Weigley, *History of the United States Army* (New York: Macmillan, 1967), pp. 396-99, and *Towards an American Army: Military Thought from Washington to Marshall* (New York: Columbia University Press, 1962), pp. 223-41.
10. Griffith, "Volunteer Army," pp. 41-43; Weigley, *History of Army*, pp. 399-400.
11. Haan, "Our New Army," *Forum*, LXV (March 1921), 297; Bond and Enoch B. Garey, *Wars of the American Nation* (Annapolis: New Military Library, 1923), pp. 199-200.
12. Bryden, "Possibilities in the Act of June 4, 1920," *Inf. J.*, XVII (September 1920), 255; Colonel Merch B. Stewart, USA, "Lessons of the War,"

Inf. J., XXI (October 1922), 373; Griffith, "Volunteer Army," pp. 51–114.

13. Carter, "Tinkering with the Army," *N. Amer. Rev.*, CCXVII (February 1923), 185; Weigley, *History of Army*, pp. 400–20.

14. Harold Sprout and Margaret Sprout, *Toward a New Order of Sea Power: American Naval Policy and the World Scene, 1918–1922* (Princeton: Princeton University Press, 1940), pp. 47–84; Captain Alfred W. Hinds, USN, "Sea Power and Disarmament," *N. Amer. Rev.*, CCXIV (November 1921), 588–93; William H. Gardiner, "A Naval View of the Conference: Fleet and Base Implications," *Atlantic*, CXXIX (April 1922), 521–39.

15. Goodrich, "The Navy and Its Owners," *N. Amer. Rev.*, CCXIII (January 1921), 28; Fiske, "The Defense of the Philippines," *N. Amer. Rev.*, CCXIII (June 1921), 723; Sprout and Sprout, *New Order*, pp. 80, 186–236.

16. Pratt, "Naval Policy and the Naval Treaty," *N. Amer. Rev.*, CCXV (May 1922), 593; Sprout and Sprout, *New Order*, pp. 100–85, 262–67.

17. On this and the following four paragraphs, see: Walter Millis, *Arms and Men: A Study in American Military History* (New York: G. P. Putnam's Sons, 1956), pp. 238–64; Sprout and Sprout, *New Order*, pp. 31–46, 100–17, 278–92; Weigley, *History of Army*, pp. 395–420.

18. Millis, ed., *American Military Thought* (Indianapolis: Bobbs-Merrill, 1966), pp. xxxviii–xxxix.

Bibliographical Essay

Primary Sources

Official Records

The *Annual Reports* of the War and Navy Departments, which contain the service secretaries' messages to Congress and statements by each service's senior officer and his principal subordinates in both the line and staff departments, provide a wealth of information on military thought and the progress of army and navy reform.

Though turn-of-the-century military officers displayed considerable candor in the preparation of those statements, the collections of the National Archives nevertheless reveal views that failed to achieve official sanction or that had to remain confidential. Most useful of those collections are the Records of the Office of the Chief of Naval Operations (RG 38), the Naval Records Collection of the Office of Naval Records and Library (RG 45), the General Records of the Department of the Navy (RG 80), the Records of the Adjutant General's Office, 1780s–1917 (RG 94), and the Records of the War Department General and Special Staffs (RG 165).

The latter two groups contain the army's war plans—documents that reveal that service's estimates of America's most probable enemies, preparations to meet those challenges, and, because army planners received little civilian guidance, service estimates of national goals and the likely means by which the government would pursue them.

237

The reports of the military attachés provide valuable clues concerning how army and navy officers viewed international developments and America's place in the world.

Memoirs and Autobiographies

Though plentiful, these tend to be so anecdotal as to provide little of value on military thought and policy. For the scholar willing to move mountains of chaff in search of a kernal of insight, however, such works are not entirely without their uses.

Among the best are: John M. Schofield's *Forty-six Years in the Army* (New York: Century, 1897) on military administration, civil-military relations, coastal defense, and national policy, to include overseas expansion; Alfred T. Mahan's *From Sail to Steam: Recollections of a Naval Life* (New York: Harper, 1907); and two books by Robley D. Evans, *A Sailor's Log: Recollections of Forty Years of Naval Life* (New York: D. Appleton, 1901) and *An Admiral's Log: Being Continued Recollections of Naval Life* (New York: D. Appleton, 1910).

Bradley A. Fiske's *From Midshipman to Rear Admiral* (New York: Century, 1919) and Hugh L. Scott's *Some Memories of a Soldier* (New York: Century, 1928) provide useful information on the preparedness debate and the two military departments in the period before the United States intervened in World War I.

On the war years, the most helpful are: Peyton C. March's *The Nation at War* (Garden City: Doubleday, Doran, 1932); Hugh S. Johnson's *The Blue Eagle from Egg to Earth* (Garden City: Doubleday, Doran, 1935); and William S. Sims's (with Burton J. Hendrick) *The Victory at Sea* (Garden City: Doubleday, Page, 1920).

Monographs

Military officers also revealed their views in books they hoped would shape civilian thinking about military policy.

Important material on the army is found in: William G. H. Carter's *The American Army* (Indianapolis: Bobbs-Merrill, 1915); Francis V. Greene's *The Present Military Situation in the United States* (New York: Scribner's, 1915); John McA. Palmer's *An Army of the People: The Constitution of an Effective Force of Trained Citizens* (New York: G. P. Putnam's Sons, 1916); Henry J. Reilly's *Why Preparedness: The Observations of an American Army Officer in Europe, 1914-1915* (Chicago: Daughaday, 1916); and Leonard Wood's *Our Military History: Its Facts and Fallacies* (Chicago: Reilly & Britton, 1916) and *The Military Obligation of Citizenship* (Princeton: Princeton University Press, 1915).

For the navy, see: James D. J. Kelley's *The Question of Ships: The Navy and the Merchant Marine* (New York: Scribner's, 1884) and Alfred T. Mahan's *The Influence of Sea Power upon History, 1660–1783* (American Century Series ed.; New York: Hill and Wang, 1957) and *The Interest of America in Sea Power, Present and Future* (Boston: Little, Brown, 1898).

Periodicals

To compensate for the bias inherent in official reports, autobiograhies, and contemporary monographs—all generally written by those who have won fame or high rank—this study made extensive use of military writing found in both civilian journals and the new military publications that began to appear after 1875.

Not counting the *Army and Navy Journal*, in fact a weekly newspaper, I surveyed in excess of one thousand articles from those sources, selecting some 350 for closer analysis. The latter group represented the work of more than two hundred officers, about half from each service. Though predominantly the work of line officers—three quarters of the army writers and 90 percent of the naval authors—the selection included a significant number by the staff as well.

Unlike official sources, the articles represented the views of all the commissioned ranks. At the time of publication, half the army writers held company-grade rank (lieutenant and captain), almost a third were field graders (major to colonel), and a fifth were generals. Of navy authors, one third were ensigns and lieutenants, one quarter were commanders, 16 percent were captains, and the remaining quarter held flag rank.

My examination of the officers' subsequent careers, however, revealed the writers to have been an influential group. Of those who remained in the service for a career, 70 percent of the army writers became generals, nearly half at one time commanded a regiment or larger unit, and the same proportion taught at a service school or civilian university. Ten became head of an army school, as did fourteen of the naval authors. Of the naval authors, 65 percent achieved flag rank, one third taught at the Naval War College or the Naval Academy, and one third commanded a fleet or squadron or served on one of the navy's major policy boards.

Although the service journals gave considerable attention to the mundane aspects of military life—from the care of cavalry horses to the sighting of naval guns—no other source provides such a broad sample of military opinion. This study thus relied heavily upon: the *Journal of the Military Service Institution of the United States;* the *Journal of the United States Cavalry Association;* the *Journal of the United States Infantry Association;* the *Journal of the United States Artillery;* the *United Service*, which appeared in three series under various subtitles; and the *Proceedings of the United States Naval Institute*.

Of the civilian monthlies, I searched the *Atlantic Monthly*, the *Forum*, *Harper's New Monthly Magazine*, the *North American Review*, and *Scribner's Magazine*. Just as the service journals made it possible to compare official and unofficial expressions of military views, the civilian monthlies helped measure the extent to which military views were shaped for particular audiences.

Manuscript Collections

These served a similar purpose, and they also indicated the degree to which military officers privately contradicted their public statements. I found invaluable the following collections of the Manuscript Division of the Library of Congress, which also holds portions of the Naval Historical Foundation collection: Tasker H. Bliss; Peyton C. March; William T. Sherman; Robert L. Bullard; John M. Schofield; Henry T. Allen; James G. Harbord; Frank R. McCoy; George V. H. Moseley; Hugh L. Scott; Leonard Wood; John McA. Palmer; George Dewey; Reginald R. Belknap; Albert Gleaves; Stephen B. Luce; William S. Sims; Charles S. Sperry; and Washington I. Chambers—all of whose careers roughly spanned the period of this study.

Secondary Works

General Studies

Of the host of general works I have consulted, the following were particularly useful: Foster Rhea Dulles's *Prelude to World Power: American Diplomatic History, 1860-1900* (New York: Macmillan, 1965), *The Imperial Years* (New York: Crowell, 1956), and *America's Rise to World Power, 1898-1954* (New York: Harper, 1955) on the general diplomatic background; H. Wayne Morgan's *From Hayes to McKinley: National Party Politics, 1877-1896* (Syracuse: Syracuse University Press, 1969), George E. Mowry's *The Era of Theodore Roosevelt and the Birth of Modern America, 1900-1912* (New York: Harper, 1958), and Arthur S. Link's *Woodrow Wilson and the Progressive Era, 1910-1917* (Torchbook ed.; New York: Harper, 1954) on political developments; and Jerry Israel's *Building the Organizational Society: Essays on Associational Activities in Modern America* (New York: Free Press, 1972) and Robert H. Wiebe's *The Search for Order, 1877-1920* (New York: Hill and Wang, 1967) for important interpretive insights.

Monographs

The following specialized studies also contributed importantly: Richard Hofstadter, *Social Darwinism in American Thought, 1860-1915* (Philadelphia:

University of Pennsylvania Press, 1945) on the influence of Darwin and Spencer; John A. S. Grenville and George B. Young, *Politics, Strategy, and American Diplomacy: Studies in Foreign Policy, 1873-1917* (New Haven: Yale University Press, 1966) on the strategic dimension of certain developments in foreign policy; Walter LaFeber, *The New Empire: An Interpretation of American Expansion, 1860-1898* (Cornell Paperbacks ed.; Ithaca: Cornell University Press, 1963), which explains imperialism's appeal to certain businessmen and intellectuals, though David F. Healy's *US Expansionism: The Imperialist Urge in the 1890s* (Madison: University of Wisconsin Press, 1963) gives a more comprehensive and balanced account; and Robert E. Osgood's *Ideals and Self-Interest in America's Foreign Relations: The Great Transformation of the Twentieth Century* (Chicago: University of Chicago Press, 1953), an insightful interpretation of American diplomacy.

Several monographic studies of America's relations with particular nations helped me compare civilian and military views on America's most probable enemies: Outten J. Clinard, *Japan's Influence on American Naval Power, 1897-1917* (Berkeley: University of California Press, 1947); Eleanor Tupper and George E. McReynolds, *Japan in American Public Opinion* (New York: Macmillan, 1937); Clara E. Schieber, *The Transformation of American Sentiment towards Germany, 1870-1914* (Boston: Cornhill, 1923); and Richard D. Challener, *Admirals, Generals, and American Foreign Policy, 1898-1914* (Princeton: Princeton University Press, 1973), which is particularly good on the relations among civilian and military policy makers.

Other works, which have examined national policy from a military perspective, have contributed more directly. The more important include: Walter Millis's *Arms and Men: A Study in American Military History* (New York: G. P. Putnam's Sons, 1956), a classic and a starting point for any investigation of American military history; Russell F. Weigley's *The American Way of War: A History of United States Military Strategy and Policy* (New York: Macmillan, 1973) and *Towards an American Army: Military Thought from Washington to Marshall* (New York: Columbia University Press, 1962); and Peter Karsten's *The Naval Aristocracy: The Golden Age of Annapolis and the Emergence of Modern American Navalism* (New York: Free Press, 1972), an excellent work on naval thought.

The professionalization of the officer corps and the reform of military administration are the subjects of two important works by Samuel P. Huntington—*The Common Defense: Strategic Programs in National Politics* (New York: Columbia University Press, 1961) and *The Soldier and the State: The Theory and Politics of Civil-Military Relations* (Cambridge: Belknap Press of Harvard University Press, 1957)—and Paul Y. Hammond's *Organizing for Defense: The American Military Establishment in the Twentieth Century* (Princeton: Princeton University Press, 1951) provides useful background on the services' Washington headquarters.

On the administrative shortcomings of the War Department and their reform, I have relied upon: Richard A. Andrews, "Years of Frustration: William T. Sherman, the Army and Reform, 1869–1883" (Ph.D. dissertation, Northwestern University, 1968); Graham A. Cosmas, *An Army for Empire: The United States Army in the Spanish-American War* (Columbia: University of Missouri Press, 1971); Otto L. Nelson, *National Security and the General Staff* (Washington: Infantry Journal Press, 1946); James W. Pohl, "The General Staff and American Military Policy: The Formative Period, 1898–1917" (Ph.D. dissertation, University of Texas, 1967); and Mabel E. Deutrich, *Struggle for Supremacy: The Career of General Fred C. Ainsworth* (Washington: Public Affairs Press, 1962).

For the naval staff, I used: Daniel J. Costello's "Planning for War: A History of the General Board of the Navy, 1900–1914" (Ph.D. dissertation, Fletcher School of Law and Diplomacy, 1968).

As the development of the services' educational systems closely relates to the movement for staff reform, I also learned from: George S. Pappas's *Prudens Futuri: The U.S. Army War College, 1901–1967* (Carlisle Barracks: Alumni Association, U.S. Army War College, [1967 or 1968]; Ronald H. Spector's " 'Professors of War,' The Naval War College and the Modern American Navy" (Ph.D. dissertation, Yale University, 1967); and Timothy K. Nenninger, *The Leavenworth Schools and the Old Army: Education, Professionalism, and the Officer Corps of the United States Army, 1881–1918* (Westport: Greenwood Press, 1978).

Institutional reform involved more, of course, than high-level staffs and schools. For studies that gave equal attention to the army in the field and the navy at sea, I used Russell F. Weigley's *History of the United States Army* (New York: Macmillan, 1967) and Harold and Margaret Sprout's *The Rise of American Naval Power, 1776–1918* (Princeton: Princeton University Press, 1939) and *Toward a New Order of Sea Power: American Naval Policy and the World Scene, 1918–1922* (Princeton: Princeton University Press, 1940).

On the influence of World War I, see: Edward M. Coffman, *The War to End All Wars: The American Military Experience in World War I* (New York: Oxford University Press, 1968); Robert D. Cuff, *The War Industries Board: Business-Government Relations during World War I* (Baltimore: Johns Hopkins University Press, 1973); and Daniel R. Beaver, *Newton D. Baker and the American War Effort, 1917–1919* (Lincoln: University of Nebraska Press, 1966).

For other specific periods, I have used: Kenneth J. Hagan, *American Gunboat Diplomacy and the Old Navy, 1877–1889* (Westport: Greenwood Press, 1973) on the late-nineteenth-century naval revolution; Walter R. Herrick, Jr., *The American Naval Revolution* (Baton Rouge: Louisiana State University Press, 1966), which places Mahan in perspective; John M. Gates, *Schoolbooks and Krags: The United States Army in the Philippines, 1898-1902* (Westport: Greenwood Press, 1973), David F. Healy, *The United States in Cuba, 1898-1902: Generals, Politicians, and the Search for Policy* (Madison: University of Wisconsin Press, 1963), and Allan R. Millett, *The Politics of Intervention: The Military Occupation of Cuba, 1906-1909* (Columbus: Ohio State University Press, 1968), all of which treat the army's work overseas; and John G. Clifford, *The Citizen Soldiers: The Plattsburg Training Camp Movement, 1913-1920* (Lexington: University Press of Kentucky, 1972), John W. Chambers, II, "Conscripting for Collossus: The Adoption of the Draft in the United States in World War I" (Ph.D. dissertation, Columbia University, 1973), and John P. Finnegan, "Military Preparedness in the Progressive Era, 1911-1917" (Ph.D. dissertation, University of Wisconsin, 1969), which examine the preparedness movement's various aspects.

On other features of the services' manpower policy, I used: Harold T. Wieand, "The History of the Development of the United States Naval Reserve, 1889-1941" (Ph.D. dissertation, University of Pittsburgh, 1953); Kenmore M. McManes, "Development of the Naval Reserve," *Military Affairs*, XVII (Spring 1953); Martha Derthick, *The National Guard in Politics* (Cambridge: Harvard University Press, 1965); Jim Dan Hill, *The Minute Man in Peace and War: A History of the National Guard* (Harrisburg: Stackpole, 1964); and William H. Riker, *Soldiers of the States: The Role of the National Guard in American Democracy* (Washington: Public Affairs Press, 1957).

Though most of the evidence came from sources too numerous to list here, several specialized studies guided my chapter on the relation between military and civilian elites: Dean G. Allard, Jr., "The Influence of the United States Navy upon the American Steel Industry, 1880-1900" (M.A. thesis, Georgetown University, 1959); Paul A. C. Koistinen, "The 'Industrial Military Complex' in Historical Perspective: World War I," *Business History Review*, XLI (Winter 1967); Armin Rappaport, *The Navy League of the United States* (Detroit: Wayne State University Press, 1962); and Alice McElin, "The National Security League: Its Work and Policy" (M.A. thesis, Stanford University, 1921).

Biographies

Several modern biographies contributed to all parts of the study. The best on army leaders are: John A. Carpenter's *Sword and Olive Branch: Oliver Otis Howard* (Pittsburgh: University of Pittsburgh Press, 1964); Edward M. Coffman's *The Hilt of the Sword: The Career of Peyton C. March* (Madison: University of Wisconsin Press, 1966); Hermann Hagedorn's uncritical *Leonard Wood: A Biography* (2 vols.; New York: Harper, 1931); Allan R. Millett's *The*

*General: Robert L. Bullard and Officership in the United States Army,
1881-1925* (Westport: Greenwood Press, 1975); Frederick Palmer's somewhat
dated *Bliss, Peacemaker: The Life and Letters of General Tasker Howard Bliss*
(New York: Dodd, Mead, 1934); and Heath Twichell's *Allen: Biography of an
Army Officer, 1859-1930* (New Brunswick: Rutgers University Press, 1974).

For the navy, I have relied upon Albert Gleaves's laudatory *Life and Letters
of Rear Admiral Stephen B. Luce, U.S. Navy: Founder of the Naval War Col-
lege* (New York: G. P. Putnam's Sons, 1925); Elting E. Morison's *Admiral
Sims and the Modern American Navy* (Boston: Houghton Mifflin, 1942); and
Robert Seager's *Alfred Thayer Mahan: The Man and His Letters* (Annapolis:
Naval Institute Press, 1977).

Index